THE OPERATOR

THE OPERATOR

The SEAL Team Operative and the Mission That Changed the World

ROBERT O'NEILL

**SIMON &
SCHUSTER**

London · New York · Sydney · Toronto · New Delhi

A CBS COMPANY

First published in Great Britain by Simon & Schuster UK Ltd, 2017
A CBS COMPANY

1 3 5 7 9 10 8 6 4 2

Simon & Schuster UK Ltd
1st Floor
222 Gray's Inn Road
London WC1X 8HB

www.simonandschuster.co.uk
www.simonandschuster.com.au
www.simonandschuster.co.in

Simon & Schuster Australia, Sydney
Simon & Schuster India, New Delhi

The author and publishers have made all reasonable efforts to contact
copyright-holders for permission, and apologise for any omissions or errors
in the form of credits given. Corrections may be made to future printings.

A CIP catalogue record for this book
is available from the British Library

Hardback ISBN: 978-1-4711-4812-5
Trade Paperback ISBN: 978-1-4711-4813-2
eBook ISBN: 978-1-4711-4814-9

Printed and bound by CPI Group (UK) Ltd, Croydon, CR0 4YY

Simon & Schuster UK Ltd are committed to sourcing paper
that is made from wood grown in sustainable forests and support the Forest
Stewardship Council, the leading international forest certification organisation.
Our books displaying the FSC logo are printed on FSC certified paper.

To the victims of 9/11 and their families
who never asked to be in the fight, but were and are.
It was in memory of you that I fought.

To the reader: The author has blacked out selected text in this book to comply with the Department of Defense Prepublication and Security Review.

AUTHOR'S NOTE

Over the past forty years, I've had much to be grateful for, including the support of two wonderful parents and the gift of my special daughters. But it was as a member of SEAL Team ▮▮ that I learned how deep friendships can be. With the ▮▮▮▮▮▮▮▮ Squadrons, I found a level of trust that, I believe, far exceeds anything that is possible in civilian life. When in the middle of a pitch-black night on the other side of the world you're about to breach a building jammed with AK-47-wielding terrorists, you have your SEAL brothers—and no one else.

For a long time, I wrestled with whether to write about my four hundred missions as a SEAL. I didn't want the book to be just about me. If that's all the story was, I wouldn't write it. Could I capture the incredible refusal to quit of my SEAL brothers? Describe what it's like to be part of a team that functions as a single organism, trained by thousands of repetitions to act as one? Explain that when any of us succeed we all succeed?

Those are the questions that kept me awake at night.

When SEALs put their lives on the line for their country, sometimes it's in obscurity and sometimes it's in the media spotlight. When the latter happens, the media often get it wrong. One SEAL never returns a hostage to her loved ones. One SEAL never liberates a town from torturers. One SEAL never rescues a man behind enemy lines. One SEAL never kills the bad guy everyone has been searching for.

When the gun fires, it's as if we all fire it. I decided, finally, to write this book to bring that truth to readers.

There are those who believe that what SEALs do should remain in the shadows. But part of what drove me as a young, in-over-his-head kid in BUD/S training were the books I'd read about this awesome military organization. My humble hope is that more than a few young men—*and* women (it's going to happen eventually!)—will put down *The Operator* with a renewed determination to do the hard things that will get them their SEAL trident. And I also hope that the rest of you who read this book will honor the service of SEALs around the world—guys who, even now, are risking everything to keep our country safe.

In telling this story, I relied on memory to reconstruct words of courage, frustration, and, yes, outrageously profane humor that I heard over the course of hundreds of missions. I've tried my best to render dialogue and events with absolute accuracy, but of course any errors are entirely my own. For security and privacy reasons, the following names in this book are pseudonyms: Kris, Nicole, Cole Sterling, Jonny Savio, Tracy Longmire, Matthew Parris, Mack, Eric Roth, Cruz, Leo, Ralph, Decker, Adam, Harp, and Karen.

TIME LINE

CHAPTER ONE

I owe my career as a Navy SEAL to a girl. I'm not the first, and I doubt I'll be the last.

She was younger than I was, a brunette with the face of a supermodel, great dance moves, and—key to my heart—a quick sense of humor. The first time I tried to kiss her, I closed my eyes too soon and I heard her say, "Uh, what are you doing?"

"I'm gonna kiss you."

"Not before you ask me out, you're not," she said.

"Will you go out with me tomorrow then?"

"Pick me up at seven o'clock," she said, then gave me a better kiss than I deserved and went home.

The next evening I picked her up at 7:00 sharp and, big spender that I was, drove her to Taco Bell. She ate a large order of Nachos Bellgrande and three soft Tacos Supreme.

Gorgeous girl, perfect figure, and the appetite of a lumberjack. I knew nothing about life, but I thought I was in love.

When I graduated high school in Butte, Montana—the same school my grandfather and father had graduated from—and enrolled at Montana Tech, the local college, this girl was still a junior. It's just one of those things; you're not going to date a high school girl when you're in college. So I stayed away, but I couldn't keep my mind off her. She went on doing her high school thing, dating and going to dances, which she damn well should have been doing. But I wanted it both ways, me having my fun

1

and her staying on hold. I simmered miserably for weeks, then finally snapped when I heard she'd spent the day with some high school boy. With a couple drinks in me I went to her house to find out what was going on, and promptly made a complete ass out of myself.

Her father, a massive Italian with black hair, a burly mustache, and a square jaw, was famous around Butte for being tough. He owned a company that jacked up entire houses and moved them whole. I was certain he would have no problem moving me. But he took pity. Instead of knocking me flat, which would have been more than justified, he gently but firmly escorted me out the door.

That kindness provoked something of an out-of-body experience. After he released his iron grip from my elbow and sent me reeling into the night, I glimpsed myself as if from a distance. It wasn't an attractive sight. I realized that if I was acting like this now, it would only get worse. I'd end up as one of those guys who hang around Butte forever, whining about the good old days.

So I knew. I had to go.

In my very limited experience, the way people got out of Butte was by joining the military. Though I'd never really considered it before, in that instant I was committed. The future, or fate, or whatever, kicked into high gear.

THESE DAYS SOME PEOPLE MIGHT call my childhood "free range." Saturday mornings I was out the door after breakfast and back only when the streetlights amped up. Kids ran in packs in my neighborhood. We ambushed each other with toy guns and played ninja warriors, leaping off rooftops and doing a bunch of other harebrained stuff I'd kill my kids for doing. We all went to see *Rambo* at the Butte Plaza Mall. That was pretty cool. Everybody wanted to be that guy blowing away evildoers with his M60. But to me, it was all fantasy, no more real than the increasingly sophisticated shooter video games that competed for our attention. The actual military was never huge in my life. I was never going to be in it, so I didn't think much about it. I just wanted to play, put on camouflage, and pretend to shoot my friends.

At first glance, Butte might not seem like an idyllic place to grow up. It's a mining town whose best years were in the early twentieth century, when every bullet in every rifle sent Over There during World War I was made of copper—most of it mined in Butte. The population hit a peak of 100,000 in 1920 and by the time I came along had dipped by about two-thirds. The residential areas mingled with pit mines, and the entire town was built on a plateau next to the biggest pit of all, Berkeley Pit, an immense, defunct, open-pit copper mine a mile wide and a third of a mile deep. Between the time it opened in 1955 and its closure on Earth Day 1982, a billion tons of ore and waste rock had been wrenched out of its depths. When the sump pumps shut off for the last time, ground water began a slow rise, leaching acids and heavy metals from the gaping wound in the earth. The water that filled the pit was toxic enough to kill any geese that possessed the poor judgment to splash down there. Eventually, the Berkeley Pit was declared the largest Superfund toxic waste site in the country.

But I was more focused on other features of Butte, specifically metal hoops that hung ten feet above gymnasium floors, and the deer, elk, and antelope that sprinted through the wild Rockies, which rose up like a frozen tsunami on the other side of town.

My dad, the son of a miner, was a stockbroker and my mom was a math teacher (I took her class three times—in seventh and eighth grades and again in high school). My parents divorced when I was six or seven. To me, having two parents who lived apart seemed almost natural. I don't remember their living together. My dad was always close by and around whenever we needed him, but the usual setup was to go with him every other weekend. That was fine with my siblings and me; all of our friends were near my mom's house and we liked to have weekends to play outside: kick the can, war, ninjas, or climbing and roof-jumping. We all played together, except the climbing and jumping. Kris, my elder sister, wanted none of that. But I could force my sister Kelley, younger than me by three years, to come along. She desperately wanted to fit in. So up we went on the roof, and off we jumped. These days I'd give my son an earful if he pulled that shit, but being a kid, I didn't think about the risk. It was just fun. Kelley was my best friend for years; I even made her sign a contract binding her to being my teammate for two-on-two football on the church lawn. She was a damn good receiver and one hell of an athlete all through college.

My older brother, Tom, was a complete dick up until he was in high school. Then some switch flipped and he became awesome. Or maybe I just stopped being so annoying. Whatever. Some magic happened and he became the funniest person I knew, and All-State in cross-country. He taught himself guitar and his first band was called The Fake ID's. That's how young they were. He still plays and has his own morning show on a local radio station.

Kris was always the most levelheaded of us, but my mom will disagree. Maybe they were too much alike, and sometimes sparks flew. Kris was always tolerant of me, easy to talk to, and the best laugher I've ever known. She was meticulous, got straight A's forever, and was gentle—when she wasn't kicking my ass, which she could do up to my junior year in high school . . . possibly longer.

My mom and dad maintained a cooperative, cordial relationship throughout my childhood. If they had any big problems with each other, they never let my siblings or me see it. The split living was actually good for my parents. My mom worked at the junior high, which was next to the high school so she could get us to school and home. She loved being a mom, but she got every other weekend off to go out on the town with her crazy, fun, and hot friends Lynn and Sue. I remember them sitting at my mom's kitchen table, sipping daiquiris and talking about what went down on Saturday night. It was too much for my tender junior high ears. I was in the next room and I had to low crawl my ass out the front door because I couldn't take it. My first mission.

We loved hanging out with Dad on those alternate weekends. He was a total bachelor but we didn't realize it. We should have guessed because our first stop on Friday was *always* to But-treys . . . a local grocery store. We needed food because he had none! He went out for most meals. So we'd go down every aisle and grab stuff we needed, going heavy on the junk food and making sure to grab ingredients for Dad's "Famous Breakfast." His scrambled eggs were and still are incredible. Cheese, mayo, butter, basil, and some secret stuff. One time we forgot milk so he added Amaretto Coffee-mate. Don't try it! We'd always end the weekend at Grampa Tom and Gramma Audrey's. She cooked like a champ; everything you can imagine. And this is where I learned my dad's trick: potato mountain and gravy lake!

As I was growing into adolescence, my dad and I developed an unusual father–son relationship, becoming more like best friends. It began when my mom moved us from up on the "hill"—where all my neighborhood buddies lived—to a place downtown, not far from the Berkeley Pit, where I didn't know anybody. I was looking for something to replace all those ninja hijinks with my friends when I saw a video—Michael Jordan's first, *Come Fly with Me.* I was instantly captivated. It begins with Jordan all alone, shooting baskets in a completely empty gym. His voice-over says, "I could never stop working on it. Each day I feel I *have* to improve." And then of course there are endless scenes of Air Jordan, defying gravity, cutting through defenders as if they're no more substantial than the atmosphere itself.

I was awed, inspired. I wasn't the biggest kid, or the best-looking, or the smartest or most athletic, but something inside me connected with that obsessive drive to keep striving. Looking back, I guess I had that all along. My favorite subject was English, and my favorite book was *The Old Man and the Sea.* I liked the way Santiago, the old fisherman, is drawn into a titanic battle of wills with the huge fish. His hands are shredded by the fishing line, he's so hungry he's eating slices of raw bait, he hasn't slept, his muscles are cramping there in his crappy little boat, but he'll die before he quits. That attitude appealed to me.

I wasn't going to hook any giant marlins in Butte, Montana, but I *could* aspire to be like Mike. There was a school right next to my new house, Greeley Elementary, with an outdoor basketball hoop. So I asked my mom to get me a basketball and she did. I would go over there every day and play by myself, hours at a time, just seeing how many free throws in a row I could make, working on my jump shot, driving left, driving right. My dad, who was about forty then, had played some at the University of Montana. He was a damn good basketball player. He found out what I was doing and he said, "Hey, do you want to start playing?"

We played at a sports club in downtown Butte. I'd still shoot by myself at the elementary school, and then he'd pick me up and we'd hit the club. I was spending four hours a day, seven days a week with a basketball in—or flying out of—my hands. When I made the school team I practiced with my teammates during the season, and when it ended, Dad's and my private season began. Dad picked me up after school and took me to the indoor court. We'd practice two or three hours; dribbling, layup drills, one on one, wildly raucous pickup games. He tried to teach me everything he'd learned, head fakes, little tricks he'd picked up on how to beat your man.

When we were finally exhausted, my dad would say, "We can't leave until one of us sinks twenty free throws in a row." He would feed me—I'd get pissed if he made me move my feet even an inch off the line—and I'd shoot till I missed. Then he'd take over. The first time it took about twenty minutes for one of us to make twenty in a row. Then we went out for a steak dinner to celebrate. The next day my dad said, "We can leave when one of us gets twenty, but we need twenty-five for the steak." Once we hit twenty-five, it went up to thirty, then thirty-five, forty. We got to where we had to make seventy free throws in a row for a dinner, and we almost always did it. I think my dad's record was ninety in a row. Mine is still 105. We were making a lot of free throws.

When I was twelve, my dad got divorced from his second wife, and my uncle Jack, his brother, persuaded him to give hunting a try on weekends to get his mind off failed marriages. There was no question I'd come with him. We went driving up the mountain in Jack's Nissan. We didn't know what we were doing at first. There are vast plains up there with magnificent animals sprinting all over at warp speed—antelope are pretty much the fastest animal in North America. Guys in trucks and four-wheelers chase them and people shoot in every direction. If I were to see it today from the perspective of a range officer at Naval Special Warfare Development Group, I'd recognize how insanely unsafe it is. But it was thrilling, and eventually we got good at it, climbing on foot to a place no trucks could go, a place where we knew the animals would retreat at the end of the night. You take up a position out of the wind and let them come to you, take them by surprise. The animals expect to be chased, not ambushed.

My first kill was a mule deer, a big buck. I remember driving up these terrible dirt roads in the dark, climbing the edge of a valley as far as we could, then walking steeply uphill as the sun rose. After about an hour, we hit the summit, which descended into a hay-colored bowl. That's where we hoped to run into the deer. There weren't any. We hung out for a while and the disappointment of not finding anything to shoot at faded. It was late fall, chilly but not bone-numbing, patches of snow here and there, and I thought: *Not bad to be sitting up on this mountaintop at the break of day, just me and my dad, as if this amazing place had been waiting for us to arrive.*

Eventually we got hungry. As we were walking back down the hill for lunch, a doe and a buck burst out of the trees into a clearing a hundred yards to our right. We were shuffling along, making a sound the buck didn't recognize. He froze right in the middle of the clearing. My dad was in front of me, right in the line of fire. He dropped to the ground and said, "Take it!" I was fortunate I didn't have time to think about it. I knew I needed to take the shot now or he was gone. The adrenaline took over. Still standing, I raised my .300 Winchester Magnum to my shoulder and barely glimpsed the buck in my scope before I pulled the trigger. My father had told me to aim for his chest, right behind his shoulder. You want to try to hit him in the lungs for a quick kill. I missed high, a lucky shot. The bullet severed his spine. That worked. The buck dropped right where he stood. We approached carefully. These big bucks can play dead. You don't want them to hop up and trample you. I stuck out my foot and gave him a nudge. The flesh of his haunch quivered, but otherwise he stayed put. I took another step toward his big antlered head, and raised the muzzle of my rifle—the same kind of rifle I'd eventually use as a SEAL sniper—to his big staring eyeball. Dead all right.

It was a bit surreal for me. He looked the same as he had just a moment ago when he was alive: pretty colors and noble antlers. But he was dead, and I'd killed him. I felt a tug of remorse. He was a beautiful animal, gone now thanks to me. But I was also proud. This was Montana. Deer were for shooting. Everybody did it. Now I was part of the club.

In the hunting seasons that followed, any residual remorse fell away. Soon it was a competition at junior high every Monday. "So and so got a buck." The real prize was the bull elk. It always seemed that someone's mythical uncle, or a miraculous shot from someone's dad, had brought down a "six point" elk. (We score different out West—you count one side of the antlers, not both. A "six point" bull has twelve points total.) That's an immense, swift, and elusive creature. They can stand five-feet high at the shoulder, and weigh almost nine hundred pounds. None of us had been good enough to kill such a bull. Some hunters had never even *seen* one.

When I was lucky enough to see one and shoot one before I turned eighteen, I felt only pride.

* * *

IN THE FALL OF 1994, the year I turned eighteen, my dad introduced me to the first Navy SEAL I ever met. His name was Jim and I was impressed with him the moment I saw him. He wasn't as big as I thought a Navy SEAL would be—an observation people make about SEALs all the time—but he was obviously in great shape. He had a clean haircut and a military bearing. What I noticed first, though, was his positive confidence. The second thing I noticed was that he always put on his seat belt. Here was this tough Navy SEAL who wasn't afraid of anything, but safety always came first. He'd never been to Montana before but figured: Guns, mountains, how hard can it be? He embraced the challenge in typical SEAL fashion—got someone to drop him off in the outback, then stayed there for three days. He walked all over hell, never seeing so much as a mule deer. I found out about that and told him, "That's not the way to do it. I got a spot."

The hike was only a little under a mile, but it was pretty much straight uphill and still pitch dark. Normally I'd take it slow, pause for a couple of breathers. Toward the top, every breath felt like sandpaper rasping my lungs, but I was thinking, *This guy's a SEAL. I can't be a pussy. I need to walk, no breaks.*

He was on my heels the whole way.

We got up there and got right into the elk—about forty of them right where I'd said they'd be. We didn't get any, but when we got back down the mountain Jim said, "You ought to consider becoming a SEAL, the way you climbed that hill in the dark."

I was flattered, but I didn't seriously consider it.

Until my ex-girlfriend's dad sent me not so gently into the night.

THE SUMMER AFTER I GRADUATED from high school I spent twelve hours a day, four days a week, shoveling crushed rock onto a huge conveyor belt in a copper mine facility, the almost total darkness relieved only by the beams of two little lamps on my helmet. I thought that would be good work for building my somewhat scrawny upper body, and I was right. But I hadn't counted on breathing in metric tons of rock dust, or scaring the crap out of myself thinking of all the workers before me who'd slipped into the conveyor belt and been converted to human pulp. My night job delivering pizzas was like a vacation by comparison.

I did think, briefly, about going out of town to college, though my idea of out of town was the University of Montana in Missoula, less than two hours down the highway. When it came to it, I just didn't have the desire. Or maybe I didn't have the courage. When you're a small-town kid from Montana, there's this sense that venturing into the big, scary outside world might pulp you as surely as that conveyor belt. Montana Tech was the safe alternative. I also had a better chance of making the basketball team there. I was a good high school player, but at 6'1" I wasn't high enough off the floor to impress at the college level. I figured I'd play my ass off on the practice team and work my way in. It went well. I had a great time, got in great shape. *Physically*. Mentally, well there was the girl.

I know now it wasn't just that. I'd just finished my first year of college basketball and was feeling burned-out. Not with playing but with the concept of practice, practice, school, and practice. The grind probably wouldn't have gotten to me if it hadn't been for the girl. I couldn't seem to get over her, and she was still in town—I could bump into her anywhere. I knew I didn't want to find myself on a barstool at Maloney's every night drinking to forget. I could already imagine the rut I could dig. It was time to do something.

My first thought was of Ben and Jim, two somewhat older guys I'd known my entire life. They'd joined the Marines and gone to boot camp together when I was still in high school. Coming home on leave, they were confidence-radiating supernovas, showing off spit-shined boots and uniforms so crisp the creases could slice cheese. I remember thinking, *These guys could kick anybody's ass in town.*

I wanted to be just like that.

I didn't even think about the possibility of combat, much less getting killed. As a freshman in high school, I saw guys who'd graduated and joined the military come back to say goodbye to their teachers before going off to fight in Desert Storm. As a fourteen-year-old, I didn't know any better so I thought the war would be a high-casualty conflict like Vietnam and they'd all die. Then I watched the war on CNN . . . piece of cake. Besides, as I weighed the idea of signing up, we weren't at war, and there wasn't one looming. I thought it would be cool to wear the uniform and sing the cadences.

Plus, I'd only be gone for a few years . . . and then I'd be back at Maloney's with a few war stories to impress the regulars.

One day in April 1995, I went to the Marine recruitment office, but the recruiter wasn't there. I remembered a funny line my Marine friends told me: "The Marine Corps is actually part of the Department of the Navy. The men's department." Which is why I thought of walking into the Navy office. I reasoned that if anyone would know where this missing Marine was, this Navy recruiter would.

He was nothing special physically, but he was very clever. Had it been years later, I would have recognized why immediately: He was wearing khakis and had anchors on his collar. He was a Navy Chief. No matter what anyone says, Chiefs make the Navy work. They do this with intelligence, loyalty, and experience. They can also be mean as hell. This Chief had quotas to fill and that is not an easy task in Butte, Montana. Especially when your office is right next to the Marines.

He looked me over skeptically and said, "Why do you want to be a Marine?"

I said, "Because Marines have the best snipers in the world. I want to be a sniper because I grew up hunting." He just nodded and said, "Look no further. We have snipers in the Navy. All you need to do is become a Navy SEAL."

I didn't even know how to swim. But the way I thought about

it was, "Hey, I'm kind of naïve, but this guy's a professional recruiter. Why's he going to lie to me?"

And it wasn't a lie. Exactly. Just a rather large omission. A
kid off a hick-town street had about the same chance of making
it as a SEAL as this recruiter had of becoming an admiral. So in
almost complete ignorance, I signed on the dotted line. It was a
deferred enrollment, which meant that I had six months before
I went to boot camp.

Which was a good thing. I could keep myself alive in the
water but not swim. I'd never attempted a pull-up. A brochure
that had been thoughtfully provided in the recruitment paperwork revealed that to even qualify for a SEAL tryout you had to
be able to do a minimum of eight pull-ups. And that's *after* you
swim five hundred yards, and do forty-two push-ups and fifty
sit-ups. And before you run.

Right then I decided to quit my job shoveling crushed rock
and devote myself full-time to getting in shape for the SEAL
screening test.

I'd been shoveling that rock for months, building my strength.
How hard could this be? Full of can-do fervor, I ran down to a
park near my mom's house that had a rusted old pull-up bar to
see how many pull-ups beyond the eight minimum I could do.
I sprang easily from the dirt depression beneath, grabbed the
pull-up bar with confidence, and heaved. One!

Gravity rudely yanked my arms back to full extension. It took
all my will to keep my grip on the bar from releasing. My brain
frantically signaled my biceps to fire and pull me back up. My
biceps replied, "Fuck you."

Words formed so clearly in my mind that I may have said
them out loud. "Oh, my God, these are hard. I need to get better
at pull-ups!"

Still, my optimism wasn't entirely crushed. *Yet.* Next I went
up to the college pool—fortunately, I still had my student ID. I
figured I'd start with a quick 1,000 meters, which is forty lengths
of the pool. By the end of the second length my arms ached and

my legs felt like they were about to cramp. I could barely lift myself out of the pool.

Okay, I was pathetic. But I wasn't defeated. Every day I worked at getting better. One day at the pool, I was lucky enough to run into a friend from high school who was getting ready to swim at Notre Dame for four years. When he saw me struggling through the water he said, "What are *you* doing in here?"

"I just joined the Navy," I said. "I'm going to SEAL school. You know they swim like a mile a day there."

He looked at me and shook his head. "Dude, you have no idea what you're getting into. There's a thousand percent chance you're not going to make it. Get back into the pool."

He showed me some basic swimming techniques and I worked hard to master them. My stepfather built me a pull-up bar in the basement of my mom's house. I would go down there, queue up Guns N' Roses' *Use Your Illusion I* and *II*, crank the volume to "liquefy," then just do pull-up after pull-up.

I didn't realize how appropriate that title was until later, but I was definitely using my illusion that I could become a SEAL to motivate myself. I began to understand something important: If you want to get better at pull-ups, do more pull-ups. That's it. And that's what I did.

One thing I had going for me was that I'd always been a good runner. I had a route that I ran, a straight shot down the street from my mom's house, past my best friend's house and my cousin's house, to a stoplight that was exactly a mile away. I always wanted to run it in no more than six minutes. At the light I'd take a thirty-second breather, then run back.

Every single morning, seven days a week, I'd get up and go down to the pool to swim for a few hours, come home, chill out and eat breakfast, knock out pull-ups, go for the run. For six months, this was my full-time job. At night I delivered pizzas.

I was really enjoying myself. And I got a lot stronger.

*   *   *

ON SUNDAY, JANUARY 28, 1996, I arrived at the Butte military enlistment processing center to officially join up. There was a Problem.

It had been some time since I'd signed my papers to enlist, and I'd nearly forgotten that in the initial flurry of paperwork I'd elected to tell the US Navy that I'd experimented with marijuana. It's true that I only tried it a handful of times, and, to be honest, I didn't even like it, but, man, did they make me feel like a sinner who needed to repent. If the me from today could give the me from nineteen years ago advice it would be, "Relax, kid. It's been about a year since you tried it; you're good. Tell them nothing. It's gonna save us all a bunch of time and nonsense. Pee in the cup, sign the fucking papers, and let's get on with the adventure."

But I hadn't been given that advice, so I found myself having a long and painful conversation with a man identified as "The Commander," promising that I would cut out my liver and eat it raw before I ever smoked the devil weed again. I'm sure he had better things to do, too, than talk to some eighteen-year-old punk from Butte. Like go and smoke a bowl of his own. Anyway, we both got through the day and I was allowed to join this man's Navy.

I still have a picture of me swearing to defend this nation against all enemies, foreign and domestic. I was wearing a red T-shirt, very classy for an official event.

For some reason the Navy had booked me a hotel room near the processing center. They were going to drive me to the airport the next day. Possibly, they wanted to keep an eye on me, make sure I wasn't going to get cold feet. It was the first time I'd ever been in a hotel room by myself. I was sitting alone in this tiny, bleak little room, my duffel bag tossed across the bed, thinking, *Why would I stay here my last night in town when I could just go down to my mom's house?*

So that night, with my family and my best friend beside me, I watched the Steelers lose to the Cowboys in Super Bowl XXX. The next morning the entire crew came out to Butte's Bert

Mooney Airport to wave me off. I was relieved to discover another recruit on the same flight, a fellow by the name of Tracy Longmire. He'd played football at the same college where I'd played basketball, and he was one of those badasses who played both offense and defense. He looked the part, too: big and mean-looking with a bald head and piercing eyes. But he was far from mean. He was a calm, reassuring presence from the moment I saw him. Even though he was only two years older, he seemed like a wise elder, humble when he could have lorded his cool over a naïve kid like me, and generous with good advice. It seemed as if he'd been there, done that already, and I was very happy he was around. As we walked out to the plane together I looked back at my family. No one said anything, they just watched me leave. Finally, I saw my brother, Tom, lean his head out and yell, "Good luck, Rob!!" I'll never forget it. He was thinking, *Good luck leaving this town and going away on your own.*

None of us could have imagined, dreamed, or even hallucinated then that fifteen years later I would confront a madman, the world's most wanted man, on the third floor of an ultrasecret compound in a country I'd yet to hear of, and that as a result people would fill the streets of D.C. and New York City to cheer.

Good luck, Rob, indeed. Good luck.

CHAPTER TWO

Tracy and I got off the plane in Chicago and boarded a bus filled with future sailors, all of whom had joined to be SEALs . . . except Tracy, who had joined to be a firefighter. He probably would have made the best SEAL on the damn bus.

Anyway, to hear the recruits talk, 99 percent of them were going to become SEALs. They'd read all of the books and thought they knew everything about being a SEAL, and they were loud as hell about it. Most of these guys could bench-press five hundred pounds, too. At least that's what they said. There wasn't a weight room in sight, so no one could prove them wrong. I heard more than one express absolute certainty he'd make it through the famously tough SEAL selection process. The worst part: I was buying it. I thought I'd prepared myself with my self-designed fitness program, but now here were these big city guys who knew so much more and were clearly better prepared.

I started to wonder, *Why did I even bother? I'm only from Butte, Montana. I'm not as good or prepared as these guys from Denver or Seattle or wherever. . . .*

At that age, it takes something special to realize this bravado is 100 percent BS. It's easy to follow the other sheep and just lie down and quit. Lie down and die. Die of shame and nothing more.

It turns out that this is *exactly* what the SEAL recruiters are watching for. They want the person who can recognize adversity, understand why his peers are folding, but have the will to say *"No.* I'm better than this; I'm not following the status quo. Nothing is scary, stress is a choice, I'm moving forward to see what is next."

It took me quite a while to realize this, though. The guys on the bus were scared, I was scared. Tracy was nervous, a curious nervousness, but he wasn't scared.

After rolling up to the check-in center at Naval Station Great Lakes, Illinois, we filed off while being screamed at by the Recruit Division Commanders (RDCs). Feel free to read that as "boot camp drill instructors." They were good, losing no opportunity to impress upon us what stinking maggots we were, but, to be honest, I'd seen *Full Metal Jacket* and other films about military training so many times I wasn't that scared of them. Don't get me wrong, I respected them and they were consummate professionals . . . it was just that Gunny Highway, Gunny Foley, or Gunny Hartman didn't show up.

Still . . . I was in a bus full of strangers watching people get yelled at by nasty guys in Dixie cup hats. I thought, *What a horrible decision I've made. I can't believe I did this.*

For a typical, small-town white guy like me, boot camp was like the bar in *Star Wars.* Everybody (except for me) talked funny. There were typical southern rednecks—the way they said "canteen" cracked me up. There were noticeable differences in accents from West Virginia, South Carolina, and Texas. We had a few guys from the Philippines, one of whom didn't speak *a word* of English, who spoke Tagalog or Filipino when among themselves. They may as well have been speaking Wookiee as far as I could tell. The two guys from Brooklyn were nearly as difficult to understand. We also had several black dudes from different parts of the country. The dude from Mississippi was probably the nicest guy in the division, and smooth—a total southern James Bond. And we had a couple guys from the inner city. Very cool guys, all joined up to get out of the neighborhood for a while. We all had one thing in common: *What the fuck did I just get myself into?*

The movies made me expect boot camp to consist of endless push-ups in the mud and running everywhere, unless you were crawling under barbed wire. But Navy boot camp isn't like that. We spent our days in the classroom learning Navy customs and courtesies, getting yelled at and cleaning up and folding—clothes, sheets, flags, anything that bends. Folding is huge in the Navy. Sailors live in tiny quarters so we needed to know how to keep our stuff tight and thin. It's amazing, the amount of folding we did. I still fold my towels the same way.

There was a cool week in which we were taught how to fight fires and what the different classes of fires are. Total Navy stuff, but I loved it. I was always big into Navy traditions. I still call people "Shipmate" . . . Love that word. I think I'm going to open a bar and call it "Shipmate's." I'll require all of the bouncers to end every sentence with that word. I can imagine them kicking a drunk out, "Get the hell out of Shipmate's . . . shipmate!"

But mostly we folded, and when we weren't learning how to fold, we were learning how to march. It turns out that it takes weeks to teach people how to walk. And walking was about the only exercise we got. They didn't let us work out at all. Here I'd spent six months getting in shape for the SEAL test, and now we were eating this unhealthy food and sitting around all day folding shit. "We're going to get fat," I'd tell anyone who'd listen. "We're going to get out of shape. We're not running. We're not doing anything. And everything we eat is covered in fucking gravy."

I was desperate to take the SEAL screening test before I turned into a 298-pound weakling. The tests happened on Tuesdays and Thursdays. I signed up for the first possible test. A bad mistake. It happened to be the day after we got all our immunizations. The Navy is famous for giving you a shit ton of shots. I woke up the next morning feeling sick as hell, bumps and bruises all over my body, my tongue twice its normal size and covered in felt. I forced myself out of my bunk and discovered I was barely strong enough to stand. I doubted I could do a single pull-up much less the eight you needed to pass.

Brushing my teeth that morning was a challenge. The test seemed somewhere north of impossible: Swim twenty lengths (five hundred yards), rest ten minutes; pump forty-two push-ups, rest two minutes; break off fifty sit-ups, rest two minutes; do those dreaded eight pull-ups, rest ten minutes; run 1.5 miles in eleven and a half minutes. In boots.

I dragged myself out to the Olympic-size indoor pool where a set of bleachers had been set up. A huge SEAL flag hung on a wall. The SEAL insignia is an eagle (representing our ability to fight from the air) perched on an anchor (representing our naval heritage) grasping Neptune's barbed trident in one talon (testifying to our ability to kick ass on the ocean) and a flintlock pistol (reminding people that we can also kick ass on land) in the other. It's one kick-ass eagle.

I stumbled up high into the bleachers and sat down facing the pool. A SEAL came out to look over the new lot. He was wearing blue trunks with the "SEAL Team Three" logo on them and nothing else. The only thing more obvious than my horrible decision to join the Navy was this man's eight-pack abs. He proceeded to walk the length of the bleachers, look us each in the eye, strut to the high dive, climb majestically, knock out a dive that Greg Louganis would have admired for more than one reason, and knife into the water like a thin blade. With almost unworldly powerful strokes he swam away, vaulted over the edge of the pool, and walked into the dressing room without a backward glance, as if he knew that not one of us deserved a second look.

I considered the five hundred bald recruit heads descending in rows before me. They turned as one to a second SEAL on the near side of the pool giving test instructions. I suddenly felt foolish. Every one of these five hundred wannabe heroes thought he could become a SEAL, along with every other guy who joins the Navy. What made me stand out?

The one non-lame move I made when I enlisted—and only because my Marine friend urged me to do it—was to insist that the recruiter put in writing that I'd get three attempts to pass the SEAL screening test. I was lucky I did.

Somehow I passed the swim. But as soon as I started doing the push-ups, which must be form perfect or they don't count, I knew I wouldn't be able to make the forty-two minimum. I was the failure I feared. I had nothing.

Except . . . I *did* have that signed guarantee of two more attempts.

By Thursday, whatever poison they'd shot into my veins the previous Monday had drained away, and I felt like a different man up in those poolside bleachers. I was once again the guy who'd spent six months preparing for this very moment. As it turned out, I was one of the few who *had* been. This would be my first glimpse of the truth that would be pounded into me in years to come: Preparation is everything.

We did the five-hundred-yard swim in heats. Of the five hundred recruits, I was one of only ten to pass.

We had a ten-minute break to change back into our uniforms, then went back out to do the push-ups. Two more fell away. All the survivors passed the sit-ups. The final leg of the test—each of the exercises for some reason is called an "evolution"—was the 1.5-mile run in boots. The minimum time was eleven and a half minutes. We lost four more.

Five hundred men who'd all convinced themselves they had what it took to become SEALs were now down to four. And this was just to qualify to attempt, and most likely fail, the twenty-eight-week SEAL tryout—Basic Underwater Demolition/SEAL, which makes the screening test look like slurping piña coladas while swinging on a shady hammock.

But I was elated. Now I knew I'd be going to BUD/S for sure. Just the thought of it excited me: I'd get to go to Coronado—a naval base that shares an island on San Diego Bay with what travel brochures call "a quaint, affluent resort city." So. Beaches, babes, beer—*and* I'd get to actually wear the green uniform of SEAL trainees.

* * *

AFTER I ENLISTED, I'D WATCHED all kinds of SEAL movies and read every book that I could find. I finally learned that SEAL does not refer to the aquatic mammal, but to Sea, Air, and Land. Clearly, someone wanted to reference the sleek and speedy animals, because they grabbed the "E" they needed from the second letter of "Sea." By rights, the correct acronym ought to be the SAL, but where's the fun in that?

SEAL teams evolved from units of Navy frogmen in World War II, who were specially trained in underwater survey and demolition. They were counted on to map approaches to beach landing sites and destroy obstacles in the path of an invading force. In the Korean War, these UDTs—Underwater Demolition Teams—were so stealthy and effective that their role expanded to include land combat operations aimed at destroying enemy railroad tunnels and bridges. As one of the UDT officers, Lt. Ted Fielding, famously explained, this expansion of duties came about because, "We were ready to do what nobody else could do, and what nobody else wanted to do."

It was for just that reason that in 1961, recognizing the changing nature of warfare, the Navy decided to turn the UDT forces into guerilla and counter-guerilla units, not limited to operating in the water and on beaches. That's where the SEa, Air, and Land came in. The first two SEAL teams were formed in 1962. Team One was stationed in Coronado and Team Two in Virginia Beach. SEALs have played a particularly dramatic role in every war and American military action since.

"Know your history, gents!" is a common phrase we use: Know from where you came. I recall being at a SEAL reunion in Virginia Beach some years ago and running into a frogman wearing a WWII veteran ball cap. He looked pretty good for being ninety-something. Trying to be smart, I asked him, "When did *you* go through Hell Week?"

"June 6, 1944," he said.

I replied, "There *was* no BUD/S in 1944," thinking I was smart.

"There was on Omaha Beach, son. Know your heritage."

Now I was going to be a part of it.

OR AT LEAST I WOULD be if I didn't screw up retaking the BUD/S test over and over. I'd noticed something the first time I took it: There were phones in the pool area, and with all the personnel concentrating on the test-takers, I could slip away and call home—a rare opportunity in boot camp. I also wanted to stay in as good shape as I could to prepare for Coronado, and folding and marching wasn't going to cut it. So retaking the test was also my best chance to work out.

Every Tuesday and Thursday I'd go down to the pool and go through it all again, get in my reps, and call home. It was a sweet deal, except that if I slipped up, had a bad day, and failed even one of the evolutions on the test, my trip to the beach at Coronado would be canceled.

I must have taken the test ten times, and, fortunately, my scores just kept improving.

One of my closest friends in boot camp was Matthew Parris. I met him the very first day in the makeshift barracks where we were divided into divisions of about seventy recruits each. Matthew and I were in the same division. I instantly looked up to him because he seemed to have his military bearing down. He was *so* Army that he had the Drill Sergeant "This We'll Defend" badge tattooed on his chest. Not surprising, since he'd been an Army Drill Sergeant who decided to start over from the bottom in the Navy because . . . you guessed it, he wanted to be a SEAL. When his enlistment in the Army was up, he walked into the Navy recruiting office dressed all in black with shined combat boots, trying to look tough, bandanna and all, and said to the recruiter: "Make me a SEAL." The recruiter regarded him with a steely-eyed squint. "Not looking like that," he said.

Matthew liked to brag, but he loved humor more, even when the joke was on him.

Matthew failed the BUD/S qualifying test the first time he took it, the day I passed. I was back out there taking the test as a workout the next week and this time we both passed. Despite the big talk, only about a half dozen guys in our division even took the test, and only the two of us passed it. We celebrated Matthew's success together and immediately became tight friends, going so far as to work out after lights went out and the Recruit Division Commanders were gone. We'd do pull-ups in the stalls in the head, sit-ups on the floor, and dips using two sinks. There were times where we'd see if we could sneak in a thousand push-ups over the course of a day.

When basic ended, we put our bald heads together and decided to choose the Aircrew Survival Equipmentman school in Millington, Tennessee, for our required post–boot camp training. You wouldn't know it from its fancy name, but the school taught those who attended how to rig parachutes, which involves sewing. A bona fide graduate of this training earns the right to be called a "stitch bitch" by his shipmates. Matthew and I didn't join the Navy to be stitch bitches. We joined to be SEALs. But we took the course because it was the shortest in duration. This would get us to Coronado the fastest and we didn't give a damn what we were called.

It turned out, anyway, that Aircrew Survival Equipmentman school was pretty cool. I had a new rack ("bed" to you non-swabbies), a bigger closet, and a pool close by that Matthew and I used every day.

And I really did learn to sew. An African-American Marine staff sergeant who was a mountain of a man taught me. Huge. I thought he quite possibly could be the toughest man on Earth. This school would be my first experience with the US Marine Corps, and this guy should have been on a poster. His cammie top had sleeves that were perfectly rolled to the middle of his huge biceps. To this day I have no idea how he fit into that. His pants were perfectly bloused into mirror-shined boots. "Eat barbed-wire and shit napalm" would have described him. His trap muscles were so big it almost looked like he had no neck and I am positive he was afraid of nothing. One time Matthew referred to him as "Sergeant," something that's acceptable in the Army. Not in the Marine Corps. It's *Staff* Sergeant. "Oh, my God, you're so fucked," one of our Marine classmates whispered when he heard that. Matthew was genuinely scared shitless as the Staff Sergeant clenched his mighty jaws, nostrils flaring, staring him down. He said nothing. He didn't need to. The man was a beast!

I'll never forget him teaching me how to wind a bobbin, something my grandma might have done.

On our first weekend pass, Matthew and I took a road trip to Memphis where we split a hotel room and proceeded to hit Beale Street. I remember coming to on a bench near a few restaurants, so drunk. We had been pounding shots. Matthew was sitting next to me with his head in his hands. A couple of waiters on break from a nearby restaurant were standing nearby, laughing about how shit-faced we were.

I heard one guy say to the other, ". . . and they're just *sitting* there."

Matthew took that as his cue to puke up a little in his mouth, hold it for a second, then spit it on his shoes.

Waiter No. 2: "Oh, *that* was nice."

We cleaned up Matthew's footwear, beat it back to Millington, and knocked out the school in just under three weeks. I invited Matthew to fly to Butte with me for a bit of leave and then we could drive my truck to Coronado. I had a great experience on the flight home: For the first time someone recognized my service. A gentleman, probably a vet, noticed that Matthew and I were in the Navy. He bought us each two beers. I thought that was very cool for two reasons: 1) I was recognized as a sailor (even though I hadn't done anything yet); and 2) beer is seven dollars on a plane.

Matthew met my family and a bunch of my friends and managed to keep his shoes dry. It was such a pleasure to be away from the Navy for a week. I didn't realize how homesick I was and how much I loved Butte. I missed getting together with my friends. I missed my sister and basketball. I missed Club 13, where you didn't need an ID to drink. I missed "The Animal House," a huge green house that my brother and a bunch of friends rented and turned into a perpetual party. I missed the bar next door called the Chaparral where we'd go to sing karaoke. I missed Wop Chops from The Freeway; regular chops at John's Pork Chops; a Welsh meat pie covered in gravy that was the specialty of Joe's Pasty Shop; and a garbage omelet served at the M&M, an old miner's bar/diner that hadn't locked its doors in more than a hundred years—seriously. I was still just a child myself, so leaving again was hard. I had *no* idea what I was getting into, and was scared shitless of BUD/S. But Matthew and I got in my truck and drove. On the way out of town we made one last stop, my sister Kris's apartment. I wanted to say goodbye to her and my nephew, Kolton. He was only two so he didn't know what was going on. I remember picking him up and hugging him and saying goodbye with tears in my eyes. I didn't know that the hardest goodbyes would come years later. I can't pick up Kolton *now*, either. He's bigger than I am.

FAREWELLS IN OUR REARVIEW MIRROR, we headed south on I-15 through Salt Lake City and didn't stop until we hit Las Vegas. We stayed in the Circus Circus hotel, but I wasn't able to do anything fun; I was still only twenty. Yes, I'd managed to get served alcohol prior to this, but that had been on airplanes and in Butte. In a pinch, I'd always used my brother, Tom's, ID. It was expired, and we look nothing alike. So I wisely decided not to try such weak shit in a place like Circus Circus. I didn't want to wake up with a horse's head in my bed.

We got McDonald's for breakfast and hit the road early. I'd been reading *Rogue Warrior* by Richard Marcinko the entire time when it wasn't my turn to drive. Marcinko was the SEAL who'd been assigned in 1979 to create an elite special operations force specifically designed to respond to terrorism and provide a way to use surgical military force when the threats come not from a foreign government, but from small, mobile networks of terrorists who can blend almost seamlessly into civilian populations. The lack of that capability had become painfully apparent earlier that year during the Iranian hostage crisis, when more than sixty Americans were held hostage for 444 days in Tehran by supporters of the Islamist revolution, only to be released at the whim of Iran's leader. An early attempt to send US commandos to free the hostages ended in disaster. The mission had been poorly conceived, prepared, and executed, and it had to be aborted due to helicopter failures before the commandos even reached their target. On retreat, one of the still operational choppers crashed into a transport plane loaded with jet fuel, igniting a huge explosion that killed eight servicemen.

Marcinko, who'd won a trunkful of medals for his valor and success in Vietnam combat actions, conceived of an elite strike force that would be like a regular SEAL team on steroids: cohesive, highly mobile, superbly equipped, and obsessively prepared. It would also be highly secret. At the time, the only two SEAL teams were One and Two, so Marcinko and the other planners settled on the name SEAL Team ██ to confuse the Soviets and make them wonder where Teams Three, Four, and Five were.

Marcinko fulfilled his orders, and then some. To be maximally effective, the new force would have to stomp all over those customs and courtesies the Navy was so fond of. SEAL Team ██ would be a brotherhood of equals called "operators," each fully involved and fully informed, and having an equal voice in the design and execution of missions, as well as maximum latitude in behavior and comportment. In practice, this created a cadre of fighters who looked more like the blue-faced warriors in *Braveheart* than anyone's idea of regular Navy. I read a great anecdote in a *New York Times* story that really captured it: A Team ▓ officer was showing an admiral around during a hostage rescue simulation on a cruise ship. After hours, he took the admiral down to one of the bars where the operators were hanging out. The officer told the *Times*, "When we opened the door, it reminded me of *Pirates of the Caribbean*." It wasn't an after-action analysis, it was a riot. The rowdy behavior, long hair, bushy beards, earrings, and regulation-be-damned uniforms hit the admiral like the shock wave from a concussion grenade. He kept saying, "These guys are in *my* Navy?"

After Marcinko retired in 1989, he became a private consultant. The next year he was charged with government contract fraud, convicted, and sent to prison for fifteen months. He claimed his prosecution was bogus, payback for the embarrassment he'd caused security officials with his ▓▓▓▓ activities. He'd have the last laugh, though: He sold a ton of books and earned big fees as a motivational speaker.

I can't judge the things Marcinko did that got him sent to prison—I wasn't around—but I think his heart and mind were both in the right place. At the end of the day his primary focus was his mission and his men.

MATTHEW AND I FINALLY ARRIVED in Coronado at dusk and went straight to the beach. We checked into a shady motel—or the shadiest one we could find in this ritzy resort area—and decided to wait until the next day to check into BUD/S. Since we were staying on the beach, Matthew and I decided to get our masks and go for our first swim in the Pacific. We'd been out there for about an hour when we noticed, off on the horizon, a bunch of inflatable boats with green "chem-lights" attached to the sides. There must have been about seven of them. They were rowing to the north and it looked as though they were attempting to row around the entire island. It was Thursday at sunset.

The boats were full of men from BUD/S Class 207. There are four classes a year, numbered consecutively from Class 1 a half century earlier. This 207th group to go through the training was completing the last evolution of their last night of Hell Week. It's called "Around the World," a complete circumnavigation of Coronado Island in these inflatable rowboats. The men had been awake since Sunday but would be done soon. Matthew and I looked at this and were in awe. Holy shit. This is real, there they are.

We checked in the next day to BUD/S. Class 208.

CHAPTER THREE

M atthew and I might have been ready for BUD/S, or at least thought we were, but BUD/S wasn't ready for us. Class 205 hadn't quite graduated yet, so we were sent to the other side of the base to live in the barracks that housed the guys who had quit BUD/S or been kicked out. They called it "X Division." These guys were miserable. Their dream of becoming Navy SEALs had cratered. Now, instead of wearing the green uniforms of SEAL trainees, these guys wore dungarees and boondockers and spent the day picking up trash and swabbing the decks. They lived in limbo, not knowing where their next duty station would be. Most likely they'd end up assigned to the fleet where they'd spend the next four years doing more trash picking and deck swabbing. It was a bleak prospect, and their attitude sucked accordingly. But they were still total know-it-alls.

You only had to be around them for a few minutes before you learned that their sorry position was everyone's fault but theirs. The training was designed to make you fail, the instructors were vindictive sociopaths, I'd be better off to just quit now before the assholes beat me down and made me embarrass myself. I remember seeing groups of eighteen-year-old dudes crowding around these quitters, hanging on every word. Despite having failed to master the challenge of Phase One, they maintained their pose as experts, expounding on everything: from where to stand in formation to where to go on the weekends. The young dudes treated it like gospel. Living with those folks was a total downer and I'm positive that more than one good guy has quit just from being exposed to the negativity of X Division. They even had T-shirts made, sort of a tongue-in-cheek shot at BUD/S. Instead of the eagle, anchor, pistol, and trident on the SEAL insignia, the shirts showed a turkey, bell, and mop. They read, "BUD/S X Division. The only easy day was every day. Ya-Hoo." At least someone kept his sense of humor.

Lucky for Matthew and me, we were reassigned after a few days to a BUD/S barracks, building 602, right in the heart of the BUD/S compound. From the air, Coronado Island looks like a giant sperm cell—a long, curving tail attached to a teardrop-shaped head. The SEAL base is like a big dash mark where the tail meets the head, projecting into the bay toward San Diego. Building 602 sits in the middle of the dash, sandwiched between SEAL Team One on one side and SEAL Teams Three and Five on the other.

But even in our new digs, Matthew and I were still in limbo. SEAL training consists of three phases. The first, which is the one in which most trainees quit or wash out, is the physical training part that ends a few weeks after the infamous Hell Week. Phase Two is diving and Phase Three is land warfare and demolition.

Before actual training begins, all newcomers tread water in a holding pattern called PTRR, which stands for physical training rehabilitation and remediation. This is also where trainees go if they get "rolled back" from one of the three phases—giving them a chance to recover from injuries or just maintain physical shape while they wait to join the next class once that class reaches the point where the student was rolled. Guys get rolled for all types of reasons: getting hurt, failing a test too many times, general sub-par performance. It's a way to keep people around while they recover from injury (rehabilitation) or get better at whichever skill they lack (remediation). There's no limit on how often a guy can get rolled; it's all about how much the instructors like you.

For new guys like us who hadn't yet been assigned to a class—

or "classed-up"—there were a few weeks of preliminary training to get us ready physically and mentally for the grueling trial of Phase One. The training was also a chance for instructors to identify guys who never should have gotten into SEAL training to begin with, and focus the kind of highly unpleasant attention on them that would ensure they didn't make it further.

I remember the first time I ever saw a BUD/S instructor go off on a student. I had heard RDCs yell at boot camp and thought that was bad. This was next-level stuff. It was one of the Chief Petty Officer instructors, they were gods to me, and he found a guy lazily running his mouth about BUD/S. He was talking loudly about how he wasn't worried about the BUD/S hype, saying he wasn't scared at all. He'd been through Army boot camp and was even a Drill Sergeant himself. He knew what to expect and had already been through the worst the military could dish out.

Unfortunately, the guy happened to be Matthew. He found out right then that his prior military experience didn't matter here. Going nose to nose, this guy with a picture-perfect black mustache—like something out of the 1890s: the style preferred by the frogmen of the UDT (Underwater Demolition Team), the SEAL predecessor—laid into Matthew to the point where it scared the shit out of the entire class. I don't remember what the Chief said, but imagine the instructor as a nine-hundred-pound grizzly and Matthew as the dude who just kicked the bear's cubs. I will never forget Matthew repeating, "Yes, Chief, yes, Chief, no, Chief . . ." He may have peed his pants. I'm pretty sure I did.

We soon discovered that this chewing out was more the rule than the exception. The instructors were loud and mean as hell day in and day out. I quickly realized that the absolute *worst* thing a trainee could do was make an excuse. That reality might seem glaringly obvious, but there are some complete boneheads out there who have a reason for everything. They get beat the worst and they *never* learn. Lucky for me, I was a fast learner. As long as I accepted that I was always wrong and they were always right, it

wasn't that bad. Whenever an instructor asked why I did something he obviously didn't like, I responded with, "Because I am
an idiot!" Deflate the situation, take your lumps, get on with life.

When we weren't eating crow served up by the instructor,
we were doing conditioning runs and spending hours in the
pool swimming. They were saving the real beatdowns for Phase
One, week one, day one. But we didn't know that yet. BUD/S
instructors like to surprise the students. At the conclusion of the
PTRR training cycle, we only had to successfully complete the
initial test we'd passed at boot camp: five-hundred-yard swim,
no fins, sidestroke or breaststroke, in twelve and a half minutes;
eight pull-ups, dead hang; forty-two push-ups, perfect form; fifty
sit-ups, perfect form; 1.5-mile run in eleven and a half minutes
in boots. You would think that everyone would be ready for this
by now. Some guys failed. Matthew was one of them.

This was not good for him. I remember being right there as
he struggled on the pull-ups. They're not as easy as they look
when you do them properly, which means extending arms full
out and hanging from the pole before pulling back up, and guys
do lose some strength after the swim. Still, Matthew had managed
six in boot camp, and they should have been a cakewalk after a
few weeks here. The pressure of everyone watching is surprisingly intense, but that usually adds adrenaline, which boosts
the number. Bottom line: Matthew was starting to lose belief
that he had what it takes, and in BUD/S nothing is more fatal.

Matthew and the other guys who failed had to go before a
"review board." Most were booted into X Division and a life of
mopping latrines. These were the underachievers who'd been
targeted the entire time for poor performance.

The board was held in a conference room right by the
grinder—the concrete-asphalt courtyard where we happened
to be working out at the time. Sitting below the office windows
of the Commanding Officers, the grinder is a place designed to
make even the slightest slip or moment of less-than-full effort
painfully visible. But I couldn't help being distracted, glancing

nervously at the door, waiting for a dejected, rejected Matthew to come slumping out. But that's not what happened. He shot from the door in a full run and slotted right into formation.

I found out later that when it had been Matthew's turn to stand, the hearing officer said, "Can you hear the workout going on outside the door?" Matthew said, "Yes, sir," and the hearing officer replied, "Go join your class."

That was a Friday. We had a graduation of sorts from PTRR, trading our standard five-point navy caps for the BUD/S helmets we'd wear throughout training, or as long as we survived. The weekend was spent chilling out and getting our helmets painted and stenciled with our name. Each training phase requires a new paint job. Green for the first, then blue for Phase Two, and finally red. Each time we painted a new color over the old, we knew we'd achieved a milestone. I'd reached my first: I was painting my helmet green. It was going to be a great week.

Or so I thought. It wasn't that I didn't know Phase One would be tougher than PTRR. I just figured it couldn't be too much worse. I figured wrong.

BEFORE DAWN MONDAY MORNING WE mustered outside of building 602 for a head count. Each class has an officer in charge, OIC in the ubiquitous military shorthand, who is a trainee just like the rest of us. Our OIC was Lt. Mike, who in addition to facing all the hurdles we faced—officers get no special treatment; in fact, sometimes the enlisted instructors like to single them out—had to begin his BUD/S career being responsible for about two hundred teenagers with practically no military experience. Poor Lt. Mike: It must have been frustrating the way we showed up. Guys were late, missing, or in the wrong crews. Head counts were off. We could all see the frustration in his face. Not only were we about to get hammered in our first PT (physical training), we couldn't even get roll call right. If we failed to get it together, we'd get a beatdown. Lt. Mike would get crushed.

I remember early on, after I'd seen what a tough position officer-trainees are in, I spoke to an ensign whose father was an admiral. I said, "Well, this has got to be tough, being an officer, because not only are you afraid of BUD/S but you have to lead everybody." He said, "Afraid of BUD/S? Why would I be afraid? There's no point in being afraid. Let that go." I thought, *Wow, that's a hell of an attitude.* It was something of a revelation to me, the first inkling I had that I needed to get over the fear, because fear is self-induced. Of course, it would take a long time for that revelation to sink in fully. In the meantime, I had to get through BUD/S.

We eventually got our roll call right, split into seven-man boat crews, and made our way, in formation, to the grinder. Even after the chaotic muster we were early—it was still pitch dark out—but the instructors were ready for us. The grinder floor is painted with sets of fins. Each student is supposed to stand on a set and the PT begins. We didn't even get to our fins, though, before we were being hit with torrents of cold water. Instructors were everywhere, holding hoses spewing frigid streams of liquid as we were supposed to be counting off. There was no hiding. They made sure that, somehow, the head count was wrong. They ordered everyone to "hit the surf." We all sprinted out of the compound and ran the quarter mile to the beach, lunging into the waves. Southern California has palm trees and sunshine, but even in June, the Pacific water temperature hovers around 60 degrees. I remember thinking, *I'm from Montana, there's no way in hell they can get me cold.* I really needed to get comfortable with being wrong.

We got back up to the grinder wet and shivering and stood on our fin marks. Like a rampaging street gang, the instructors split up and searched for the weak links in our herd, in this case guys who'd cheated and hadn't gotten completely wet. They found a few unfortunates with dry patches and escorted them back out to the beach for "special attention." Another quarter-mile run and another cold plunge, this time featuring total submersion. Still dripping and shivering properly this time, they were ordered to make a "sugar cookie," which meant rolling on the beach until every square inch of their bodies was covered with the grit of crushed volcanic rock and shell that makes up California beach sand, turning them into human sandpaper and making the mandated "bear crawls" and "wind sprints" up and down the sand dunes all the more painful.

Not that it was much easier for the rest of us on the grinder. An instructor who appeared to be on speed led us through hundreds of push-ups of endless variety: military, diamond, dive-bombers; followed by an equally varied array of painful ab exercises. That SEAL I saw at the pool in basic training? Now I knew where his eight-pack came from.

As we sweated and sucked air, instructors swarmed us, screaming nonstop. If a guy failed mid push-up, it was like wolves on prey. Three or four would bend over, screaming in the guy's face. It was total humiliation. I even saw young men cry out of fear. After a few minutes of being told what a piece of human shit he was, the weak link was ordered to hit the slushy. That is a rubber raft full of ice water. A barrier over the top of the water in the middle of the raft ensures that the student being punished goes in, headfirst, all the way. Needless to say, it sucked.

And we hadn't even eaten breakfast yet.

The beatdown went on for an hour. It was a total shock. Beatdowns didn't mean instructors were punching you in the face, but they might as well have been. When PT ended, an instructor yelled, "Hit the surf, get to chow, be back ready to run at seven fifteen!" So after another plunge in the frigid Pacific, it was run a mile to the galley, jostle among two hundred other guys for food, run a mile back, and be ready for a six-mile conditioning run in a little over an hour.

Have a wonderful 1-1 day.

We started our trek to chow wet and sandy, moving at a kind of trot we called the "BUD/S shuffle." This was the minimum speed at which we were permitted to go anywhere. God help the man who is caught walking. I was beat, shaken to the core, and shocked to see the sun just rising over San Diego. Keeping this up until past sunset seemed a complete impossibility.

Even as I reflected on impending doom, I knew I was thrilled to be there. I had no certainty I was going to graduate—if I were being honest, it seemed a long shot. I told myself it didn't matter. I was living my dream to even attempt this.

I would never quit. I was certain of that. Everyone I knew back home told me I couldn't do it. *There's no way; it's too hard and you're not a tough guy, you're too skinny, too slow, and too weak. Those guys will eat you alive.* The only person who really believed in me was my dad. Even my mom and siblings talked behind my back about how I'd never make it. Proving them wrong was my motivation. That, and something BUD/S did that was both diabolical and brilliant. When you quit, you have to put your helmet in "the quitter line." Your helmet has your class number and last name on it. There was no way in hell I was going to put my father's name in a line of quitters: He was the only one who believed in me.

BUT EVEN IF I DIDN'T quit, failure and injury loomed as a constant threat. I had so far to go, twenty-six weeks, and I knew that 80 percent of those shuffling along beside me wouldn't make it. I'd never wanted anything more in my life than *not* to be one of those guys.

Looking back after all these years, chow time that day is a blur, just like all of the other times we ate during training. The whole process was as mechanical as a fighter jet refueling in midair. I can't remember how anything tasted, but I do remember this: There was no food shortage.

I've seen a lot of movies about SEAL training, many filled with silly fantasies. The most ridiculous scenes occur in a movie called *G.I. Jane* in which SEAL trainees have to eat out of trash cans, or are forced to skip meals. The reality is quite the opposite. For me, it was all you can eat, and quite a selection: everything from a huge salad bar to appetizers to four entrees, coffee, soda, whatever we desired. The last thing the instructors wanted was for guys to go down from lack of calories. The problem was finding a good balance. Yes, we were starving at lunch after three tough evolutions, but if we stuffed ourselves and had a six-mile conditioning run right after, the result was predictable. The runs were bad enough without puking. I remember watching guys just pee down their own legs in mid-stride. You sure as hell can't ask to go to the little boys' room, and you'll get drilled for whipping it out, but you can pee your pants if you want. So you definitely didn't want to be peeing and puking at the same time. It's just bad for morale.

The rest of Day 1-1 is veiled in a haze of exhaustion and emotional shock. I'm sure we did the BUD/S shuffle back to the grinder and went right into another kick-in-the-nuts evolution. I'm sure that was followed by another and another, then a shuffle back to the galley for mini sandwiches. The first week was designed to scare us and show us what we'd be doing for the next twenty-six weeks. The only thing I remember clearly is meeting our class proctor the evening before Day 1-1. I'm not sure if it was part of the job description for a class proctor, but this guy took it on himself to be our protector, going to creative lengths to get our heads right and give us the best chance of surviving BUD/S. His name was Instructor A, on the surface a textbook image of a chiseled Navy SEAL. He had strong features and a square jawline. His blue UDT/SEAL instructor shirt looked like it was painted on. "Extra-medium," he called it.

We were all seated at desks as though we were in high school, dead silent. Most of us were nervous. He walked slowly down the aisle to the front of the class, eyeballing us each individually along the way. Then he turned to face us, scanning the classroom from side to side. The room sank into an eerie silence made of equal parts fear and anticipation.

Finally, he spoke in the rich and resonant voice of someone they hire to do voice-overs in historical documentaries.

"Lookin' good today, gents!" he said, pausing to make sure we'd all taken the bait. "Not you, me!"

Nobody laughed. We were way too afraid to laugh.

He then said, "Never mind my perfect physique, I'm not here to intimidate. I'm here to motivate!"

Again, we didn't know what was going on. We all recognized the humor but didn't expect it. All the other instructors were the meanest guys on the planet.

After more time staring over the class without ever once breaking a smile, Instructor A said, "I know what you're thinking: I look a little tired. That's because I am. I was up all night because I had to get my wife out of jail. She was arrested yesterday for shoplifting!"

What the hell?

Then he said, "We were leaving the mall together, she had her arm around me . . . security thought she was trying to steal an anatomy chart!"

This was the kind of guy he was, all the more impressive for the contrast with every other part of the BUD/S experience. He believed in something that I would come to believe throughout my entire career. Morale is the key to everything. There is nothing wrong with keeping people happy. Granted, this environment was an odd place for him to do it: The instructors should have been trying to make us quit—for the simple reason that those who refused to quit against all reasonable odds were the only ones who could do what SEALs needed to do.

I guess Instructor A thought, as our proctor, that there was enough hate to go around. I'd be willing to bet that there were several guys who wouldn't have made it through the entire program without that little gust of support coming from Instructor A. He meant what he said about being a motivator.

"I'm never going to ask you to do anything impossible," he told us. "But I will make you do something very hard. Followed by something very hard, followed by something very hard, day after day after day, for eight straight months. And that sounds like a lot, to get from now to eight months from now, but don't think about it that way. That's not the way you achieve a long-term goal. Get up in the morning, make your bed, brush your teeth, little victories. Get to five o'clock PT, finish that, from PT get to breakfast. From breakfast try to make it to lunch, from lunch make it to dinner. After dinner, get back to your room into that bed that you made and do the same thing all over again. All you need to do to get from now to eight months from now and graduate is not do one thing: No matter what, never quit and you'll be just fine."

That thought was what kept me going many times during Phase One, and especially when I first confronted the BUD/S obstacle course, one of the highest and scariest in the world, requiring a combination of endurance, upper-body strength, and steel-sphinctered fearlessness. Instructor N, a complete freak of nature physically, showed us how it went down. He was what an instructor should be: lean, fast, strong, and pissed off. He would flawlessly demonstrate each obstacle only once, and then it was our turn.

If you've ever seen those *American Ninja Warrior* competitions on television, you'll be able to picture the course—without the padding and the primary colors. A lot of climbing, jumping, balancing, and leaping over huge logs. One of the most daunting obstacles involved a fifty-foot-high cargo net secured between two telephone poles. You climbed up one side, crossed over, and climbed your ass down. The first time I crossed over the top, it felt like the wind was going to blow me over and I had to will myself to lift one leg up and over. Eventually I got so good at it, as did every BUD/S student, that I'd cross with my chest, flip both legs over at once, then climb down using only my hands and arms.

But achieving that level of ease took *months*.

Actually, the scariest obstacle was the "slide for life." The first time I saw Instructor N demonstrate it, my brain yelped, *Oh, no!* This is an obstacle that is four stories high. I know that because that's exactly what it is: A four-story building with no walls, only floors and beams in the corners. The task is very simple: Climb from the sand up to the first floor. Then climb to the second, then the third and fourth. There are several different ways to climb up but the easiest is to stand on the edge facing outward, reach up to the next level so that your hands actually go up to full extension, and behind your head, grab hold of the floor of the next level. Then, still facing out, you pull both legs up in a reverse-somersault. If you do it right, you'll find yourself on your belly on the next level with your head just peeking over the edge. Once you do that all the way to the top, there's a very thick rope connected to a pole on the back of the fourth story. From there, the rope goes at a forty-five-degree angle off the front edge all the way to the ground about forty-five meters away. The student's job is to use the rope to get down, knowing there was nothing but the hard ground below him.

The first few times we did it, we'd sit on the edge of the building, grab the rope, wrap our legs around it, and start to shuffle down. We quickly learned—and by quickly I mean after a few weeks—that there was a better way. Put your body on top of the rope with most of it against your chest, head facing down; bend one knee out and wrap the foot from that leg back over the rope for more stability, leaving the other leg straight out for balance; then, keeping your chest centered on the rope, pull yourself down, hand over hand, using your arms.

The discovery of that technique came too late for Matthew. I didn't see what happened, but I heard it. It was the very first time we attempted the slide. He was a few places behind me when, somewhere on the rope, he fell off and did his best impersonation of a sand dart, flying headfirst. The sound was sickening, a gasping shout then a heavy thud. I was only several meters ahead of him so I briefly looked back, not knowing it was Matthew. I couldn't see much; a group of instructors and medical staff had closed in. *Someone just got proper-fucked,* I thought.

He must have been able to angle his head up at the last minute, because he messed his shoulder up really bad but didn't break his neck. Either way, his dream of being a SEAL plummeted to earth along with the rest of him. He was medically dropped from training that day. Over the course of my seventeen-year career, I saw him only a handful of times after that. Our time as stitch bitches paid an unanticipated dividend. He became a rigger in Naval Special Warfare—the first rigger on the Navy Parachute Team—and quite the skydiver himself. He was actually the first Navy rigger to make the Navy jump team, the "Leap Frogs." I was proud of him.

Most likely, it was a matter of chance that Matthew went down that day and I didn't. A little gust of wind, the rope quivering at exactly the wrong time. Whatever, my good fortune gave me time to learn. I eventually got to the point that I actually enjoyed doing the obstacles. I could run through them all in just over six minutes, which isn't bad, but more than half a minute short of the record, which at that time was held by a SEAL named Neil Roberts. He was just a name to me then, someone who could do something amazing, but he would have an important role in my future.

OF COURSE IN BUD/S THERE *is* no future, except for the next intimidating evolution, the next beatdown. The next time they throw you in the pool to drown.

No joke. This is something that forced a lot of people out. They called it "drown-proofing," a skill we practiced most days for the first few weeks. By practiced, I mean "tried not to die." They tied our hands behind our backs and our feet together and then tossed us in the pool. We exhaled to sink to the bottom, then kicked off the bottom to break the surface and get another breath. Then exhale and back down. They call that bobbing. You do that for ten minutes at a time. After that you have to float for five minutes without touching the bottom at all. It may surprise you to learn that it's really hard to float tied up. After that, you swim—and by swim I mean wriggle like a worm—to the edge of the pool and back without touching the bottom. Then you do five more minutes of bobbing. The big finale is, they put a mask down at the bottom of the pool and you need to go down and get it with your teeth and show it to them. It's a lot of time to be tied up in water over your head, and time moves extremely slowly when you think you might drown at any second.

But even more than "drown-proofing," what really stands out in memory is the four-mile timed runs. In the beginning, the time to beat was thirty-two minutes. It had dropped to twenty-eight by the end of training. For some reason, running always came naturally to me. At least, it came naturally when I was twenty and weighed about 180. When I eventually bulked up to 230, running was no longer my thing. Being able to carry my huge teammates was. Anyway, at BUD/S I was always near the front for the timed runs and the conditioning runs. I was never in the "Goon Squad," which was the group that couldn't keep up. They always got "extra attention" both during and after the runs: wind-sprints, bear-crawls up and down the dunes. They got their asses handed to them all the time. I never envied them, but I didn't feel too bad for them, either. Running is not technique. It's all heart, "put-out," . . . and breathing.

Anyway, one day just before one of our four-mile timed runs, I announced to the class, "You know, I think I'm gonna win this today."

My friend Dave, who was often the class motivator, said, "O'Neill, if you win this, you can have a weekend out on me!"

The instructors came out with the vehicles and we waited in a fat line. One truck drove down two miles and stopped. That was the turnaround point. We would run by and yell out our names to be marked off. Don't want any cheaters! At the signal I took off. I ran as fast as I could, figuring that if I built up enough of a lead at the turnaround, no one would try to catch me. I got to the truck at about eleven minutes, an insane five minutes ahead of pace.

As I started back, I saw the rest of the class for the first time. Leading the pack were the two fastest guys in the class: Mark and Jimmy. The turnaround was about two hundred meters behind me before we crossed paths, and that was when I realized, "Holy crap, I can actually win this thing!" I ran for another minute or two before passing the bulk of the class. I remember seeing Dave in the front of that pack and he was yelling, "Yeah, O'Neill, go!" He later told me that he loved seeing this big dude in a white T-shirt with a bright pink face, hauling ass toward the class.

I finished first in just over twenty-four minutes, which is really good for wearing boots and pants and running in the sand. I think it also helped that I grew up five thousand feet above sea level and wasn't quite used to the fullness of the oxygen in California. I won most of the runs for the next few months before some others began to pass me by. To give you an idea of how fast we were, at the very end of BUD/S we ran a 5K. It was the first time any of us had run on pavement in running shoes in eight months. We were used to running in boots in the sand. I ran it in 15:15. That's damn near All-State speed. And I finished third.

I miss being twenty years old.

A comical side note: I prepped for that first race I won by smoking a cigarette. Smoking is nasty and no one should do it, much less if you're about to compete in a four-mile run. But it was a way for me to relieve stress during BUD/S. Drinking wasn't an option most nights. So we had these Singaporean exchange students from the Singapore military, there to observe our training methods: Tan, Shory, Oh, and Tan. No kidding. They'd sneak out behind the infirmary and burn smokes all the time and I decided to bum one right before the run. Most in the class saw me do it and I gained a reputation for "hiding behind medical and smoking with the Singaporeans." It was true, too, but it didn't matter to me. BUD/S was hell and we all did what we needed to do to get by.

*   *   *

ONE OF THE MOST IMPORTANT stress relievers was humor. I realized something at an early stage in my SEAL career: SEALs are funny. I first discovered the strategic use of humor during one of the most comical times in training—well, comical for the instructors anyway; terrifying for the students. Room inspections.

Room inspections are legendary at BUD/S. They are conducted every Monday and just suck. A lot of students stay in their barracks all weekend during the first few weeks of training and do nothing but clean. They strip the wax from the deck, then re-wax it. Then they buff it and wax it and buff it. They don't realize that there is no way in hell that they're going to pass, no matter what they do. *Nobody* passes the first inspection.

The best advice I can give anyone aspiring to be a SEAL is this: Go out and have fun on the first three weekends. Sweep the floor, make your bed, and organize your locker. But have beer on Saturday, recoup on Sunday, and enjoy yourself. Don't waste your first few weekends in your room on a fool's errand. There are girls in San Diego, for God's sake. Go find a few. You will not pass!

And for officer trainees: You may not pass a room inspection the entire time you're there! Go out and compare academy ring sizes or study vocabulary or improve your stamp collection. Do whatever officers do. You're not passing, either.

My roommates, Matt, John, and Mark, stayed in the room all weekend and cleaned the shit out of it. I decided that my time would be better spent at the mall watching movies and eating trash food. I lived for getting in my truck and turning right on the strand to the Carl's Jr. in Imperial Beach. I'd order these huge burgers with barbecue sauce and onion rings on them. That's one nice thing about BUD/S: You can eat anything you want, it's not going to matter. You're going to lose weight.

But my roommates were pretty pissed at me when I showed up on Sunday and hadn't done anything. I told them that it was a waste of time but they didn't believe me. We cleaned the remainder of the day and went to sleep. The next day, we had 0500

PT, as usual, and then we ran to the galley. The inspection was at 0730, so we had time to get back and put on our "Inspection Uniform." This consisted of boots that were spit-shined so aggressively you needed sunglasses to look at them and "greens" pressed and starched so stiff you could snap them in two.

At 0730 precisely, we stood at attention in front of our open lockers, our UDT vests (which we hadn't even used yet) laid out on our bunks. In a perfect world, the instructors would come in, we'd announce, "Room so and so ready for inspection!" and they'd see their reflections in our immaculate floor and notice that all horizontal surfaces were dust free and that our beds were perfectly made with hospital corners. They'd then inspect our lockers while noticing that everything was in alphabetical order and that all of our uniforms were in line. Then they'd see our vests, check the CO_2 cartridges and actuator, and detect no corrosion. They'd tell us that we were model students in the best BUD/S class ever and that we were free to change out for the next evolution.

Nope.

Our room was on the top floor, the third, and just off the stairs. The instructors started on the first floor so we could hear the mayhem going on below. They were going room-to-room crushing people. I could hear students running to the surf zone, I could hear lines of guys doing eight-counts, I could hear the sheer evil coming out of many, many instructors. I think they brought in extra instructors from other phases of training just so they could assist in the fun. SEALs get bored.

Here is how our first room inspection went down: Nine instructors came in like a fucking hurricane. Our senior guy, Matt, was trying to pipe up with, "Room so and so ready for inspection!" He got out, "Room . . ."

All we heard was, "DROP!"

We were knocking out push-ups before the inspection even started. The line of instructors came rolling in. One had a jar full of sand he threw at the ceiling, then started yelling at us in disbelief. "How in the hell did you get *sand* on the ceiling?!" What goes up must come down . . . so sand covered our immaculate floor. We did more push-ups for that. Some sand fell on the bed and we did push-ups for that. They spilled salt water on our UDTs and told us that they would definitely be rusted. We were beat for *future* rust. They stepped on our boots and told us they were scuffed. We were ordered to hit the surf in our inspection uniforms. These shiny-ass boots would never sparkle again.

I actually think back to these times, these inspections, as my favorite evolutions. Even though I was terrified of the instructors, it sort of humanized them. It was all a game and I could tell. These guys must have laughed their asses off afterward in the office. They were messing around, probably trying to one-up each other. I would even venture to say that they bet money on who could make someone cry first. But all the while, the students' fear was real. They were facing potential dismissal from the program for screwing up. At least, that's what they believed and it was enough to make them take the instructors' upset seriously.

But this sense of humor that I saw in the instructors stood out to me and I had an idea. We'd tried to be perfect the first three weeks and all we'd gotten was a larger dry-cleaning bill. We'd never reach perfection. But there was a way to pass, or so I thought. We didn't need to impress the instructors, we needed to distract them.

Instead of wasting our weekend cleaning, we wasted it shopping. We purchased two huge platters and filled one with cans of Copenhagen and the other with PowerBars and cookies. We hung pictures of our girls (and girls we only dreamed of) in our lockers and had music playing on the stereo. That was a big "no-no," but what the hell? What were they going to do? Beat us?

We loaded "horizontal surfaces" with candy bars. We laid out porn mags and gun mags, opened to just the right pages.

With Tupac blaring, we waited for the commotion to hit us. They were close, we could hear them working their way through the building; the guys getting crushed, the screams outside. Holy crap, this might have been a bad idea. We could get dropped for insubordination. Too late now.

The pack entered. The first instructor in line stopped dead in his tracks, hearing the music. Another one froze behind him. Not a word was spoken. The lead instructor looked at the four of us and asked, "What in the Good Christ are you thinking?"

We were scared to death. Then he said, "That is entirely too *little* volume for TUPAC!" He walked over to the stereo and cranked it! He then walked over to Mark, who is about 5'5", and looked down at him. This was the point where we usually started getting the shit beat out of us. With Tupac blaring, he eyeballed Mark but instead of yelling, "Drop!" he casually said, "Dance."

Instantly, Mark started throwing down. He was doing the robot, he was twerking, he was going off the chain. The other three of us stood at attention, not believing what was happening, and too shocked to laugh. I started thinking, *Holy shit, it's working!*

The remainder of the instructors came in and actually slipped out of character. They were laughing at Mark, staring at us, and then noticing all of the "bait" we'd placed. It was a huge violation, but they didn't care. They strutted around the room, grabbing Gatorades or sodas and munching on candy and PowerBars, picking up our magazines and checking out guns and chicks, filling their pockets with tobacco. One instructor even ran his hand across a high windowsill and a Snickers fell into his grasp. He said, "Oh, you've gotta be shittin' me!"

They finally ordered all four of us to dance and we did. When they caught their breath from laughing at us, they said, "Congratulations. You passed inspection."

After the instructors left, we were sort of breathing hard but we'd done it. We all started to high five and change out of our inspection uniforms and into our working uniforms. But as a result of what had occurred something had sunk in: Don't be afraid to think outside the box. There is never a perfect plan. Impossibilities only exist until somebody does it. We thought this way, gave it a shot, and won. Mission success.

That elation lasted for about thirty minutes. We watched other classmates get their asses handed to them for a while. Then we got to the next evolution and BUD/S was in full swing again. It was refreshing to finally achieve a little victory. But the worst was still to come.

CORONADO IS A NAVAL BASE. Seals are aquatic animals. And the first two letters of SEAL refer to the sea. Not to mention that SEALs evolved from Navy frogmen.

So all this time spent on dry land (or rolling wet bodies in dry sand), running, doing PT and the obstacle course, and cleaning our barracks might give the wrong impression of an excessively land-based Phase One. During the early days at BUD/S, a ton of time was spent at the pool. Though my swimming had come a long way, I still dreaded this and feared it would doom my chances of making it through to graduation for one painfully simple reason: sunburn.

I am a very white man. I mean white like a sheet. It got to the point that when instructors would mess with me about my skin color, I'd simply say, "I just got off an eight-month deployment on a submarine."

But to me, the lack of melatonin was as serious as cancer. The pool is outside and the sun in San Diego is for real. I had to wake up at least thirty minutes earlier than I normally would just to slather on sunscreen. And even so, I had to reapply it at frequent intervals during the seemingly endless hours we spent at the pool. We would swim laps for about thirty minutes just to warm up. Then we'd do drills and tests, especially in the first few weeks. The instructors were still trying to weed people out so they'd come up with stuff to scare folks.

One thing we did was called the "beehive." Instructors forced the entire class to the center of the pool as close to one another as possible. Imagine 170 guys—by this point, we were down from the original two hundred—all crowded together in the deep end of an Olympic pool. I'm talking skin on skin, to the point that we couldn't swim. Guys started to sink under the mass of bodies, and those on top would inevitably use those below as hand and foot holds to stay afloat. Dudes really freaked out. I quickly figured out that if you got pushed down, the only safe way out was to stay calm, hold your breath, and swim to the bottom. Then you could look up, find the outside of the "hive" and surface at the edge. It was really pretty simple, but water scares people. So does drowning.

It's rare, but SEAL trainees and actual SEALs have died during pool-training exercises, despite monitoring by medical staff. Fear can sometimes be the right reaction, the rational one. And a large part of becoming a SEAL is learning how not to let fear get in the way of accomplishing the mission. In this case, the mission was to stay in BUD/S. The beehive caused a lot of mission failure. I watched more than a few guys swim away from the hive, pull themselves out of the pool, and quit, then and there.

I would survive the hive, but another pool evolution almost got me. It was a simple one-length sprint. The catch was this: If you won, you were done and got to sit out. If you lost, you swam again. By now we had about 150 guys. You can imagine how long this shit was going to take. One more thing to consider: A lot of the guys in BUD/S were collegiate swimmers and water polo players. At the very least, they swam in high school. My dumb ass had just learned how to swim. I knew I was going to be swimming many, many laps.

To make matters worse, the instructors decided to mess with me. They told me that they "were concerned about my sensitive skin." They told me that to be safe from the sun's harmful rays, I'd need to wear my white T-shirt during this pool evolution. Obviously, they didn't give a rat's red dick about my getting sunburned, they were just bored and it was my turn in the barrel. So I was losing races that I probably would have lost anyway, but now I had a T-shirt billowing out and acting as a parachute, increasing my drag in the water.

After about ten races, knowing that I couldn't take 150 races—

which, given the rate I swam with the shirt on, was the way it was headed—I decided that I'd respectfully ask permission to take off my shirt so that I had a chance. The instructor who I calculated would be most likely to give me a break was a mountain of a man by the name of Joe Hawes. He was a huge, ripped, black bald dude who'd played a commando in that movie *The Rock* with Nicolas Cage and Sean Connery. He was scary looking, but "nice," at least in comparison to his fellow BUD/S instructors. He was also the first African-American SEAL I'd met. So after deciding I had no other recourse, I went up to him and said, "Instructor Hawes, may I please take this T-shirt off so that I can at least compete to win? This thing is really slowing me down."

He stared at me for several seconds. I could see that his mind was spinning like a roulette wheel, and I knew I'd gambled recklessly just by asking. He looked down long and hard at his very dark skin, then looked back at me with a squint that somehow managed to suggest the lifelong burden of living in a racist world. He paused and did the same thing again.

Finally he said, "I tell you what, take your shirt off but I must warn you. I was in your shoes once. I took my shirt off. You're gonna hate yourself!"

SEALs are damn funny.

I won the next race and got out.

I'm only mentioning this little victory because it was so rare in BUD/S. BUD/S isn't about winning, it's about getting your butt kicked over and over again and being able to get up, bend over, and get your butt kicked again. You never knew what was coming next, and if you thought about that, the anticipation only made things worse. In fact, I'd say that fear of what was next was almost inevitably fatal. You just couldn't survive that kind of thinking. BUD/S was so bad, so hard, that nothing else mattered but doing what was right in front of you. If a guy doesn't want to be a SEAL more than *anything* else in life, he can forget it. More than *anything*. I saw guys who hadn't made it into SEAL training off the bat so they went to the fleet. Once there, they met a girl, got married, had some babies. Then belatedly they got "their shot." Too late. If a guy had any priorities other than completing BUD/S, forget it.

When I was growing up jumping off rooftops and just doing whatever else kids do that make their mothers wring their hands and beg them to be careful, I'd say, "Mom, stop worrying. I'm here to do something special. Don't even worry about me."

I don't know where that came from, and I didn't think I was being serious at the time, but looking back on it I did feel some vague sense of destiny. Maybe that started when I was shooting free throws with my dad. At first, even twenty in a row seemed nearly impossible, but somehow I accomplished that. And then I got the idea of making a hundred in a row, and I actually did it. It was all tied up with feeling my dad's faith in me. I kept moving the target back and somehow getting there. Surviving SEAL training had become the new target, the most impossible to attain of all. I suppose the whole ordeal was the ultimate test of whether I was marked for something different. If I failed, I wouldn't just be showing my father's faith to be unmerited, I'd know once and for all that I was nobody special.

At some point in the first four weeks of Phase One, I remember thinking, "I know that I have a past, although I can't really remember it. I know that I came from somewhere, though even that is blurry. What sucks is that I don't have a future. I'm never going anywhere. I'm just here. I'm in SEAL training and it's never going to end. I'm going to be cold and wet for the rest of my life. That is until it gets so hot that I can't bear it. Then I'll *be hot* and wet . . . until it gets cold again."

That's what BUD/S days are like. There are no positive outcomes. You wake up: BUD/S. You get tortured. You go to sleep, maybe, at night . . . you dream about BUD/S. You wake up: BUD/S. Then there are the lucky few who get up thirty minutes early to put on sunscreen. Then you get tortured. That is what life is. There's no ending, and no beginning. There's only an eternity of suffering. And this is after only two weeks!

I know it sounds like hell, but Hell hadn't even begun.

CHAPTER FOUR

On the fifth Sunday of Phase One, they put us all in tents on the beach. I shared my tent with my new swim buddy—one of those "rollbacks" who'd already washed out once and was getting a second, or possibly third, chance with my class. From the beginning of Class 208's PTRR days, this guy had been one of the chief know-it-alls, spewing whatever he thought would make him look important—which mostly consisted of gripes and negativity about the training process: Everything about BUD/S was bullshit—except for him. It wasn't that he was incompetent, he could actually perform physically, so much so that most of the class bought his line.

I'd had the same swim buddy since the beginning, a great guy named Monte, but for some reason, just as Hell Week was about to cut loose, I was assigned this guy. Maybe it was a devilish handicap the instructors had engineered just for me, like the T-shirt-clad sprint in the pool. Whatever. There we were, this know-it-all and me sitting in the tent on our racks. You could hear the scattered murmur of quiet conversations seeping through from the tents all around us. Nobody was sleeping. We all knew Hell Week was coming, but we were unsure what it actually entailed. Suddenly my new swim buddy, this dude who'd always acted so macho and confident, said to me, "Hey, O'Neill, man, I'm really scared."

I thought he was joking. "Ha, ha, seriously, what's up?" I asked.

"No man. I'm very, very scared. I don't want to do this!"

I was bowled over, but I tried to calm him down. "You're going to be fine," I said. "We're all in this together."

He said, "No man, I can't do this."

On cue, explosions. Instructors running into the tents screaming and spray-firing automatic weapons loaded with blanks. Welcome to Hell Week, the Hollywood version of SEAL training, the part we'd all seen on TV, and so cool to see in person. This was it!

The explosions came nonstop, deafening and breathtaking, like being inside the climax of a fireworks display. Shock waves slammed through my body. Instructors swarmed, ordering us here and there; students sprinted wildly, pinballed by other instructors screaming contradictory orders—to the surf zone to get wet and sandy, to the grinder to do push-ups and get soaked with the hoses. We were all desperately trying to stay with our swim buddies. Losing your buddy is about the worst thing a SEAL can do. So of course instructors were ordering swim buddies in opposite directions, then beating them down for not sticking together.

This chaos was designed to see how guys can handle the stress of not knowing what in the hell is going on but feeling that they *should* know. It went on for a few hours that seemed like days. The poor officers in charge of getting head counts had no chance as people ran frantically around looking for their lost buddies. Through all the confusion, guys were being berated by instructors breathing fiery outrage: *If you aren't good enough here, can't even manage to find your buddy in a piddling training exercise, you certainly won't make it in the Teams!* Guys bought it, too. Some quit right then. I thought it was nuts. We hadn't done anything hard yet! My swim buddy disagreed. He quit about ten minutes into it.

There would be moments—hours, days—ahead when it was hard not to envy his choice.

After the long beatdown, when we finally managed to as-semble our boat crews, we were ordered to grab our boats and paddle through the surf zone a mile north to the waterfront of the glamorous Hotel del Coronado, one of the ritziest pieces of real estate in the country. About one hundred yards of beautiful sand separate the balconies of the hotel and the massive rocks at the surf break. It makes for a great experience as a guest: the smell of the ocean, the cool breeze, and the sweet sound of waves crashing over jagged, razor-edged rocks. It's quite a different experience as a BUD/S student.

My senses scrambled by the breakout, my muscles already fatigued, I didn't make the connection between this line of rubber boats paddling past the Hotel del Coronado and the almost identical formation of SEALs in rubber boats Matthew and I had seen from the other side, the beach side, when we first rolled into town. I could barely recognize the boy I'd been, standing on that beach less than a month earlier. The scant weeks between then and now had become an impenetrable border between what I'd been and what I was becoming.

It would have been nice to reflect on that, but I had more immediate concerns. The rocks were coming up fast. Guys in our class had all read books about SEAL training and heard the horror stories about this particular evolution from previous classes. Our goal was to "surf" the wave and use its momentum to carry us to the rocks. Once we got there, our lead guy would jump out, quickly find footing, and get some distance from the boat. Then someone else would throw him the bowline. He'd cut the slack and hold the boat on and off while the rest of the crew jumped over the side onto the uneven rocks, trying to find a balance point so they could grab a piece of the side of the raft. From there our job was simple: Get the boat up and over the rocks and onto the sand on the beach. Sounds easy. The problem is that the waves don't stop coming. They keep slamming over the stern, into the boat, onto us.

We'd been warned: "The one thing you *never* want to do is get in between the boat and the rocks. Guys have been squeezed until their backs break when the waves hit them."

As the sound of the surf crashing on the rocks grew to a

constant roar, we backed our paddles to maintain position until we were given a signal from an instructor, then dug in with our paddles, pulling the boat into the dip before a rising swell of water.

Southern California was having some of its biggest surf in years. Guys were getting knocked all over the place and the boats threatened to run broadside against the rocks, which would have spelled disaster. Our lead guy jumped out and slipped, almost going down. Somehow he regained his balance and lunged for the rope just in time to keep the boat off the rocks. He pulled tight, and we all jumped out. We got slammed, trapped, and battered as we tried to maintain our cadence: "READY, UP . . . HEAVE!!! READY, UP . . . HEAVE!!!"

After several minutes and multiple bruises, we finally worked the boat over the rocks and onto a gorgeous stretch of beach. We broke into a group smile despite our exhaustion, just uncomplicatedly happy to have survived. That's when the instructor came by and said, "Great job, Boat Crew Two! Now do it again!!"

This was going to go on for hours. A half dozen more men quit before it was over.

Except, there *was* no over in Hell Week. It just went on and on. We'd be doing regular BUD/S stuff, pull-ups, push-ups in the sand, jumping in the water, rolling in the dunes, just like before, except in Hell Week, *everywhere* you went, you carried a boat. On your head. While running. All. The. Frigging. Time. The rubber rafts SEALs use might be listed on inventories as "Inflatable Boat *Small*," but the sucker weighs 320 pounds. This would become a form of brutal torture in the days ahead. Boat crews even carry their boat to the galley, which is a mile away. Think about that: Students get to run six miles a day just to eat meals. Eight miles a day during Hell Week because there's a fourth meal. That's a lot of running even without a big "small" boat on your head. And that's just to avoid starving. The boat goes everywhere, including to the "O" course, where we had to haul it through every obstacle. Well, not the cargo net or the slide for life. Guys would almost certainly die.

The constant bouncing and scraping gives your neck horrible kinks and I'm sure that most SEALs will have terrible lower back pain when they reach their sixties. It rubs so raw that a bunch of guys start to develop bald spots by Thursday. The boat becomes your worst enemy but it must also be your best buddy, right? Why else would you bring it everywhere?

At any moment, day or night, we might hear the instructor yell the words we dreaded second most, "Prepare to up-boat!" followed by the words we dreaded most. "UP-BOAT!" This is where we would, as a team, lift our boat in an awkward "snatch" and rest it on our heads. That alone was painful after a few days, but nothing compared to what we knew was coming.

"Extended-arm carry!"

On command we hoisted the boat up as high as our arms could reach. Then we stood there, arms burning. The instructors usually made us stay in that position until some guys started to fail and more weight was added to the rest of us. Eventually every guy would fail and the boat would come back down on our heads, or worse, we'd drop it completely. Failure was inevitable, but the instructors acted as if we were the first crew in the history of BUD/S to do it so miserably. They'd scream at us, kick sand on us, make us do a few hundred more push-ups while they shoveled sand on our backs and necks with our oars. Then they'd make us stand back up beside the boat.

"Prepare to UP-BOAT!"

The issue this time was that there was an instructor standing in the boat adding to the weight.

"You weak fuckers better not drop me!" he'd scream. "UP-BOAT!"

We lifted again, fighting the exhaustion from the beating we were taking. We managed to hold the instructor up for a while, but in a period of time impossible to measure, our arms gave out and we dropped him. So now the instructor hammered us in disbelief that we'd just tried to hurt him. This went on for some time.

I began to understand that the instructors wanted to see how we behaved as a team. If guys started yelling at each other for not "carrying their weight," the whole team would disintegrate. I watched finger-pointing destroy crews during Hell Week, and later saw the same tendency ruin careers. That's why the course is designed the way it is. The SEAL brass doesn't want guys who blame others on the teams. The goal is to find guys who, no matter what, work together as a team and, most important, *never quit.*

In Hell Week, everything was a race. We'd be up in the sand dunes, all standing in a column, and the instructors would point out a landmark and tell us to race around it, there and back, three times.

The boat crews were divided by height. This might seem random, but in fact it was supremely practical. Crews of similar height meant that at least the weight of the boat would be equally distributed on everyone's head and the boat itself would remain level as we hauled to hell and back.

But it sucked to be one of the short guys. We called the shortest crew the "Smurf Crew." Every class called the short crew that same name and I've never heard a good story involving the Smurf Crew. I've only heard of pain, suffering, and humiliation.

Predictably, the taller guys ran the fastest; it was usually Boat Crews I, II, and III—numbered tallest to shortest—competing for the land races. I was in crew II, and we competed for pretty much every race with I and III. The Smurfs were always getting crushed. Water, land, anything, the Smurfs would finish last and always get extra attention from the instructors. Some of the instructors were short, too, which meant that they'd once been Smurfs themselves. That didn't matter; they didn't let up on the Smurf Crew, probably taking out on them the frustration they themselves felt back in the day. If you ever meet a SEAL who's short, chances are he's as hard as woodpecker lips because he was a Smurf.

When we weren't racing on land or in the surf, we'd do "Elephant Walks" where we began by lining up by height, Boat

Crew I in the front and the Smurfs in the back, our boats touching bow to stern all the way down the line. These walks were about the speed of a slow jog with the instructors all around us yelling through megaphones, making this awful screeching feedback by yelling too close to the mouthpiece. It would have been unbearably annoying even without the siren, which came standard on Hell Week megaphones.

Flogged by screaming, screeching, and sirens, we were ordered to keep the boats touching in a single-file line, "Nut to Butt," and walk around California. It sounds easy but it sucks, just like everything else about Hell Week. The boats get ridiculously heavy after days of this, and guys are bitching at each other about keeping their heads under it to share the weight. Naturally, the Smurf Crew can't keep up so they're in the back, getting abuse from the instructors.

The boats felt so much heavier as the week went on that we were convinced the instructors were filling them with sand while we were in the galley. We actually started standing watch on our boats as we ate. Not that it would have mattered if we'd caught them red-handed. Anyway, they *weren't* doing that. We were just getting really tired.

We also started getting shin splints. The overstressed ligaments in between shin and kneecap began to feel like razors sliding beneath the skin. My knees got so bad I wondered if I could keep going. I knew I wasn't going to quit, but the pain of every step was so severe I began thinking it was possible I'd simply pass out at some point. Before that happened I learned that if I stretched out my hamstring the pain would diminish. I started doing that every day and the pain actually went away. But a lot of guys couldn't deal with it, couldn't run at all, and they quit.

When a guy quit during Hell Week, he was immediately taken out of whatever evolution we were doing, brought back to the barracks, and cleaned up. The next morning a formation of quitters would be marched to a big bell that was set up right outside of the first-phase office and the guys would ring the bell three times each and then place their helmets in a line called, in case anyone had missed the point, "the quitter line." Every morning that bell would ring and ring like school was letting out. All anyone had to do to quit was ring that goddamn bell whose sound seemed to follow us around everywhere.

WHEN PEOPLE SAY MAKING IT through Hell Week isn't physical, it's mental, that's sort of true, but the mental part is talking yourself through the constant physical pain. It was painful the entire time; extremely painful. There were times I'd be running on the beach with a boat on my head and my knees screamed with so much pain that I was mad at them, yelling, "Why would you do this now?! I can't quit because of sore knees!!" I'd broken my pinkie toe in the pool on the Friday before Hell Week began. That may not sound like a big deal, but even if you're a hundred percent, Hell Week sucks. This is where the mental comes in. You can convince your body to do anything. Things are only impossible until someone does them. Tape your toe to the other toes, stretch your ass and your hamstrings to loosen your knees. Rub some fucking dirt on it, walk it off.

Right before Hell Week, Instructor A pulled me aside and said, "You're about to go to war for the first time and the enemy is all your doubts, all your fears, and everybody you know back home who said you couldn't do this. Keep your head down and keep moving forward no matter what, never quit, and you'll be fine."

That really hit me. I flashed back to that mine I'd worked at in Butte. I was having lunch with a friend and another guy. My buddy pointed to me and said, "Yeah, this guy's going to the Navy in a few months. He's going to be a Navy SEAL." The other dude looked at me and said, "Oh, you're never going to be a Navy SEAL. You'll never make it." When I heard Instructor A give that little speech, that stubborn thing in me just flared up, and I held on to it as resolutely as I held on to the boat, taking one step and then another, doing whatever they told me wherever they told me to do it, covered in cold salt water, sand and sweat, and body stink.

Oh, yeah, and you don't sleep. In the five days of Hell Week, from the kickoff on Sunday evening through the final evolution on Friday afternoon, you're lucky if you drift off for twenty minutes once a day, wherever you happen to be, half collapsed on the beach or up to your knees in the surf, head nodding until an instructor screams you awake. We were always exhausted, always hurting, always cold.

Once a day the instructors got us naked and put us through what's called DeCon. It's really just a hose-down with cold, fresh water, but it gets the sand off. No small thing when you've been caked in it nonstop for twenty-four hours and it's penetrated every wrinkle and crevice of your body. You soap up, put on a clean pair of tri-shorts, which are kind of like spandex boxer briefs, and walk to the doctors' office. They check you out. You're chafing in every joint and bleeding out of every orifice, and maybe your body temperature isn't recovering from the constant exposure to cold. The docs don't want to lose any students to hypothermia, broken bones, or runaway flesh-eating bacterial infections from all the cuts and scrapes, but otherwise they aren't too picky.

As we left the checkup they gave us a handful of petroleum jelly to use on our chafing. Every part of our bodies had been rubbed raw. What they gave us never could cover it all, but that didn't matter. There was only one place we were going to use it. Something terrible happens to a man who wears heavy cotton clothes that are soaking wet all of the time with salt water while he is constantly moving. The wet clothes/salt/sand rub on his skin constantly. Eventually a rash forms. Then it gets worse and worse. Then it starts to bleed after a few days. It takes some serious mental strength to put up with this pain in the ass, literally, on top of ALL the other stuff.

Needless to say, a man's "junk" gets chafed really badly, too. And that hurts worse than anything. So all of the jelly goes on Hell Week nuts.

After you lube yourself up, they hand you clean clothes, clean boots, and clean socks.

I remember putting on my boots. My hands were so cold and stiff that I couldn't tie the laces. I looked over at the guy standing beside me in his tri-shorts. He was cold and miserable, too, just hating life. I read his name tag. I said, "Hey, Sterling, will you pee on my hands?" It's a safe way to warm them up. He looked down at me for a perfectly timed beat, then said, "Well, yeah, man, if you're into that sort of thing."

I was like, "No, that's not what I meant!"

I'd never spoken with this guy before he peed on my hands. He's one of my best friends to this day. He was as miserable as the rest of us. He just thought humor would be a nice change of pace.

Nice to meet you.

Getting dressed in clean dry greens was an intense relief—for all of thirty seconds. The first instructor who saw you step out of medical—it didn't even matter if he was on duty—ordered you to get right back into the ocean and told you to then take a nice roll in the sand. The "sugar cookie" was back. And Hell Week was full bore again.

We drilled nonstop until the sun started to go down. That was the only time the instructors would let us put down our boats and stand beside them. We stood there, soaked, feeling the wind getting colder as the sun dipped into the ocean. We did this every night and it was the one time when the instructors didn't try to inflict chaos. They wanted a moment of calm, not out of compassion, but so we could use our own minds to mess with ourselves. As the wind picked up, cutting into the cold flesh through our wet clothes, only one instructor would speak: "Say goodbye to the sun, gents. It's going to be another long, cold, wet night. All you have to do is quit and the pain and cold stops."

They'd up the ante by offering dry clothes, warm food, and coffee if we would only give up. It was that simple to quit. And the instructors wanted us to quit. They never came up empty.

There'd always be a few rings of the bell before the sun set. Then we went on with the night.

On night two, the survivors elephant-walked over to the "Steel Pier." When we arrived, the instructors ordered us to put down our boats and jump in the cold water to perform some "life-saving" drills. Basically we stripped off our clothes and tied knots in certain parts and blew into the garments to inflate them. It was old-school Navy stuff for "man overboard," but we were just doing it to get cold. After a few minutes of that, we were told to throw our clothes up on the pier and tread water in our skivvies.

This is where the mind fuck came in. Guys started to believe that they were actually getting colder because their clothes were off, though that wasn't really true in the water. Again, truth didn't matter. Only belief mattered. And some guys got out and quit because they stopped believing they could make it.

We stayed in there for about thirty minutes, treading water and watching quitters. Then we were told to get out, but the instructors weren't done with their fun. Once out, we were ordered to lie down, bare legs and backs, on the cold steel pier. Now this actually did make you colder. You could hear bodies shaking against the hard deck of the pier. Just in case we weren't cold enough, the instructors sprayed us with the hoses. More guys quit. Then they told us to roll over on our bellies. Still more quitters. It sucked like this for a while, then we were ordered back in the water for more treading. Then back on the pier for more cold steel and cold hose water.

I run into a lot of teenagers now who say to me, "I want to be a SEAL." I'll say, "What are you doing to prepare for it?" One of the common answers I get is "taking cold showers," because they've heard about the steel pier evolution. I'll say, "All right, here's the deal, stop doing that right now. Don't ever do that again." They always ask why. I say, "Let me explain it to you: If I told you that in thirty days I'm going to kick you in the nuts as hard as I can, and to get ready for it, you had your best friend kick you in the nuts every single day until then, guess what, it's still going to suck when I do it. You don't get used to it. Take every warm shower you can from here to the time you get there."

So the steel pier taught me something. It was a pretty merciless event and I want to say that most of the quitters from Class 208 came from right there.

I HAD AN AGREEMENT WITH a friend of mine named John: If one of us felt like quitting, we'd find the other so we could get talked off the ledge. When they finally let us off the pier for the last time, I couldn't find John anywhere. Hell Week went on as usual until breakfast, when we ran our boats to the galley. It's the same galley where the regular Navy guys eat, and we'd sit right next to them, only we'd be wearing our training greens and they'd be in their blues or dungarees. I was going through the line and there was John, right in front of me, in dungarees and a light blue shirt. I said, "What the fuck, dude?"

He said, "I couldn't do it anymore."

"Why didn't you come find me?"

"Because you would have talked me out of it," he said.

Off to the fleet he went.

That was Wednesday morning. And here's the irony: Wednesday morning is the key to Hell Week. If you live to see the sunrise on Wednesday, you'll make it. Probably. The instructors realize that if you've made it through sixty hours of brutal physical punishment with no sleep to speak of, you've most likely got what it takes to be a SEAL. And they know that for any human, this is where the dementia kicks in. It's unavoidable, and their attitude shifts accordingly. From Wednesday morning on, instead of trying to make guys quit, they're more likely to talk them into staying. I don't think we did anything all that difficult after Wednesday. Of course, having been awake for three days and covering hundreds of miles with boats on our heads, we found just keeping upright really difficult. But the instructors definitely eased up. At least, I *think* they did. Truthfully, I can barely remember.

On Thursday night, the last night, we did a final evolution called "Around the World." Students race their boats around Coronado Island, starting and ending at the BUD/S compound. It takes all night and is a ton of rowing. We rowed and talked. It was kind of peaceful without the sound of instructors screaming at us through megaphones accompanied by that horrible squelching sound. During the row, just past Naval Air Station North Island, I spouted off to my crew, "Hey, guys, is that an aircraft carrier over there?"

"No," they kind of mumbled.

"Good!" I said. "Then I won't ask why there is a dragon on the flight deck. I'm on a high, by the way!"

At some point we pulled to the shore and were given "mid-rats"—Navy for midnight rations—and we sat on the beach eating. The instructors were there, and seemed like they were sort of over it, too. They weren't really yelling at this point, just sort of complaining at us. Once we finished, we were back out on the water rowing through the bay about halfway to Imperial Beach. There was a designated spot on the man-made peninsula where we could cross the highway. That was fun. Groups of six guys, all drunk on exhaustion, carrying boats while trying to avoid traffic. On the Pacific side of the Silver Strand, we got back in the boats and finished our row up to the compound. The sun was up and we thought we were done for sure. Need I say that once again we were wrong? An admiral was supposed to be there to bring an end to Hell Week but, naturally, he was late. So the instructors had to get creative.

The good news: We were finally able to leave the damn boats. The not-so-good news: They ran us straight to what were known as the "mud pits." The mud pits are probably the place where the devil takes his mistresses. They're not quite a hundred square yards in a fenced-in area. It is easily the nastiest, smelliest sewage mud in the Lower 48. Students have actually been medically retired due to flesh-eating bacteria. *Really? I wonder where they caught that?* This place is disgusting. At first, they made us wade into it until we could tread mud. Then they ordered us to put our heads under. There is a damn sewer drain in there, *seriously*. I wasn't sure if it was importing or exporting but it smelled awful. Then we got to play the rope game. There are two parallel ropes, one low and one high, over the pits. Students get on, feet on the lower rope, hands gripping the high one, then try to cross while instructors shake them off. No one has ever made it across and no one ever will. It's just fun for the instructors to watch the students fall in the shit. Hey, why not? They all went through it, too.

The admiral finally showed up about noon. He walked in with his entourage and for us it was like witnessing the Second Coming. We were all saved. Hell Week was over.

He gave some "rah-rah" speech and officially pronounced us done. Then we got in a line, covered in filth, and he came by and shook each of our hands.

I'll never forget what he said to me: "Congratulations, O'Neill, you made it through Hell Week. Now wipe the shit off your face."

What an asshole.

We were all escorted back to medical where we were given our final cold shower. Seriously? From there, we put on skivvies and were given two buckets of water each to stand in. The water was warm. So shocking. I thought I'd melt right into those buckets.

Finally we were given fresh UDT shorts and our first brown shirt. Everyone who has yet to graduate Hell Week wears a white T-shirt, even under his greens. A brown shirt is the first rite of passage on the way to becoming a SEAL. By this point, I was so sleep deprived from five and a half days of Hell Week I no longer had a firm grip on where I was or what I was doing. As it happened, my father had been in contact with his SEAL friend, the guy I'd taken hunting up the mountain a hundred years before. Now he was back in Coronado. He asked, "How's Rob doing?"

"I don't know, I haven't heard from him," my dad said.

"Well, good. It's Wednesday. If you haven't heard from him that's a good thing. He's still in it."

That meant I'd probably make it through the week, he said.

My dad asked my mother if she wanted to surprise me by making the trip to California. They both really wanted to see me because the idea of SEAL training scared them shitless. Of course, we didn't know that there'd be much graver things to worry about in the years to come.

As luck would have it, when my parents arrived at the base they ran into my favorite instructor, Instructor A, who told them he could sneak them into medical to see me.

Standing there in my underwear, waiting to get checked by a doc, I saw Instructor A approaching. "Hey, Rob," he said, "put your hands up and face me. I'm going to document how you're chafing." He had one of those little disposable cameras, and I still have that picture. The chafing was truly impressive. But he'd really taken the picture to distract me from the fact that my parents were walking up. I must have heard something because I turned and spotted them. They were both looking at me with tears in their eyes. My dad's tears were probably tears of pride, and my mom's most likely tears of concern as she beheld the chafed, bruised, and battered body of her son.

I was merely amused by the clever turn my imagination had taken.

My dad said, "You're not dreaming this, Rob, we're really here."

"Sure you are," I said.

I turned around and walked into the clinic, where I was examined and told I was good to go. Instead of a handful of petroleum jelly, this time I was handed the entire tube, followed by a sixty-four-ounce Gatorade and an entire large pizza. Take it up to your rack and eat it, they said.

"How much time before our next evolution?" I asked. "Will I have time to eat all of this?"

The doc responded, "There are no more evolutions. Hell Week is over."

I didn't believe him. Hell doesn't end.

I was escorted up to my room. Some of my four roommates

were there already. Amazingly, three out of four of us had made it, which was the inverse of the class as a whole. We ate our pizzas, drank our Gatorade, took warm showers, doused ourselves with petroleum jelly—doubling up on the Hell Week nuts—and got under the blankets. All of the mattresses had been put on the floor. No need to freak out during our first eight hours of sleep in a week, fall off the top bunk, and break our damn necks. Ha, ha. The thought struck me as hilarious.

And that was it. Ten hours later I woke up to a note that one of the sentries had left in my locker. It informed me that my parents were waiting to take me to breakfast. They actually *were* here. I wondered if the dragon would be joining us.

CHAPTER FIVE

After Hell Week, students have what is known as a "Walk Week." It's the only time we were allowed to walk anywhere and there were no timed evolutions or tests. A guy's body gets so broken during Hell Week that at least a week is needed to recover. More, actually, but a week is what they gave us, nine days if you count the weekends to either side.

Then, broken bodies healed or not, it was business as usual, only now the days would be even longer. We would still do our evolutions each day, but the evenings were spent studying hydrographic reconnaissance and WWII-era Underwater Demolition Team (UDT) tactics—which basically meant charting underwater approaches to invasion-site landings on beaches.

We would separate ourselves by twenty-five meters each, perpendicular to the beach, and swim out as a group, measuring the depth with primitive little "lead-lines" or heavy sinkers on the end of thick fisherman's line. Utilizing this eighteenth-century technology is tedious, and basically useless in the twenty-first century when a submarine can map the whole deal with a few blasts from a side-scan sonar. None of us would ever use this skill again.

Didn't matter. They kept us up late most nights reading off the markings from our recon and making pretty maps that no one would ever read. No doubt we spent two weeks doing it only because the instructors knew that it sucked. *They* had to go through it, why shouldn't we?

While the instructors were busy torturing our brains, they also made sure to torture our bodies. Our first evolution on the Monday after Walk Week was a timed ocean swim. After a man undergoes the ordeal of Hell Week, he's prone to have a phobia of Mother Ocean for some time. I still have mine and don't care if I never get in salt water again. Bet you didn't think you'd hear a SEAL saying that. I actually had people ask me, while I lived in Virginia Beach, if I wanted to "go to the beach this weekend." I told them I'd rather go to Nebraska. No one has ever been attacked by sharks while sitting on a barstool or singing karaoke.

We were all a little concerned as we stood in line facing the water, ready to be inspected. My favorite instructor, Instructor A, walked in front of us. He was casually strolling and sort of smirking. He could walk slowly because there were only about thirty-three of us left out of the original two hundred. He could sense our anxiety as he announced in an uncharacteristically subdued voice, "First time in the ocean since Hell Week, eh, gents? Kind of *spooky*, isn't it?"

It took me a few weeks to realize how funny that was.

Only one other thing really stands out to me from the last two weeks of Phase One. We were getting a briefing on some sort of reconnaissance gear and the class instructor said, "Okay, gents, you'll need to pay attention to this part of the instruction because you'll be the one in your platoon responsible for this. And most of you *will* make it to your platoons because you made it through Hell Week."

This was the first time I'd ever heard anyone discussing my possible future as a SEAL without leaning hard on the phrase "in the unlikely event." What a great feeling.

Now we were ready to start learning how to dive. I know there are a lot of divers out there who fondly remember the amazing experience they had learning how to dive. I'm sure they couldn't wait to go again, and as often as possible. Well, this is the Navy, boys and girls, and I assure you that we can make anything fun suck. Especially during SEAL training.

Naturally, there was still 0500 PT on the grinder, still the mile run each way to chow and back. Then, delightfully sweat-soaked, we got to exercise our brains in the classroom, learning diving physics and diving medicine. It's very important to understand things like Boyle's law and the partial pressures of oxygen and nitrogen and their effects on the human body. Once you understand that volume and pressure are inversely related, and that a full breath of air at a depth of thirty feet will expand to twice its volume at the surface—popping your lungs like an overstretched balloon—you tend to pay attention when you're told to exhale hard on the way up from a dive. You don't, your lungs explode. The compressed oxygen in your brain expands, too, forming bubbles and causing an arterial gas embolism. All of which means you probably die. Good shit to know.

We were also learning how to "jam" our bottles, or fill our SCUBA tanks with air. This was pretty straightforward: being able to read pressure gauges and understand which of the thin copper pipes went where and how to turn them on and off and equalize pressure. In second phase it's common to hear a student yell, "Bleeding down!" followed by a loud, short hiss of air. Then you know he's just opened a hose or gauge. If the student screws that up, though, and hasn't properly turned the bottle off, the loud hiss will continue. Instructors know this sound well and will be on that student like vultures on roadkill. He'll find himself in the front lean and rest position doing forty push-ups. That's the minimum cost of messing up in second phase. It's fifty in third phase.

We also prepped for the written tests we needed to pass before qualifying to get in the water. These tests are infamous, a surprise stumbling block that can get guys who think they're through the shit rolled back to the next class. Nobody who survived Hell Week had to go through *that* again—too cruel even by SEAL instructor standards. But anyone flunking the tests would get bounced back to PTRR limbo until the next SEAL class arrived at the point where they'd fucked up, then they'd join in. SEALs are physically adept but they need to be smart, too. If you can't study or take written tests or understand physiology, you probably won't make it.

We all knew that we'd moved past the hardest part of BUD/S. But the instructors still didn't like us and certainly didn't owe us anything. All we'd done was get to the end of first phase. They'd done that years ago and then gone on to Teams and deployed. We weren't even "meat" to them yet. They still beat us and loved it. And they were still BUD/S instructors so they were creative as hell. One of the worst beatings I ever received at BUD/S was also easily the most annoying: We'd done something stupid and the instructor lined us up on the "second phase grinder." We were in off-set rows on the cement facing him. He sat on the podium with a megaphone and said, calmly and in a monotone, "On your backs."

That meant we had to lie down as fast as possible on our backs with our feet closest to him. Then, "On your feet." We jumped back up facing him.

"On your belly." We fell down again, this time on our stomachs with our heads closest to him.

"On your feet. On your belly. On your feet. On your back. On your belly. On your back. On your feet. On your back. On your belly. On your back. On your feet."

Each command was calm. Each separated by about three seconds. We did this approximately forever. At first, I was annoyed. And then I was pissed. Then sweat was streaming off my head, chin, and fingers. Then there was a pool of sweat. Then I started to bleed. Two hours into it, it stopped just like it started. The instructor looked at us as if nothing had happened, a bland look on his face.

He raised the megaphone to his mouth and, just as calmly, said, "Go to chow."

Flop around like beached fish for two hours. Run a mile, eat. Run a mile back, find a way to focus on memorizing depth and pressure tables. Nothing to it.

*   *   *

IN FACT, MOST OF US *did* pass the tests, qualifying us to go on to another notorious part of BUD/S: "Pool Week."

We thought something called Pool Week would be fun. But that was only because, for people smart enough to pass the written dive test, we were extraordinarily stupid. The week started with us running to the pool a little more than a mile from the BUD/S compound. No big deal, except we were running with old school–style "twin 80s" SCUBA tanks, which weigh about sixty pounds.

Twin 80s have double hoses, each feeding over a shoulder and into a part of the diving gear called a regulator, which has a rubber bit that fits into the diver's mouth. The right hose is for inhaling and the left for exhaling. It is an archaic method and is only used to screw with the students: These double hoses are easy to tie into knots while the student is diving. You didn't read that wrong. I'll explain later.

To begin, we were taken to the shallow end of the pool and lined up in two columns, one facing the other. While wearing our masks we bit down on the mouthpiece with the air valve turned on. Then we sat down on the pool bottom for our first experience of breathing underwater. Unbeknown to us, we were using the worst of the hoses and actuators. The exhalation tubes on most of the rigs leaked. When we exhaled, water rushed in and fouled our next breath, giving us the sensation of drowning. Because most of us were diving virgins, we had no idea that it shouldn't feel like this. It felt scary, claustrophobic, as if we were waterboarding ourselves.

None of this was accidental. The instructors wanted to see how we dealt with the panic. They were screaming and taunting and calling us "pussies" just to add to the stress. If guys stood up to try to get air, they were hauled out of the pool and treated as if they potentially had a gas embolism and later made to sign safety violations and threatened with banishment to the fleet.

Technically, an embolism would be possible at a depth of four feet but highly unlikely. They were just beating us up.

I didn't stand up, but I still remember the miserable feeling of drowning for about twenty minutes. I managed to figure out how to exhale out of the side of the actuator while spitting out some of the leaking water and swallowing the rest. Others figured it out, too. The whole time I was thinking, "Jesus, people do this for fun?!"

In truth, the fun was just getting started, and no real fun-lover should miss what was coming at the end of Pool Week—the pool competency test, known as "pool comp." The cover story for pool comp was that it tested whether a diver could handle a "surf hit" as he dealt with heavy surf. I say that's a handful of bullshit: If you're dumb enough to try to breathe compressed gas through the surf zone, you deserve a big air bubble in the brain. Say hi to Darwin for me.

It won't surprise you to learn that in reality, pool comp was simply another excuse for instructors to beat the daylights out of the students while also scaring the snot out of them.

To prepare, we were taught procedures and techniques: If there's a problem with the breathing apparatus, first reach back and make sure your air is on. If that's not the issue, you need to take off your bottles—what we called the air tanks—to visually inspect them. Make sure you do it properly: Weight belt comes off first and then is placed across the back of the legs as the student kneels on the bottom. Chest strap is released first, then the waist strap. The bottles are lifted up and over to be checked for knots. If there are knots, untie them. When they're untied, get some air. Hold your breath and put the bottles back on. Fasten your waist strap first, then your chest strap. Put your weight belt back on and continue with your dive.

If you can't untie the knot, you must set the bottles down, look over at your instructor, and give him a thumbs-up to indicate that you want to surface. Once you get the okay, you must put your lips on the pool floor and "kiss the deck," and then begin a controlled ascent while constantly exhaling. The smooch of the pool bottom is to make certain that students have to surface from at least nine feet down—which means proper exhalation on the way up is necessary to avoid lung issues. I'm sure the instructors also enjoyed making us suck face with rough concrete.

Once a guy surfaced, he *immediately* had to yell, "I FEEL FINE!" There was an important safety reason for that: If someone surfaced incorrectly and experienced an embolism, he'd have a hard time pronouncing the letter "F." It would sound more like an "M." Or so they told us. Anyway, not saying those words instantly upon surfacing resulted in immediate failure.

The test, which was on a Friday, required us to swim from one side of the pool to another, back and forth, in the nine-foot section of the pool. We went in alphabetical order, six guys at a time. The rest sat on the side of the pool quite a distance away with their backs turned so they couldn't see what was happening. I remember sitting there with my bottles on, going through the procedures in my head. About twenty minutes into it, I heard my first "I FEEL FINE!" followed by "So and so . . . FAIL, get out of the pool!"

Again, "I FEEL FINE!" . . . Again, "FAIL, get out of my pool."

This went on as they got closer to the "O's." Finally, I heard, "O'Neill, get up here."

I asked permission to enter the pool and it was granted. I began my swim, back and forth, excited to knock this out and be done with it. Barely a minute into my swim I got crushed. My mask was ripped off my face and my fins were removed roughly. My air was also turned off. I suppose this could happen in the surf zone. I waited for this "simulation" to end as I held my breath. I calmly reached back and turned my air on. All good. I could barely see without my mask but I could breathe, so I continued my dive by crawling on the floor instead of swimming. Most divers would do that in the ocean, right?

After a minute of this, I was hit hard again. The regulator was pulled from my mouth and I could sense the instructor tying a knot in the hose. I waited the thirty seconds or so, calmly holding my breath. Once he was gone, I reached back and turned my air on. This made the hoses buoyant; they popped over my head where I could see the damage. The left hose had a major knot in it that I couldn't untie. The right hose had been knotted, too, but apparently not as badly because the sudden increase in air pressure when I turned the tank back on had forced out the knot. Now it was leaking air, and at least I could breathe, but not without taking in water with every breath. Fortunately I had experienced this feeling of drowning all week and could easily handle swallowing a little water with each breath for the next fifteen minutes. The whole time I was hoping SEAL candidates don't do in pools what little kids do in pools.

So far so good and I was far from feeling panic. I continued back and forth for the next fifteen minutes, getting hit hard every now and then. I saw four more knots but I managed to get them all undone by following procedure. Some came undone when I turned my air back on, some didn't and I had to remove my tanks and untie them manually.

I got hit a fifth time, I could feel the instructor using his feet and hands on this one. We'd heard from the guys who'd gone before us that when the instructors wanted to make you fail, they'd tie a knot so tight it was impossible to get out. They called this their "whammy knot." That's what I feared was happening beside me as the instructor gave my hoses special attention. When he finally finished, I reached back and turned my air on. Nothing. Weight belt off, undo chest strap, undo waist strap, pull off tanks, and inspect. I tried to get even a little air but there was nothing coming out. I tried my best to undo the knot but it wasn't happening. After holding my breath for about a minute while working the knot, I finally decided that this was it. I turned to the instructor and gave him the signal to surface. He gave me the okay. I kissed the bottom of the pool, turned my head to the side, and began to exhale. I did this all the way to the surface and took a huge breath of California air and then yelled, "I FEEL FINE!"

From behind me I heard my instructor yell to the recording instructor, "O'Neill, FAIL. Failure to follow instructions."

What?

"Get out of the fucking pool, O'Neill!"

I got out of the pool and grabbed my abandoned gear from the diver who'd retrieved it. I sat down, steaming, and listened to more people fail for about an hour. It was my turn again. Same result: Fail.

I think the instructors intended to be especially hard-ass on a Friday—knowing they could torture us by making us worry all weekend about it. If a student performed flawlessly in every respect, they'd grudgingly give him a pass, but any hesitation, even the slightest slip, equaled failure. By the end of the day, only half the class had passed.

I knew I'd have another two shots on Monday. If I failed then, I'd get rolled and have to wait in PTRR until the next class started second phase. If I failed with that class, Class 209, I was out and would never be a SEAL.

From the moment I heard that awful word "fail" echoing across the pool, a loop tape began to run in my head: I *must* pass this. I can't get rolled. I *need* to get through BUD/S on the first attempt!

This was going to be a lovely fucking weekend.

WE WERE GIVEN ACCESS TO the gear and the classroom and fully utilized it. On Saturday I practiced nonstop until the sun went down. After, I went to a buddy's room to watch *Heat*. It had just come out and everyone wanted to see it. I watched it through to the end. As the credits rolled, I realized I hadn't the slightest idea what the movie had been about. The entire two hours, I'd been thinking only about pool comp. I eventually did watch *Heat* again after BUD/S. Damn, that was a great movie. That was the first time Hollywood included "mag changes." A realistic gunfight for a change.

So the weekend sucked, especially Sunday night. Sunday nights always sucked at BUD/S. But this Sunday the usual misery was amplified by that lovely loop tape running nonstop. *Must ... pass ... can't ... get ... rolled.* I felt like an X-Man getting his butt kicked by Magneto.

Monday was a great deal for the guys who'd passed on Friday. They were assigned their "single hose regulator"—the modern kind recreational divers use—and were working on regular diving in the deep end of the pool, maybe even having ... *fun*—or at least that's what I was thinking, aching with jealousy as I sat with my back to the pool waiting for my name to be called. I listened as some passed and some failed and then I heard my name called. I walked over and asked permission to enter.

I drew an instructor who was a notorious dick. I was not excited. We did the same routine: He crushed me, punched the mask off my face, and turned off my air. I got the air on and kept going. He slammed me against the bottom and tied my stuff in knots. We went at it for a solid thirty minutes. I decided that I was not going up until I was about to drown. I went through about eight knots until I got one that was impossible. I worked it for about a full minute and then decided that I couldn't get it. It was time to surface. I gave the thumbs-up to the instructor and permission was granted. I kissed the deck, exhaled all the way up, slowly, and surfaced. "I FEEL FINE!"

The instructor didn't say a word. He tapped me on the shoulder and I turned around. He stared at me for a few very long seconds without indicating anything. He didn't smile, he didn't frown. He just stared.

"I should fail you for keeping me down there so long. You untied three of my whammy knots," he said, then looked up and announced, "O'Neill, pass."

It was sad to see the guys who failed twice that day. Three had been in my boat crew. The one who shocked me the most was Dave. He'd been the voice and spiritual leader of the class since Day One. He'd been in a class several months before 208 and gotten hurt before Hell Week. So he'd been rolled into our class. He knew the drill but wasn't a loudmouth. Okay, so he *was* a loudmouth but he was a great one. He was a motivator and a true "swim buddy." He knew all of the instructors' names and made sure we did, too, when we'd call them out or give them a "Hooyah." He'd been instrumental in keeping me positive during Hell Week, and I owe my survival in large part to him. I'm sure a bunch of the guys felt the same way.

On that Monday, he failed pool comp for the fourth time. I remember watching him leave the pool in his brown shirt, shorts, and tanks. The rest of us were sitting there on the opposite end watching. He turned around and yelled, "Good luck, 208!" A true class act. It was predictable, and just, that he ended up graduating with Class 209 and went on to one of the SEAL teams on the West Coast.

THE EVER-DWINDLING NUMBER OF CLASS 208 students moved on to the actual dive training. At first we'd just swim out on a bearing for a few hundred meters, then surface to see if we were close to where we thought we should be, correct any mistakes, and take a new bearing back to the beach. Soon the dives became a bit more challenging: We'd swim multiple bearings and try to find different "targets," counting our kicks to measure distances. It was nice to finally be learning some actual Navy SEAL shit.

Even better, we began diving beneath the undercarriage of big Navy ships, and learned about the assembly and placement of limpet mines that could take out any one of them. Gliding silently under the monstrous keels, past propeller shafts and propellers and rudders that seemed forged for a race of giants, felt surreal, almost magical. I always paid attention to the massive seams of the ship, as well. It's possible under that massive amount of steel for your compass to lose all sense of magnetic north and spin crazily. If that happens, you find the welding seams of the ship and follow them out from underneath. No one wants to drown while swimming in circles under a bunch of shipmates.

Doing several of these dives every day would be enough of a workout for most people, but not us. Our SCUBA training was supplemented by the PT, of course, which never stopped. One night the instructors were keeping us up, beating us down until almost midnight. We were desperate to get to bed since we knew we'd be waking up in about four hours. We didn't dare gripe aloud, but our tormentors looked like they could hear our collective silent groan. One said, "See that hoop over there? If we have anyone in the class who can make a three-pointer, we'll secure the beating right now, and you can go to bed."

I heard myself saying, "I can do it."

It had been quite a while since I'd made a free throw, it was late, I was beat, and with all my classmates looking and the stakes so high, it was far more pressure than an arena full of screaming spectators. But what the hell.

"Get over here then, hotshot. Let's see what you got."

As I walked up to the three-point line, someone in the ranks mumbled, "He played in college!"

What an asshole. The instructor smiled. "Okay, O'Neill," he said. "You can shoot this three-pointer but you got to make it on your knees."

As I got on my knees, I could feel everyone's eyes on me. I just chucked it up there. What else could I do?

Nothing but net.

Despite my lucky shot, our respite was brief and insufficient. Nothing could save us from the most dreaded part of second phase—the 5.5-nautical-mile swim (which works out to more than 6.3 normal people miles).

We did ours on a Friday. It would be our only evolution of the day and then we'd have the weekend to recover. Thank God. But, as I mentioned, the second-phase instructors didn't like us. As we were getting our swim brief, the lead instructor announced, "Gents, the currents have shifted today so instead of swimming south to Imperial Beach from here, we're loading up the buses, driving to IB, and swimming back."

He was full of shit because the current *never* went that way. They just wanted us to suffer, trying to swim over six land miles against the current. As I was imagining creative ways to kill him, he said, "You'll be conducting the 5.5-mile swim. . . . I'll be in one of the safety boats with my sandwiches, my bucket of KFC, and my Cokes conducting the 5.5-mile picnic! I'll be throwing chicken bones at you the whole way, chumming the water."

I was laughing. He was a dick, but that was funny.

"If you think there aren't great white sharks out there, you're lying to yourself."

I stopped laughing.

We pulled on wetsuit tops and loaded the bus. It took a long time to get there in a freaking bus going fifty miles an hour. And now we had to *swim* back. Against the current.

After we arrived, we lined up in two rows facing our swim buddies. I'd been reunited with my original first-phase buddy, Monte. Monte was then and still is perpetually hilarious. Not this day. I faced him and the ocean. He faced me. I was watching him, thinking, *I've never seen anyone look more miserable.* I'm sure he was thinking exactly the same thing about me. I didn't like swims. Two nautical miles was plenty. Now we were about to do five and a half.

Instructor Picnic gave the order and we backed into the water, then started swimming toward Coronado. Did I mention this was in the ocean? It was immediately obvious that we were pushing against a strong current. This was going to be a long-ass day. All I remember is kick, stroke, glide, breath, kick, stroke, glide. The beach was concave so, rather than follow it and have to travel farther, we headed out into the ocean on a beeline for the compound. Every swim pair did this and the tactic spread us all way out. There weren't nearly enough safety boats to monitor us all. At one point we stopped and Monte, a California surfer, said, "Bro, we're like three miles out to sea."

I had my back to the beach at this point so I turned and looked. He wasn't lying. There were no boats near us and no other pairs, either. We were hungry and thirsty, but had nothing. "This sucks. Let's go."

We swam on. Like we had a choice. Five and a half hours into it we were finally close to the surf zone and swimming up the beach. Monte and I had switched sides a mile or so back and now I was facing the beach, and guiding us along it. We were opposite the "O" course so we knew that we only had a couple of hundred meters to go. At this point I could see a big commotion on the beach. An officer in his khaki uniform was screaming at us—all of us. A few instructors were yelling through bullhorns for us to get out of the water. "What the hell?"

The officer was the XO of the entire command. A man of his exalted rank shouldn't have been out there and certainly shouldn't have been yelling. Something had happened. We assumed a medical emergency so we hauled ass to the beach. I can still remember the feeling of my feet touching sand in the shallows. Finally! Only two pairs had finished the course. We were two hundred meters shy, but I didn't care. It was over, we were out, and it was the weekend.

We later learned that the XO had discovered the instructors had purposely made us swim against the current. He knew that would put us dangerously close to the hard limit of the human body's ability to withstand exposure to cold water. Plus, we were so spread out that if anyone went down, he wouldn't have been pulled out in time. It was a very dangerous stunt they'd pulled, and I'm sure the instructor staff got an earful from the boss. We got some satisfaction imagining that.

I was in a great mood all weekend. Now that the 5.5-mile swim was behind me, there was nothing to prevent me from becoming a Navy SEAL.

My underage buddies and I hit Tijuana that weekend, and hit it hard. We came back to work a little poorer and a lot hungover, anticipating an easy day in the classroom. We sat at our desks

Monday morning, still laughing at our buddy Jimmy, whom we'd dragged back across the border shit-faced and minus his flip-flops. He's half Asian and has brown skin, so we ended up spending more than a few minutes explaining to the border patrol that he was in the US Navy, not a barefoot illegal.

Just then one of the instructors came running in. He'd obviously been present for the "earful" from the boss about Friday's aborted swim. He said, "Classes are canceled for the day!"

Say what?

"Since not all of you finished the mandatory 5.5-mile swim on Friday," he said, "we're doing it again right now!"

Oh, fuck *me*.

It couldn't be true.

But it was. And there was more.

"This time, gents, we're not sure of the current," he said. "So we're going to swim halfway to Imperial Beach and then back!"

What a dick! They knew damn well, again, which way it was going. They could have let us swim with the current and be done in a few hours. That wasn't going to be the case and it was time to get our rubber on.

Once again I found myself in formation, face-to-face with Monte and the water. Didn't we just fucking do this? I remember how disheartened he looked. His hood was a bit tight so it made his pouty face look chubby. As I looked him over, I got nervous. Where an emergency flare should have been fastened to the end of a big-ass knife on his cargo belt, he'd taped instead a king-size Snickers bar. I laughed my ass off, but said, "Dude, if they see that we're both fucked!"

Monte said, "Bro, if you don't say anything, I'll split it with you!"

It was insane! After all we'd been through, was I really going to risk getting ripped from BUD/S over two thousand calories of chocolaty peanutty goodness?

Why, yes, I was.

Luckily for us, the instructors were so freaked about almost getting fired, they never noticed. The swim was miserable, the water was cold, the whole thing sucked again. Except for my portion of the Snickers at the halfway point. That was delicious.

To this day, I think making us do the 5.5-mile swim for a second time was the meanest thing anyone has ever done to me, with the possible exception of terrorists shooting at and trying to blow me up. That shit was definitely mean. But we did the swim for a second time and, this time, we all finished. I was relieved. I thought that would be the last hard thing we did, but only because I never learn.

CHAPTER SIX

San Clemente Island is a twenty-one-mile-long apostrophe of land, essentially the ridge line of an underwater mountain thrusting nearly two thousand feet above the Pacific seventy-eight miles west and slightly north of San Diego. It's officially uninhabited, and owned in its entirety by the Navy. The only development is the Naval Special Warfare compound. This is where SEAL training reaches its climax. If it weren't for the live ordnance frequently exploding in its vicinity, it would be an excellent place for a camping trip. The surrounding water is the clearest I've seen, a shimmery blue-green that resembles a cut and polished aquamarine gemstone. I could see down to a depth of twenty-five feet, even at night. There are lobsters and fish everywhere. The whole coastal area is a breeding ground for great white sharks, notorious for occasionally mistaking humans in wetsuits for sea lions, their favorite cuisine. It wasn't uncommon for half of a four-hundred-pound sea lion to wash up on the beach where we trained.

Still, shark attacks are extremely rare, and no SEAL has ever been bitten by a shark. Swims go on even when fins are spotted. The manual's only advice is "use caution." But there's another apex predator on the island, as well—SEAL instructors. Because this small plot of land is far removed from the Coronado command structure, the instructors feel they have something close to free rein. They have a motto for the last forty days of training: "No one can hear you scream." There are no days off and nothing else for the instructors to do except relentlessly torment trainees.

We all thought that Phase Three of training would be fun because we'd finally get to play with some of the Navy's toys. The course covered land warfare tactics, weapons training, and demolition. And some of it *was* fun. Before we got to the island we hit Naval shooting ranges in San Diego and learned land navigation at Mount Laguna on a multiday "camping" trip. Both experiences were challenging in an entertaining way, especially since we were all on an extended high from the knowledge that we'd almost certainly become SEALs.

The fun stopped at San Clemente Island.

We landed on the island in the early evening and split up into teams. Each team had a room with bunk beds. Once we put our gear away, we were brought into the classroom for a lesson the instructors said would feature "shark appreciation," followed by a "shark appreciation swim." At night.

We watched about two hours of the best of Shark Week and then were told to get our wetsuits on for a swim in the bay. Usually swim pairs spread out and guys race to win. This swim was different: We all swam huddled close together in beehive formation. I guess we were hoping for safety in numbers. In retrospect, that might have been counterproductive, inasmuch as we resembled a large, poorly swimming school of tasty-looking fish. It was a relief to get out of the water.

The next time we went swimming, we were packing, loaded down with haversacks full of C-4. Even the great whites knew better than to fuck with us. We practiced blowing up WWII-style obstacles old-school frogman style by holding our breath, free diving down, and tying as much boom as possible to the obstacle before returning to the surface for air. It was up to another two pairs to swim down with a wheel of detonation cord. We'd do practice burns to see how long the cord took to burn down, calculate the delay we wanted, then measure out the proper amount. After it was wired and set, we lit the fuse and everyone got clear to watch the show. Seeing several hundred pounds of C-4 going off underwater for the first time is a thrill. Water doesn't compress, so it shoots several hundred feet in the air. You see the plume, then you hear the boom.

We blew shit up underwater for a few weeks, then moved on to weapons and small unit tactics. I'm aware that this still sounds like fun, but remember, we were miles away from humanity, and at the mercy of inhuman SEAL instructors. We quickly understood that their terror would reign for forty days and forty nights. There was no way we were going to get a day off. With no distractions, the instructors got bored. When they got bored, we got beat. Every day we did pull-ups in full gear and had to sprint up a mountain we called "frog hill"—just to get to breakfast. After all we'd been through, though, the PT stuff was more annoying than painful. Even the fourteen-mile run was more a scenic island tour than a form of torture.

The problem was that the instructors found infinite excuses to send us sprinting two hundred meters to the beach to get wet and sandy. No matter how fit the students were, cold and wet always won. And if you actually messed up, you got crushed. Even if you were in the general vicinity of someone who messed up, you got crushed. That's what made my island experience so hellish.

Once again, my old swim buddy, Monte, and I were split up and randomly assigned to different teams. And once again, I drew the short straw with my new buddy, a guy I'll call Parker. After gutting out Hell Week, Pool Week, and the two 5.5-mile swims like the rest of us—which theoretically should have meant he was fireproof—Parker, for some reason, began to melt down on the island.

He'd been my roommate since we'd moved to building 618 in second phase and would be again once we returned from the island for graduation week. We'd had no problem getting along. He was very funny and the biggest Jimmy Buffett fan I'd ever met.

His performance had never been an issue. He was extremely fit and had been cruising through just fine. The problem was that he had a girlfriend in San Diego. Having her nearby on weekend leave must have been holding him together. Once we left for the island, he lost it. He began falling short in PT. He got busted trying to turn around early on one of the runs up frog hill—by the students, thank God for him. He was noticeably not performing to third-phase standards and we began to get concerned.

One time, he forgot to put the buffer spring in his gun, an essential part of the recoil and recovery mechanism. The gun won't work without it. At the rifle range, an instructor asked him if he'd completed an inspection of his weapon and a "function test." Parker lied and said yes. Failing to do the test is an unpardonable sin. Lying about failing to do it is grounds for immediate ejection from training. It was also unbelievably stupid. Of course, the instructor attempted to perform the same test. There was no spring, so no tension.

I have to think that Parker was so exhausted and worn down that on some level he wanted to get tossed out. But the instructors liked this guy, plus they hesitated to boot anyone so deep into training. Instead of going nuclear, they decided to punish him by making him get wet and sandy every hour on the hour for twenty-four hours.

The problem for me was that although we were on the island, *no* man is an island in the SEALs. We always have our swim buddies, even when we screw up. I'm all about a team effort, but getting punished for someone else's incompetence and laziness over and over gets old. Every time Parker screwed up, the instructors said: "Sucks to be you, O'Neill." It sure did. The island was tough enough without being perpetually cold, wet, sandy, and sleep deprived. I'd been beat down over and over for him and it was starting to piss me off.

Then something odd happened. A group from SEAL Team Three came out to the island to train in some water demolition drills. They stayed in a better compound, much nicer than ours, just a few hundred meters from the BUD/S compound. As opposed to several plain barracks with no common areas, it was a state-of-the-art, one-story hotel. It had big-screen TVs, a big kitchen, and a bar. There were fire pits outside and plenty of room to work out. Team Three also had freezers that needed to be taped shut because they were so full of lobster.

But they trained in the same bay that we did. On one of their drills, the underwater charge didn't explode. The SEALs also failed to follow rule No. 1: "Two is one, one is none." They didn't put a secondary initiator on the charge for redundancy. Because there was now unexploded ordnance underwater with no way to blow it, they needed to wait a minimum of forty-eight hours before they could send in a guy to reattach an initiator. It took that long to be sure the charge wouldn't blow when someone came to fix it. Since the very large unexploded charge was just off the only accessible beach on the island—most of the coastline was sheer rock cliff—there was nowhere else to do the dive training. This was great news for Class 208 because that meant *nobody* could get in the water for a few days. What a sweet deal!! Then Parker screwed up again.

This time he didn't thoroughly clean his weapon and there was a bunch of carbon in the bore. The instructor started to say, "Get wet and sandy every hour on the . . ." when it hit him. "Oh, shit. You *can't* get in the water."

I was so sick of being punished because of this guy, I blurted out, "Let me hit him with the hose every hour on the hour."

The instructor laughed and agreed. As had happened with the room inspection, I'd come up with something unexpected and entertaining, so the instructor decided to go with it. Of course, it wasn't very loyal of me to suggest it, but this dude was killing me. The other students were fed up, too, and they appreciated my creativity. The only flaw was I still had to wake up every hour to do the hosing.

I don't think Parker blamed me for it. It was pretty obvious that he wasn't himself and the instructors didn't want to kick him out yet. He just needed to be rolled back to Coronado to get his mind right, which he did. He graduated with Class 209.

For forty straight days we shot and blew stuff up and swam and learned. It was the first time in eight months that our bodies were allowed to heal a little, so all the working out, instead of constantly tearing us down, was finally building us up. We could only eat what they served in the galley, which meant no junk food and no booze. I remember looking at myself in the mirror before a shower and wondering how in the hell my Pillsbury Doughboy mid-section got this six-pack.

A few weeks before our stint on the island was over, we were handed "Dream Sheets" to fill out. We were told to fill in our name, rank, and BUD/S class, along with our top three choices for team assignment. It really boiled down to whether I wanted to go to even-numbered SEAL teams on the East Coast, or stay out here in Coronado with the odd-numbered teams. I chose the East Coast. Team Two was the oldest team, and had the richest history. It had been the SEAL team that had been deployed to the Bosnian War. True, deployment to that conflict had just recently ended, but I figured that part of the world might provide the best chance of putting to use all my combat training.

The truth is, I was choosing blindly. None of us were exactly sure what SEAL teams did, but we had an idea that there were all kinds of covert ops going on.

There was one thing we were sure about, though: DO NOT PUT "SDV" ANYWHERE ON YOUR DREAM SHEET!

SDV stands for SEAL Delivery Vehicle. It's a mini-submarine that can carry a SEAL team long distances and deliver them to targets undetected. The swimmers can emerge beneath ships, sneak onto beaches, or sail far up rivers for clandestine insertion into cities. It sounds cool and looks good on paper, but get this: These are not airtight vehicles. They're flooded with cold water and dark inside. It's like sitting in a coffin full of water.

I'd had enough of being cold and wet for long periods. Plus, since you're *always* diving, there is no time for other Navy SEAL activity, the fun stuff: skydiving, shooting, setting off big explosions, etc.

Reasonably, no one wanted to be an SDV crewman, but the Navy still needed to fill the slots. So if you even *breathed* the letters "SDV," you were going and for a long-ass time.

When it came time for us to get our first SEAL assignments, we all sat together in a classroom, listening as an instructor went down the list: So and so, SEAL Team One. So and so, SEAL Team Eight. So and so, SDV Two. You could hear the grumbles from the class anytime the dreaded letters were read. We had about eight guys go SDV before my name came up. The instructor was so used to saying it, he actually said, "O'Neill, SD . . . excuse me, SEAL Team Two."

In the blink of the puckered ass it took for that slip, I must have said, "Oh, fuck me" about nine times, followed by a *"Yes!"* SEAL Team Two it was. My first choice. My true swim buddy, Monte, and I went out back that day and had our picture taken together. I still have the shot: I held up two fingers for SEAL Team Two, he held up one finger. Guess where he was going?

Flying back to Coronado was such a kick-ass feeling: It was Friday, we had two days off, and Monday would be the first day of our last week in BUD/S. That was when it really sank in for the first time: I was going to graduate and become a Navy SEAL.

My family came down to watch me graduate the following Friday. The thirty-three survivors of the original two hundred members of Class 208 were sitting together wearing their dress blues, waiting for the graduation ceremony to begin, when Instructor A walked in. Most of the class hadn't seen him for months, as he was a first-phase instructor. Back then, each week right before Friday liberty, he'd stand before us in the same classroom where we'd first met. With that marvelously rich voice, he'd read off, in alphabetical order, the last names of guys who hadn't failed an evolution all week and ask them to stand. He'd then announce that the men standing were this week's "BUD/S Studs."

Now, in that same voice, he asked us all to stand and said, "When I read your name, take a seat!"

He started to read off names in alphabetical order, most ones we didn't recognize, and the list was long. He read off about 170 names before he was done. We were all still standing.

He let us take it in for a moment of heavy silence, then said, "Those are all your quitters. The men standing are the BUD/S Studs from Class 208. Congratulations."

It was very cool of him to do that and something I'll never forget.

NOBODY CAN PREDICT WHO'LL MAKE it through BUD/S. The brass tries to figure it out; they bring in psychologists and boost the number of guys beginning the process, hoping more SEALs will be left standing at the end. They tweak the design to create more equal opportunity for minorities, but all that happens is that the instructors do to the students exactly what was done to them, and always 80 percent don't make it. We have more white SEALs simply because more white guys try out. Eighty percent of white guys fail, 80 percent of Filipinos fail, 80 percent of black guys fail. And the irony is, the Navy doesn't *want* an 80 percent failure rate. There can't be too many SEALs. We're always undermanned.

From the beginning of boot camp, the instructors try separating guys who want to be SEALs. They put them together, feed them better, give them workouts designed to prepare them for BUD/S. These promising rookies get in better shape, are better nourished, and are psychologically primed to go. Then they're sent to SEAL training and 80 percent fail. No matter what the Navy process tweakers do, they can't crack it. You'd think the Olympic swimmer would make it. You'd think the pro-football player would make it. But they don't—well, 80 percent don't.

In my experience, the one category of people who get reliably crushed in BUD/S are that noble demographic, the loudmouths. They're usually the first to ring the bell.

As for who will make it, all I can say is: Are you the person who can convince your body that it can do anything you ask it to? Who can hit the wall and say, "What wall?" That strength of mind isn't associated with any ethnicity or level of skin pigmentation. It's not a function of size or musculature or IQ. In the end, it's sheer cussedness, and I'm guessing you're either born that way or you never get there.

AFTER GRADUATING, I CELEBRATED WITH my family in BUD/S style by going to Tijuana. My family couldn't believe how cheap the Oakley sunglasses were. It broke my heart to have to tell them they were fake. They didn't believe me anyway.

We all went back to Butte for the Christmas holiday. I can't tell you how pumped I was. I'd just finished BUD/S, had orders to report to SEAL Team Two, and had a stop at jump school—Basic Airborne at Fort Benning, Georgia.

When I checked in there in early January, I wasn't sure what to expect. I knew that the other students would be about my age, but I wondered what they were like. Would they be huge, tough Army guys? I was curious, but it turned out they were more curious about me. They wanted to know about SEAL training and if the movies and TV shows were accurate. Naturally, I said they were *exactly* right. Just like the movies, that's us.

It was only when I saw my brothers from BUD/S Class 208 that I realized how much I'd missed them, even after only two weeks. We'd finished the world's most difficult military training together and we had the kind of bond usually forged by going to war. We also may have been just a teensy bit full of ourselves.

We knew that even if we failed jump school, our team would slap our wrists and send us right back. Guys from other branches didn't have this luxury; if they failed, they were out. We were the military's version of made men. We were also in the best shape of our lives, cocky as hell, and really good-looking.

In jump training, before a student could eat, he had to do five pull-ups on the bars outside the chow hall. Our guys would be on pull-up number thirty before the airborne instructor—they were called "black hats" because they all wore black ball caps with a conspicuously shiny parachutist badge pinned on them— would yell at us to knock it off. I remember one hilarious black hat who shouted, "You don't think I know who you are . . . Navy SEALs . . . Damn Terminators!"

Another cool instructor pulled us aside and said, "I know what you all just did. We get you guys every other class or so. Keep in mind, I have a job to do and this school is a big deal to your Army, Marine, and Air Force brothers and sisters. Be professional and don't give the black hats too hard of a time!" He laughed and yelled, "Drop!"

We got in the push-up position or "front lean and rest," obligated to do our ten push-ups and count 'em out. Keep in mind: During third phase of BUD/S, every time we were "dropped" the number was fifty. We were used to doing thousands per day.

Our senior man became the cadence and the rest of us would "count."

"Down . . . ONE!"

"Down . . . ONE!"

"Down . . . ONE!"

"Down . . . ONE!"

We counted to one about thirty times before the black hat yelled, "RE-cover!"

We did. "Assholes. Get back with your class!"

They were good to us and we were good to them . . . for the most part. I remember telling one of the black hats about my first jump. "That was the coolest thing I've ever done!"

He must have been amused by my wide-eyed enthusiasm, which I'm sure he'd seen a hundred times before. The jump door had looked small but the outside enormous; a big, fake movie screen full of sky on one side and trees on the other. Jumping out was a loud rush followed by "holy shit" and then the most peaceful calm. And a really hard landing. It actually took me three weeks to master how to land. And I was happy about that. The longer it took, the more jumps I could make.

Anyway, none of us encountered any major issues and we all graduated on time. I was given my jump wings—a cool pin of silver wings curving out from a parachute canopy—and I was very proud. Jumping out of a plane changes your life, and I wanted to get the full treatment: "blood wings."

I'd heard about it from instructors, SEALs, and the 82nd Airborne. They all talked about it as a rite of passage ... "back in my day ..." It had been officially prohibited, but I knew it still went on among the hardcore. You might be able to guess what it involved.

I went to the office of my favorite black hat and knocked on the door. There were three other black hats in there. I handed him my wings, having removed the stoppers on the sharp pins. He said, "What do you want?"

I said, "I haven't earned these yet. I know what you guys do at the 82nd."

"Hazing is illegal, O'Neill."

"Pin me."

We looked at each other for a second. He nodded and came closer. He stuck the sharp pins on my left breast with his left hand and punched the jump wings into my chest. He shook my hand. I looked at the other three black hats and said, "Well?"

They all came over and, one at a time, punched the wings in farther, smiled, and shook my hand. Now I was Airborne.

Time to drive to Virginia Beach for the first time in my life. Time to check in with the legendary SEAL Team Two.

CHAPTER SEVEN

My very first night in Virginia Beach, four of the guys from 208 and I went to Peabody's, a famous "18 and up" club. I liked the music inside but wanted to get some fresh air so I grabbed a beer and walked outside. Too bad there was no balcony.

I was twenty years old, and I was used to Butte, Montana. Turns out in the normal world you can't buy a beer and drink it on the sidewalk. I'd barely taken a swig when a hand clamped down on my arm. It was a city cop, and he was pulling me into his car.

I was thinking, *Okay, here I am, not only do I have an open container, but I'm underage.*

The horror of the situation opened like a trapdoor. If you're arrested on an alcohol-related charge your first day with a SEAL team they're going to kick you out. All the months of sweat, blood, sand, and wetness flashed by in review. I'd just pissed it all away because I was less than a year shy of twenty-one.

I thought of my older brother, Tom's, expired license tucked into my wallet. I'd grabbed it when I was a senior in high school and had kept it with me when I left Butte. Not only was it expired, but the unsmiling face on the license didn't remotely look like me. I figured, *Screw it. I've got nothing to lose,* and reached for my wallet. I gave the cop the license and turned my face away as he looked it over. I waited for him to crush me, but he just jotted the info on his clipboard and calmly handed it back. "Stay inside next time, Montana," he said.

A couple weeks later I got a call from Butte. It was Tom, wondering why he'd gotten an open-container violation ticket from Virginia Beach.

"I've never even been to Virginia Beach!" he said.

SEAL TEAM TWO WAS BASED at the two-thousand-acre Naval Amphibious Base on an inlet of the Atlantic called Little Creek Cove. The team itself occupies a two-story building with a weight room, a locker room, and some offices downstairs. Upstairs are what we call platoon huts, which are essentially clubhouses for the eight sixteen-member platoons.

I checked in on a Friday, knowing it would be a short day and figuring it would give me a chance to orient before Monday. Christian, a buddy from Class 208, and I moved into a shared room in the Navy barracks because we weren't getting a housing allowance and couldn't afford any rent with our meager paychecks. We even ate at the Navy galley, not my first choice, but we were poor.

When I walked in the first day I was still three months of additional tactical training and a two-hour oral exam away from being a full-fledged team member. That cocky self-confidence from getting through BUD/S and airborne school? Vanished. I didn't know what to say or how to act around these guys.

So, of course, the first SEAL I encountered just happened to be the biggest hard-ass of all the hard-ass instructors from my BUD/S training in Coronado: Instructor Woodie. Even his name sounded mean. He was a big barrel-chested dude, a complete physical phenomenon who emitted visible rays of intimidation. Just a legendary asshole at BUD/S. The standard punishment of making guys run from the "O" course over the dunes into the water to get wet and sandy wasn't nearly mean enough for him. He would make us low crawl on knees and elbows like human snakes through the sand to the surf and then back a couple hundred meters, over and over, until men up and quit. There's no counting how many SEAL hopefuls he managed to force out of the course like that, changing their lives, all because he was such a prick.

Or that's what I thought at the time. While screaming at us as usual one day he actually explained himself. He wanted people who could put up with the most ridiculous bullshit, who would never quit and would do anything to succeed, because the guys who made it through would eventually end up serving with him, probably in a war.

When I walked in and saw him there, I might as well have been back in Coronado in the middle of Hell Week. Like an idiot I said, "Hooyah, Instructor Woodie!"

He did a double take and said, "What the fuck are you talking about, dude? You're in a SEAL team now, there's no hooyah, there's no instructor this. I'm Woodie."

I managed to say, "Okay, cool. Woodie," but it took me a while to get used to calling him that. He turned out to be one of the nicest, most caring, big-hearted guys I ever knew. A true mentor with an infallible sense of humor, he was always willing to explain to a green kid tactics and how the teams worked.

There was a refreshing sense of equality and mutual respect among SEAL team members—even between officers and enlisted men. We called officers by their first names and weren't saluting them all the time. They were the ones with the college degrees—a guy had to have one to be an officer. But the officers recognized we'd been through something far more demanding than four years of college—BUD/S. When it came to actual missions, the officers were the organizers—and the ones responsible—and the enlisted men designed and executed the tactics. But there was a lot of back and forth between all of us. There were programs for enlisted guys who wanted to become officers, but I never felt the need, even though they made more money. I liked where I was.

After Instructor Woodie—sorry! I mean, after *Woodie*, the second person I met was a guy named Neil Roberts. He had reddish blond hair like I did, and his name echoed mine in reverse. But

I certainly didn't take much from those trivial similarities. He immediately impressed me as the ultimate SEAL. He still held the record for the "O" course at BUD/S, and was always finishing first in the team workouts. He was something I could only aspire to: extremely squared away in every aspect, from his impeccable physical condition to how clean his locker was. Everything he did was done with efficiency and purpose. Right away he looked over my gear and explained what should go where and why, and what I didn't need. A very serious but generous guy.

That first day he took me to lunch at an Arby's across from the base and treated me as an equal. Both the stacked brisket and onion ring sandwiches and his respect were unexpected treats for me. I remember thinking, *These are some impressive people.*

On the verge of becoming a SEAL myself—the very cool official designation was Naval Special Warfare Operator—I was still naïve. I assumed what most people who'd never been in the SEAL teams did: that SEALs were busy all of the time going on covert ops. I pretty much thought that anyone in the building wearing a Trident—a gold pin with the eagle, pistol, and trident insignia—had several kills and probably a bunch of those with knives. In 1997, that was pretty much the furthest thing from the truth.

No SEALs had seen real action since the invasion of Panama, when guys from SEAL Team Four got in a major gunfight on Paitilla Airfield going after corrupt dictator Manuel Noriega's getaway plane. Three SEAL platoons had parachuted into the ocean with their inflatable boats, motoring the rest of the way to the airfield. Because their rules of engagement required them to challenge Noriega's guard before shooting, they had to give away their presence. The Panamanians responded by opening fire from a hangar, killing four and injuring seven of the fifteen SEALs in the lead platoon. The Panamanians rushed in reinforcements to support their resistance, but were no match for the remaining SEALs.

That had been in 1989, eight years earlier—the same year the

Berlin Wall came down, and the beginning of an all-too-brief Pax Americana. Then some Team ▮ guys got in a few fights in Somalia during the *Black Hawk Down* days. Aside from some very peripheral involvement in the first Gulf War, that was about it. Even though the daily morning muster began beneath a sign that said, "Are you ready for war today? You should be," SEALs hadn't fired a shot in anger in years. But nobody ever admitted that around civilians, even to their closest non-SEAL friends. We'd pull the old "can't talk about it" crap, leaving the impression of untold secret missions. We actually referred to the whole charade as "Living the Lie."

There is an old saying in combat units: "Train like you fight!" We used to make fun of it because we knew the truth. We started saying, "Train like you train!" because that was all that was going to happen.

Anyway, when I checked into SEAL Team Two, I treated everyone with a Trident with respect, which was definitely due. Even if these guys hadn't been shot at, they'd all gone overseas willing to fight. They just hadn't been given the opportunity yet.

During the first few months with Team Two we new guys were in a kind of limbo. We couldn't become actual SEALs until we underwent thirteen weeks of additional tactical training, but the training classes only happened a couple of times a year, and we had to wait until a new one started. In the meantime we would work out every day with the entire team. This wasn't the agony of BUD/S. We were rested and in shape, and the four-mile runs could end with several coolers of beer and a comedy-filled bus ride back to Little Creek. SEALs are very funny, as I was learning. I knew I needed to up my game.

But Tuesday still sucked. Every Tuesday we swam two miles in the ocean no matter the weather. If it was a hundred degrees and sunny, we swam. When it was snowing with ice on the water, we swam. We all hated it to the point that it became comical to see what kind of excuses guys could come up with to get out of it. We saw it not so much as shirking as an ingenuity competition. If you were in need of a dental appointment, schedule it on Tuesday morning. Same with medical appointments. I always laughed when I came into the "Team Room" on a Tuesday morning and saw several guys in their cammies and not their PT gear.

"Where are you guys going today?"

"Dental!"

Guys who hadn't properly scheduled an appointment were expected to go to their lockers or "cages" and put on their wetsuits. This left time for an attempt at escape and evasion. Some guys walked into the locker room and just kept walking out the back door where they jumped the fence to the parking lot. Others hid in their cages; one cut a hole in the ends of three kit bags, then sewed them together, end to end. He could crawl in there and nobody would think to find him because it just looked like three bags on a shelf, all too small to fit a living human.

Even if you failed to vanish, it wasn't too late. We'd take a bus to a spot near Lesner Bridge, then swim from there to the Chesapeake Bay bridge/tunnel. While the bus was loading, guys would pretend to urgently need the bathroom, then sit on the toilet until the bus left. They'd actually run after the departing bus in wetsuits, shouting and waving, pretending to be upset that they'd miss the swim. Hilarious.

The platoon chiefs didn't think it was quite as funny as we did. For our transgressions we'd see our weekend leaves canceled, and get bad evaluations. But, hey, we were creating a tradition.

I discovered another fun tradition in those first days. With the entire team assembled, we new guys were asked to stand up front to "tell us a bit about yourself!" Before I could get out my full rank, the entire team yelled, "Shut the fuck up!!!" The more senior operators added their own random comments like, "Eat shit!!" or "Blow it out your ass!!" The guys laughed heartily. When the yucks died down someone piped up with, "Seriously, tell us about yourself."

Repeat.

It was an extended and mostly good-natured kind of hazing.

They called us "new meat," or collectively, "meats," and we just had to grin and bear it. After a few months, a spot in a tactical training course finally opened, and not a moment too soon. The thirteen-week course consisted of more advanced versions of the training we'd had in Coronado and on the island. We rehearsed combat diving in Puerto Rico, and land warfare, weapons, and tactics at Fort A.P. Hill in Virginia. Even after that, I was still on probation. The command observed everything from our social interactions with the rest of the team to how we performed in PT—including the dreaded two-mile swim. Which meant I wouldn't be hiding in any tricked-out gym bags or riding any toilets. When the command thinks you're ready, you're given a two-hour oral exam in front of the senior enlisted SEALs. The test was intense, and took months of study. They could hit you with anything, or several things at once, like making you do a timed assembly of a machine gun while answering questions about the properties of electric versus nonelectric fuses.

My board was nearly a disaster because I'm always such a smart-ass. That morning I was dressing for PT in the cage with a guy I hadn't seen before. He was another redheaded dude, maybe ten years older than me. He said his name was Mark, and he asked if he could borrow a PT pad. I gave him one.

I didn't see him again until we were out on the obstacle course. We had a guy named Art who is one of those top one-percenters—just a complete freak of nature at everything he does. Swims fast, runs faster, excellent shot, all-around super SEAL. I was still trying to prove myself in this elite group, so when Art moved out front as usual, I took off after him. I busted my ass to catch up, but there was no way. When we got to the part of the course where you had to step in and out of a series of tires, I started skipping some, trying to make up some time. As we were running through a tunnel I heard someone yell, "Hey, you can't skip any tires!" I looked back to see who the jerk was: Mark, the new guy.

We make three big loops around the "O" course, and on the second loop Art and I were way out front, but I was still behind, so I skipped the tires again. Mark, half a loop behind us, coming the other way, saw this and yelled at me again, "I told you, don't skip any tires."

"If you were fast enough," I yelled back, "you'd have seen me skip every other monkey bar, too, asshole."

I finished the "O" course a close second and didn't give Mark another thought. I was too nervous to think of anything but the impending test. Finally it was time. I walked into the boardroom and looked at the review panel seated before me. In the dead center of the panel was the redheaded guy, Mark. Turns out he was the incoming Command Master Chief, the new boss. I stood there, trying not to groan out loud. "It's the guy who cheats on the 'O' course trying to get his Trident," was the first thing out of his mouth. "Do you need to cheat to win, O'Neill?"

"I do if I want to beat Art!" I was trying to be funny. Mark didn't laugh.

He grilled me pretty hard on that, but I got my Trident that day. I was now a Naval Special Warfare Operator, a hot-damn Navy SEAL.

CHAPTER EIGHT

I t had been almost two years since I'd enlisted in the Navy, and I'd yet to set foot on a ship. That little gap in my nautical résumé would be remedied big time by my first deployment. We drove down to the Marine base at Camp Lejeune and boarded the USS *Austin*, one of three ships constituting the Mobile Amphibious Ready Group. The Austin was a classic Navy transport ship from the 1960s, 569 feet long with the capacity to carry almost a thousand troops. We set sail for Rota, Spain, and were out to sea for about fourteen days. Until then, I'd never been out of sight of land for more than a few hours at a time.

We weren't responding to any particular world crisis, we were just part of the projection of American military might around the world, something that is happening every minute of every day of every year. That's the "Ready" part of Mobile Amphibious Ready Group.

It was my first experience around Marines. I was impressed. Fresh out of SEAL sniper school at Camp Atterbury, Indiana, I'd learned how to shoot while accounting for wind and distance, how to lead while accounting for a moving target, how to determine distance by using tiny dots in my sight—called mil dots—and making quick geometric calculations, how to spot for another shooter by learning to actually see the path a bullet makes through the air, and how to camouflage myself and move stealthily enough to get within feet of the target without being seen. I got pretty good at all that, too, making top 20 percent in a class of capable snipers.

But I had nothing on the Marine snipers. The sniper course that Naval Special Warfare puts on was designed by a Marine, Gunnery Sergeant Carlos Hathcock, who may have been the most famous sniper in history with ninety-three confirmed kills in Vietnam and probably three times that many that weren't officially confirmed. He once took out an enemy sniper at long range, striking him in the eye through his own telescopic sight. He perfected the art of stalking and camouflage. According to an obituary I saw—Hathcock died in 1999—he once covered a thousand meters of open terrain by crawling inch by inch through the brush, unseen even when he came within twenty feet of the enemy. He crawled for three days and nights, but he got his man, a Vietnamese general. The Marine snipers on the ship were right on top of all his methods, worthy successors. We had a blast talking about utilizing mil dots, reading range charts, and all the stuff that warms a sniper's cold heart. Then we'd go up in helicopters and shoot at barrels floating in the ocean. Sniper bonding activities.

As for the on-ship routine—the sleeping in tiny berths stacked three high, the constant rocking back and forth—I quickly got used to it. I even kind of liked it. I developed a real appreciation for the fact that there are people in the Navy who have harder jobs than SEALs. They bust their asses on those ships, working long hours with no recognition. Naval sea power and forward defense is the key to global stability. There are a lot of folks busting their butts every day with little thanks.

A machinist, for example, will labor for a good portion of the day in the dark with the machines and the heat and then have four hours of watch. It made me think about something I'd noticed in BUD/S. A lot of the guys who quit were guys who'd never been to the fleet. The guys who'd seen life in the fleet were the last to quit because they understood what it was they'd have to go back to. That understanding helped me later in my career because I ended up doing two more deployments on Navy ships, and I'd always tell my newer guys, "Look, I had a tendency to be cocky when I was younger, too, but don't give these guys shit on the ship. They work harder than you do."

Especially when at sea. As SEALs, we didn't have a job aboard. They say that when you're at sea, the acronym SEAL turns from SEa, Air, and Land to Sleep, EAt, and Lift. The ship had a cramped little weight room and a couple of treadmills. The rolling of the ship in the waves added an element of interest to running on the treadmills. Now you're sprinting, now you're running uphill, now you're sprinting. We worked out a lot. We played cards and board games. We didn't have any video games then, and only very poor Internet, so email was rare. It was a cabin fever setup, but the upside was we got to know each other really well.

And of course, we found creative ways to keep up our two-mile swim, because how would we carry out our "can't talk about 'em" missions without regularly fine-tuning our swim stroke? In the middle of the Atlantic Ocean, we lowered our inflatable boat over the side—not the small one we'd learned to love in Hell Week, but a big, semi-rigid boat about thirty feet long—and motored two miles away. Then all of us but the boat crew jumped out and swam back. It was badass out there. We're talking about eight thousand feet of the cleanest water you've ever seen. Before we set off, one of the boat guys handed me a cigarette because I'd said I wanted to be the first guy in the history of the world to smoke a cigarette in the middle of the Atlantic Ocean. I did it, too.

After our sea voyage, since there was no war going on, we had a nice little tour of Europe, including Spain, Italy, and Greece. For this boy from Butte, Montana, that was quite an eye-opener. I got a kick out of all the little differences. This was before the euro, so each country had its own currency. Some had depreciated so drastically they must have been running the printing presses day and night. I loved pulling nine million Turkish lira out of ATMs.

Our only mission was to engage in prearranged exercises with various NATO allies. Not that it was entirely risk free. Our training always involved an element of danger—and it would get even more dangerous in the future. On one exercise, another sniper and I went up in a Vietnam-era Huey to toss barrels into the ocean and shoot them from the moving chopper. We wanted to see how fast we could put enough holes in them to make them sink.

The pilot was this very cool Marine captain we flew with a lot. Those old Hueys had windows that pushed down like on a school bus—you squeezed the clip that retracted the lock and pushed them down. He'd be flying the thing while chain-smoking cigarettes and tossing them out the window as we were blasting away at the barrels. It was very white trash, and a hell of a lot of fun.

While the pilot was smoking and we were shooting, all of a sudden we heard this loud boom. I instinctively turned to look in the direction of the sound and saw ragged remains where the engine had been. I did the math, and it didn't take long: There was only one engine. I looked back at the air crew chief. He was strapping himself in. I looked at the other sniper. He was peering out through the door as if he was thinking of jumping. I knew I had to make a decision: *At what point do I jump?* Did I want to risk getting caught in an exploding helicopter or was it better to take a long leap into the ocean? I looked again. We were clearly too high, at least five hundred feet. There'd be no recovering from a jump like that.

The first thing this Marine pilot did when he heard the boom was calmly put his smoke up to his mouth, take a final, long drag, exhale, flick the butt out the window, and say, "Fuck." Then he set about maneuvering his crippled bird toward our ship, which seemed a long way off to me. He kept yanking all his levers and practically willed us toward it. The vessel came up fast but we were falling faster. The chopper hit into the stern with barely enough altitude to skid forward instead of slamming into the hull and falling into the ocean.

We all climbed out, unhurt. The bird was down for a while but somehow they got it back up. Mechanics are awesome.

The next week, we were at a base in Italy doing exercises in old Navy H-53s, the big, oily helicopters with the huge rotor. Our ship had left port without us, and we were about to catch a ride on an H-53 to meet back up with it. We weren't happy. *Saving Private Ryan* had just come out and we wanted to stay at the base and watch it. Our bad attitude must have been pretty potent, because the chopper blew an engine on takeoff and we had to crash-land right there. This crash happened too fast and too low to even think about jumping or take a final drag on a cigarette. There was another loud boom and the chopper just dropped straight down. We were able to soften the landing by utilizing "autorotation." I'm not sure what that is but, like I said, pilots are cool. The good news was, we were alive and unhurt, and back at base just in time to catch the opening credits of *Saving Private Ryan.*

Then, finally, we got a bit of real-world work. We'd been planning a big exercise in Albania when we got intelligence that al-Qaeda was plotting to attack senior officials there. I remember someone mentioned the name Osama bin Laden. The Navy flew us in to the embassy in Tirana, Albania, to help provide security. My friend Mike Johnson and I went on patrol on the embassy grounds. We were wearing plainclothes, just like in the movies, and I remember thinking how cool that was when a car rolled past the embassy gate spraying automatic weapons fire. It was just some punk kids making noise. The whole thing barely raised my heart rate. But that was the first time I'd ever been fired on.

We ran at the car, but they took off.

I didn't have even a moment of hesitation about the possible dangers. We'd been training for this for so long. Even knowing a few guys had gotten hurt in Bosnia and Kosovo, you wanted to be one of those guys in the real action because they instantly get legendary status. I wanted to be that guy, I wanted to be the best one there.

But I wouldn't see any action, not on this deployment. When the big event finally came off—the president of Albania meeting with a bunch of admirals—they flew us in again. We found high ground on the roof to set up a sniper position, with a spotter across the way. I actually made a range chart so I would know how to aim at various potential targets if I needed to. I ended up with nothing to show for my prep work but the usual sunburn. That was the end of the deployment pretty much. When we landed back in Virginia Beach, the first thing we all wanted to do was go to Taco Bell.

IN EARLY 2000, I WENT on my first deployment to the Middle East aboard an aircraft carrier. The mission would make headlines worldwide. Here's how it was reported in the *Baltimore Sun*:

> On a still night earlier this month, a Navy Seahawk helicopter sped across the dark waters of the Gulf of Oman and hovered above the Russian-flag commercial oil tanker *Volganeft*, anchored just off the United Arab Emirates. Suddenly ten SEALs—black-clad commandos carrying M-16 rifles and machine guns—clambered up to the deck and rounded up the crew. Scrambling up to the bridge, the commandos found documents claiming that the 4,000 metric tons of oil on board—the equivalent of 29,200 barrels—had been pumped in Iran. But satellite-based navigation records revealed that the tanker's route began in Iraq and that charts of the voyage had been erased. Commandos interrogated crew members, who told different stories about their route and where they stopped in Iran. Evidence seized aboard the *Volganeft* on Feb. 2 included a sample of the oil. A US laboratory tested the sample. Several days later Defense Secretary William S. Cohen announced the results: The oil came from Iraqi wells, a flagrant violation of United Nations sanctions.

I was one of those black-clad SEALs. It was the first helicopter-borne vessel boarding I know of. I trained for it, but had never heard of anyone doing it for real. My job as sniper was to stay in the hovering chopper and cover my guys as they were making their move onto the tanker. Of course, it was a merchant ship not a warship. I wasn't sure if I'd have to blast somebody, but I was ready if it came to it. It was also one of my first experiences around interrogations. All we had to do was get them talking, and as the article said, they all had different stories.

We took command of the ship and steered it to Oman where we turned it and the crew over to the authorities. This operation was supposed to be our little secret, but there we were on the news.

The next year, we deployed to Kosovo from a staging point in Germany. Even though the conflict had ended in 1999, there was still a need for peacekeeping. We'd alternate different platoons from Germany to Camp Bondsteel, Kosovo, to conduct reconnaissance and surveillance. We'd hide in the mountains and observe the locals, making sure there were no signs of aggression. We learned two things: Clandestine R&S teams get compromised by unassuming locals most of the time, and it sucks to walk through minefields. Plugging your ears does nothing.

IN LATE SUMMER, WE'D JUST gotten back from Kosovo. I was sitting around the office with a half dozen of my teammates. We were looking forward to a few weeks of routine downtime: muster in the morning, PT, train a bit, and be done by 1600. Then we'd go back to our barracks, which had been upgraded for complete comfort over the previous year, clean up, and go to the Irish pub.

I was thinking about a pint of something at the pub and typing an email to a girl I'd met in Lithuania to plan her upcoming visit, barely aware of a CNN financial report droning on the TV hanging from the ceiling. At 2:49 German time, the show transitioned from a commercial to a "breaking news" logo, and there was a stunning image of one of the World Trade Center towers in New York belching black smoke from a massive hole in its midsection. I stopped typing and watched, thinking, "What the hell?" A witness jabbered nervously as the tower billowed smoke. A passenger jet came slicing out of the flawless blue sky on the right side of the screen and flew directly into the second tower. A massive fireball rose up behind the streaming smoke from the first tower. The commentator, who hadn't even noticed, or hadn't been watching, continued his interview as if nothing new had happened. But we saw it. We saw it, but could barely believe what we'd seen.

Everyone was going, "Did you see that? Did you see that other plane?"

It couldn't have been more than thirty seconds before someone said: "Osama bin Laden. This is al-Qaeda. We're under attack."

I thought, *Holy shit, our lives just changed, man. This is it.*

Like everyone else, we stared at the television the rest of the day. We didn't know how the world was going to respond. We didn't know if we'd get the call: "Get your shit on and leave immediately." But that didn't happen. It turned out that a plan had to be pulled together first. Our deployment soon ended and we flew home. It was weird seeing all the flags flying and sensing everyone's tension. Everything looked different now.

I'D NEVER REALLY PLANNED TO make a long career of being a SEAL, but things had changed. We were actually going to war. In fact, SEAL Team ▇▇ almost immediately flew out to Afghanistan. Soon after, they were working to bring down the Taliban regime—the same regime that had sheltered al-Qaeda as it trained its suicide soldiers and plotted against America. I wanted to join Team ▇▇ on the front lines of this new war. I put in my paperwork to apply for it, but first I had to do one more deployment with Team Four.

It was an exciting time. We'd been training for this for years, and now the skills we'd worked so hard to obtain were what our country desperately needed. We pictured these assholes with the long hair and big beards we'd seen in footage of Taliban fighters, the mujahideen with their muffin-top hats and Kalashnikov rifles who'd chased the Russians back to Moscow. And now our guys were already over there in the mountains just fucking them up.

We returned home from Germany that fall for another training rotation in Virginia Beach, and by March 4, 2002, we were gearing up for our own deployment to the Mediterranean. I was in the air loft at Little Creek, packing parachutes, when someone came in and said, "Hey, did you know Neil Roberts?" Neil was the second guy I'd met when I'd joined SEAL Team Two four years earlier, the guy who had so impressed me with his fitness and generosity. Right away I didn't like the question's past tense. "Why?" I asked. "What happened?"

"They told us he was killed in combat."

We didn't know the whole story, but rumors started to fly about how he'd fallen out of a helicopter that was taking heavy fire from rocket grenades on top of a mountain called Takur Ghar. People said the helicopter had to take a hard dive down the mountain, leaving him to fight it out by himself against a swarm of enemy.

Operation Anaconda was the biggest pitched battle in Afghanistan since the failed attempt three months earlier to kill bin Laden, who'd been entrenched with his fighters in caves in the mountains of Tora Bora.

By March, al-Qaeda and Taliban insurgents had regrouped in the Shahi-Kot Valley in eastern Afghanistan. Our intelligence estimated that between 150 to 200 fighters were wintering there. This was only the first error of what would become an error-plagued operation. It turned out the real number was between 500 and 1,000, and they were expecting an attack.

On March 4, Neil and his fellow SEALs were assigned the mission of establishing an observation point on Takur Ghar's ten-thousand-foot-high peak overlooking the valley. Normally, they would have landed in a more protected area and hiked to the peak, but the chopper that was supposed to ferry them into battle had an engine malfunction. They had to wait for a replacement. Since they needed to achieve their position before daylight, they no longer had time to make the hike. Instead they'd land directly on the exposed peak, a much more dangerous proposition.

An earlier flyby by an AC-130 gunship had reported that the peak was clear of enemy fighters. The gunship flew off to provide close support for another battle, leaving the mountaintop blind. When the chopper carrying Roberts and his team arrived shortly before 3:00 a.m., the crew observed footprints on the snowy peak, then an anti-aircraft gun, which opened fire. A withering hail from machine guns, automatic weapons, and rocket-propelled grenades blasted into the helicopter, damaging the engine and control systems. The pilot fought the dying hydraulics and the helicopter began to buck wildly. Roberts, preparing to unload, possibly slipped on some grease and fell toward the open ramp. One of his teammates saw him tumbling out the door and tried to pull him back, but ultimately Roberts's own weight of two-hundred-plus pounds plus his eighty-pound pack and twenty-seven-pound gun were too much. He slipped from his buddy's grasp. The pilot tried to return for him, but he could no longer control the craft and had to execute a controlled crash down the mountain, slamming to earth about four miles away.

That Roberts survived the fall and continued fighting is suggested by a drone video feed showing a lone fighter holding off a swarm of enemies ninety minutes after he fell from the chopper, right up until he went down and was dragged away—just seconds before his remaining teammates returned in a second helicopter to attempt a rescue.

Neil's would-be rescuers landed in the same hornet's nest of heavy fire as the first chopper. They were immediately pinned down and began taking casualties. Ultimately reinforcements, aided by air support, fought a furious seventeen-hour battle to take the summit, killing scores of enemy at the cost of six more

Americans dead and four wounded. A helmet believed to belong to Roberts was found with a single bullet hole in the back. I doubt anyone will ever know all the details for sure, but we also recovered the weapon Neil was carrying—it was called a SAW, for Squad Automatic Weapon. We had it mounted above my desk as a memorial. The barrel is bent at a sharp angle—he'd fallen so hard it bent the damn barrel. It would have been useless when he needed it most, so he'd kept fighting with what he had, a few grenades and his pistol. When that ammo was gone, I have no doubt he fought with his knife until the end came.

Before going on this mission, Neil had written a letter to his wife to be opened in case he didn't make it back. In it he said, "Although I sacrificed personal freedom and many other things, I got just as much as I gave. My time in the Teams was special. For all the times I was cold, wet, tired, sore, scared, hungry and angry, I had a blast."

When I got the news that Neil had died that day, war became real to me.

CHAPTER NINE

To try out for SEAL Team ▓ I needed to fill out a form called a special request chit. You fill out a chit for everything in the Navy, from taking leaves to going on liberty to moving off base to even getting a tattoo. I guess I missed that last part several times.

Anyway, you submit the chit to your leading Petty Officer who, if he approves it, submits it up his chain of command to the Platoon Chief, who brings it to the Command Master Chief. Each must agree that the petitioner has a good shot at making the team. If the Command Master Chief says you're good, then the Commanding Officer's going to agree, and you're in. Not to the team, but to the screening process.

The conventional SEAL teams are filled with tough, capable warriors. But they don't have the experience and haven't yet proven themselves to be the best of the best, the guys wanted for the most sensitive, secretive missions with the most at stake. The screening and training process take the better part of a year. There's the initial screening, which determines if you'll be selected for the more extensive screening that determines if you'll be selected for the eight-month training/selection process that gives you a fifty-fifty shot at actually making it.

So, piece of cake.

Team ▓ conducts a few screenings every year. Guys have to complete a vastly amped-up version of the physical test that conventional SEALs have to pass. Every distance is longer, every time faster, and every exercise has more reps. It's a pretty serious test. If you pass that, then you go before a board of senior officers and enlisted in a room where they grill you for an hour about your array of service medals, your tactics, your experiences, your bosses, your home life, your finances, and how much you drink—and knowing SEALs, they might find "only a little" as disturbing an answer as "a lot." Basically, they want to make sure they feel comfortable with you before they invite you to an additional three weeks of screening.

I sat before the screening board in late spring 2003 and was immediately intimidated. All the men staring at me had seen combat. *Real* combat. And they'd all lost men, brothers. They were more serious than the SEALs from my base, more professional. Older. They didn't joke around, they cut to the point. Why should you be here? What do you offer? You're not trying out to be a Navy SEAL, you're attempting to become a SEAL Team █ operator. Can you handle it? They even had the administrative chief in there going through my service record, making sure the ribbons I was wearing were in order and nothing was missing. Making damn sure I wasn't wearing anything I hadn't earned.

I got invited to the class that began in March 2004. I had almost a year to wait as I continued going on training and a deployment with my conventional SEAL team. We cruised the Mediterranean hoping to get into the fight in Iraq, but it didn't happen.

By then, my living conditions in Virginia had improved considerably. I was sharing a kick-ass condo on the beach with two of my team members, impressing women, and generally living the SEAL dream. The winds of change blew in with a phone call from my sister Kelley, still living in Butte, who'd just bailed from a bad relationship and desperately wanted to leave town. I could relate. I said, "You know what you should do, just move in with me in Virginia Beach."

I flew up to Montana, fixed her car, a shitty little blue Nissan, and we drove back to Virginia Beach on an epic road trip. Before we even left town I discovered she had no money. Well, *almost* no money. She literally had one dollar. I said, "It's bullshit I have to pay for everything, but you won't spend that one dollar—on one condition. We're listening to Elvis Presley the whole way."

So we did. We had fun on every mile and took our time. It's a thirty-four-hour drive that we stretched over six days. In that week on the road, Kelley drove a whopping four hours total—so I could get some shut-eye. In those four hours, she managed to get a speeding ticket in Iowa and run the car into a ditch in West Virginia. A deep ditch. A bib-wearing redneck showed up out of nowhere with a tow truck, asking, "Y'all need a tow outta that ditch 'er sumthin?" Kelley, pissed off and embarrassed, said, "No, bro, I got this!! . . . Of course we need a tow!"

When we got to Virginia Beach, I wrangled her a job at a sports bar called Hometown Heroes. I knew the owner, so I hooked her up. I swear I didn't do it just to get an inside track with the cute young blonde named Nicole who worked there as a waitress, but I did ask Kelley to put in a good word. Nicole wanted nothing to do with me. Smart kid. Also fun, bubbly, and free-spirited. I pursued her for a long time with nothing to show for it. She didn't even know what a SEAL was at first, so she had no idea how little quit I had in me. Finally she caved, probably just to shut me up. She also didn't know how close I was to filling out a special request chit.

We got married about a year and a half later and bought a house. I was starting to see the outlines of a different life, one with more responsibility.

Selection screening began with more physical tests, even tougher than the preliminaries, but since the candidates were all seasoned SEALs, the main focus of the screening was on psychological evaluation—they needed to feel certain that a candidate could function at the highest level under the worst possible conditions, like if you fell from a helicopter on a mountain peak surrounded by heavily armed enemies. This was no joke.

I made it through, and went on to the next phase. The first

three or four weeks were devoted to skydiving. They switched it up later—made it the *second* training section—because the skydiving training was expensive and too many guys were washing out in the next part, which was close quarters combat. But I was happy to start by jumping out of planes. I was on a high to begin with.

Immediately, I noticed we weren't in Kansas anymore. We enjoyed the perks of SEAL Team ▇▇'s budget, which meant that instead of leaping out of a battered Korean War–era C-130, as we did in SEAL Team Two, we were flying down to Arizona to a posh facility outside of Tucson.

WE STARTED THE DAY EARLY with a twelve-mile run, then spent the rest of it skydiving. We began with what's called HALO—high-altitude, low-opening—jumps, which involve a very long free fall and the chute opening just high enough off the ground to keep the jumper in one piece. The trickier variant is HAHO—high-altitude, *high*-opening—jumps, which involve opening chutes almost as soon as the jumper has left the plane. Thirty of us would exit the plane one after another, pull the chutes, and try to get in formation as a troop—picture twenty guys under canopy, each guy ten feet behind and ten feet above the guy ahead of him. It's what we call a "stack." These chutes aren't the traditional ice cream cone tops, but rectangular, almost like the wing of a plane. You can guide the chute, fly it. In HAHO jumps, it's possible to travel in formation as a troop at a horizontal speed of twenty to fifty miles per hour (depending on the wind) and land ten miles away at an exact spot no one has seen before except on a map.

A troop of flying SEALs is really cool, and really dangerous. The stacking maneuver requires extreme caution and rigid adherence to basic principles. For instance, whenever we'd do a HAHO jump, we always went to the right as we left the plane. Always. This was an unbreakable rule. We'd want everyone turning in the same direction. If two jumpers—each weighed down by about a hundred pounds of equipment—bump going the same direction, it's scary as hell, but it most likely won't kill them. If they bump going in the *opposite* direction, it's catastrophic. In that circumstance, they'd hit each other at a speed of twenty miles per hour—equivalent to slamming into a brick wall at forty miles per hour. Both jumpers would die on impact, probably cutting each other in half. Even if the jumpers don't hit each other, they can cross each other's lines. Not good. They'd wrap up in a big ball of silk and plummet toward the earth thinking about how painful it is to get part of their arm cut off by constricting chute cords, and how it sucks that they only have forty-five seconds to live before smacking into the mountain.

No matter what precautions you take, it's just flat-out dangerous. Later in my career, we lost two guys in one month during jump training. We all felt the risk. After a while, though, you stop being scared, replacing the fear with a constant aware-ness that shit can really go sideways. Want to learn to accept your mortality? Jump in formation from planes in the total blackout of a moonless night, and do it repeatedly. The upside: It kept us well fed. After a day and a night of jumping, one of us would inevitably say, "We've got to have steak tonight because this could be our last night on Earth."

On one jump I was testing a new kind of high-performance chute, designed to move faster through the air. The chute was moving so fast, my head got pinned in the cords and I couldn't get to the release. I was caught in this death spiral for a long time. It actually got to the point where I said to myself, *If you ever want to see your family again, you* need *to get rid of this thing. It needs to happen.*

To this day I can't tell you how I managed to get freed up, but I pulled and the goddamn thing flew out of there, this beautiful, fully inflated canopy. I looked at my altimeter and saw I was at about 4,500 feet. If I hadn't pulled my canopy when I did, at 10,000 feet, and waited until the usual 5,500, I would have hit the ground before I ever got untangled.

When I landed, I ran into one of my friends. He said, "You look like you just saw a ghost. What happened up there?" I explained it to him. I remember saying, "Jesus, we need to fix this or else someone's going to die. We need to fix this system. These two don't match up."

Only nobody did, and it would come back to haunt me in a particularly cruel way.

But I survived that day, just as I survived the rest of the jump training—none the worse for wear and possibly a few pounds heavier from all those steak dinners.

THE NEXT PHASE OF TRAINING, the most famous and the most difficult, is called close quarters battle (or CQB) training. This prepared us for an intimate and especially dangerous kind of fighting—entering buildings occupied by an armed and very hostile enemy, often complicated by the presence of civilians and/or hostages. The target might be a house, a hotel, or a ship—all situations in which you have to breach exterior barriers and defenses, then operate in cramped spaces, any one of which can be a death trap.

We'd practice our moves—like a violent, high speed ballet—hundreds, thousands of times.

Instructors would be watching our every move. At the end of the day they read out your scores, lingering on every lack of awareness and every safety violation. At the end of the week they'd turn the tables on us, say, "Make a list right now: top five, bottom five in the class. Go!" I never had a problem ranking the top five because I could just look around the room and think, "This guy's a stud, this guy's a stud, stud, stud . . . ," but then I'd get to the bottom five and think, "Shit, everyone's good." So I'd end up putting myself at the bottom and then just throw four other people under the bus. We all did that.

It all gets in your head to the point where you'll be having a great day, thinking nothing can go wrong, and then in a fraction of a second you fuck up, and they take your gun away and run you through it again, this time with a broom, just to make you feel like an asshole. You always know the next fuckup will get you booted—because guys were getting booted right and left.

One morning, after a few hours of kickboxing, I was talking with a guy about what we were going to do in Memphis that night. It was Friday. All we had to do was get through a few hours of CQB; it had been a great week and it was almost over. In the fourth room on our last run, we were on the same wall after coming through a corner door. We turned right. Two other guys were on the opposite wall. There were three toilet stalls in front of me with the doors closed. Simple: I walk to them, open the door as I lean my back against the wall, one of the guys on the opposite wall shoots if there is a threat inside. Repeat on the next stall. Repeat. Simple. The only problem was, when I opened the first door, my buddy right behind me took three shots basically right next to my head. The bullets went inches in front of my face. Three times. I took a deep breath, exhaled, looked him in the eyes, and then looked at the two guys on the opposite wall. Their mouths were wide open. They couldn't believe he'd taken those shots. As I went to the next door, I pointed at one of the guys on the opposite wall and yelled, "*You* shoot this time!"

"Cease fire!!" an instructor yelled. I looked up. He was staring down at me from his observation post in the rafters. "I'm sorry I didn't stop that, O'Neill. When I saw him shoot, I swallowed my whistle." He pointed at me and the two guys on the far wall. "You three, get out of the house!" Then he pointed at my buddy. "You!! Unload your weapon and stay behind!"

He was on a plane home that afternoon. I never saw him again.

It's all a well-thought-out strategy. They want to know: Are you a person who can make a mistake under high pressure and forget about it? Or do you dwell on a mistake and then make a bigger mistake? Are your wounded ego and self-doubt going to jeopardize the entire team?

We need someone who can make life-and-death decisions

rapidly and keep moving no matter what. One of the ways I like to put it is: The instructors take the stress of combat and try to put it in a training environment. Because it's *not* actual combat, just training, people can more easily see that the stress is in their head, self-induced. But that's entry level: Ultimately, SEAL commanders are trying to find the people who can realize that *all* stress is self-induced. Even when bombs are going off and people are trying to kill you. Worrying doesn't help keep you alive. In fact, it can get you killed. Can you put that bag of bricks down and forget about it, or are you going to let it ruin your day?

In CQB especially, it's very important to understand what your buddies are doing, where the team is going, what makes the most sense. Communication, not talking, is key. It is a very difficult process that will get you fired if you screw up. There isn't time for people who can't think fast or who cave to pressure.

BY THE TIME WE FINISHED training, I thought it wasn't possible that we'd get any better or faster. I'd soon find out how wrong I was.

Another cool part of training took place in Washington State at the Survival, Evasion, Resistance, Escape school. The highlight was a war game exercise. The scenario: We were told one of the squadrons was going to jump into a hostile country and we were supposed to get to the drop zone, meet up with them, and drive them out. We had maps of the fictional city and a dossier of briefing notes concerning logistics, local government agencies, and communications. As we were driving in, we were pulled over by a fleet of screaming police cars. Officers in foreign uniforms yanked us out of the car at gunpoint and shoved us into vans. These guys were totally into the role—waving their guns dangerously and screaming at us with heavy foreign accents, even babbling among themselves in some strange language.

They brought us in, separated us, and aggressively interrogated me. This is one of the schools where they're allowed to put their hands on you, so they slapped me around, beat me up a bit, put me in cuffs and a prison jumpsuit, and locked me in a cell. It's not like a cell in an American prison. It's about the size of a high school locker, barely enough room to sit down if you put your knees up to your chest. All they gave me was an empty coffee can to dump in. My guess is they kept us in there maybe two and a half days—but your sense of time is the first thing to go.

Periodically, they'd drag me out for another interrogation. Sometimes I'd get the designated asshole and he'd smack me around, then throw me back in the cell. Sometimes I'd get the nice guy and actually find myself feeling a rapport with the guy. I'd think, *Shit, this is real*. Only later did I realize they're teaching you how to do good cop, bad cop.

Either way, I got thrown back in that school locker of a cell. I couldn't sleep because they were playing these awful recordings of children screaming over and over, or when they weren't doing that, this ridiculous foreign music I heard so often I began to think the words were English. I couldn't see anyone, but I began to think I could recognize my buddies by their coughs, so I realized, okay, my friends are here, and we started trying to communicate as if we were real POWs. Our first attempts started out as knocks and then turned to whispers, coughs. The guards would get pissed but they couldn't tell exactly who was doing it. One time I heard a guy yell "Noonan!!," right out of *Caddyshack*. Hearing my bros laugh kept my morale high.

They make you stand the whole time, but you'd hear guys sliding down the wall to the floor. Then you'd hear the guard outside screaming, and the next thing you knew your door was opening and someone was throwing a bucket of cold water on *you*. You're thinking—maybe even saying: "What the fuck, man?"

"Your buddy next to you sat down so we're punishing you."

Soon enough, I'd hear the guy on the *other* side of me slide down and—blam!—the cell door was opening and again with the cold water. By this time I'd be exhausted from standing and not sleeping, and from freezing my ass off, too. This went on for hours at one point until I finally said to myself, *This is bullshit*, and sat down. The guard slammed open the door. "You're sitting down! Pick a friend."

I said, "Fuck you, hit 'em both."

As I've said, I lost all sense of time, but it seemed like I'd been in there forever when they pulled me out again. I thought, here comes another beating, but instead they finally broke out of their roles and showed me around. I was still in some other reality even then. But they showed me an American flag and read off the Bill of Rights or some other patriotic shit. When I showed signs of coming out of it, they sat me down and showed me a compilation of my interrogation videos and took me through them point by point—what you're supposed to say and not supposed to say, how to layer your story so that if you do lie, you can keep your lies straight. It was interesting, though I don't think a lot of it is applicable because if we get captured we know damn well our head's getting cut off, if the bad guys are nice.

ABOUT HALFWAY THROUGH THE EIGHT months, we were training on a big Navy ship pretty far out at sea where we could blow stuff up and shoot live fire. The ship was sparse on amenities. In fact, there were no bunks—we just put a mat down in whatever cubbyhole we could find and slept in a sleeping bag. There was also no cell phone coverage. Very bad timing, since my wife was extremely pregnant. One morning, I woke up and was getting ready to train when the Master Chief of the class came up to me and said, "Hey, O'Neill, you're out of here."

My jaw dropped and my eyes blazed. I said, "What the fuck? We didn't even start training! I'm out? What did I do?"

He said, "Oh, no, no, no. Nothing like that. Your buddy called. Your wife's at Portsmouth, she's going into labor. We've got boats coming out to get you."

My first thought was, *Oh, thank God I'm not kicked out*.

My second thought: *Holy shit! I'm going to be a father*.

The boat they'd sent was damn fast, and we set some kind of nautical record hauling back into shore. I jumped into my car and broke every speed limit from there to the hospital in Portsmouth. I made the birth of my daughter with five minutes to spare.

Fortunately, we were back in town for a week or two after she was born, so I was able to be there when my wife and daughter came home from the hospital. But I still had to get up for 5:00 a.m. workouts and then train straight through to 7:00 p.m. With a brand-new baby, it was like an hour of sleep at night and then freaking training. Hell Week all over again.

Nicole really had no idea what she was signing up for when she married me. But she was cool with it. Her family was local, and we had a great support structure made up of the famous SEAL wives network. They were good at taking care of each other. Back then, not a lot of guys were dying in combat, so Nicole didn't worry too much about that aspect of my job. As a new mom, she didn't really have much on her mind besides that totally immersive experience.

I successfully completed training by December 2004. We ended up with thirty-five guys out of the sixty or so who'd started. For those of us who'd made it through, squadron placement worked like the NFL draft: Each squadron would get a turn to pick. The squadron that got first pick the previous year would pick last, and so on. Every squadron has members who help supervise the training, so they function as scouts, giving their group an inside scoop on the candidates. There's also an official top-down list based on all the instructor evaluations, as well as those painful peer evaluations.

We all went into the "draft" with a favorite squadron in mind. Maybe we already had friends there, or we liked the squadron's reputation—each unit had its own characteristics. My quick take on it was that one squadron was known to drink quite a bit, be physically tough as hell, and smoke cigarettes. Another was the team that was the most likely to look out for their guys by telling senior officers and other services to go fuck themselves.

The squadron I wanted was the work-through-lunch, get-off-hungry-type team. Hardworking, really professional—and combat hardened.

The squadron was known for its exploits during Operation Anaconda and Roberts' Ridge. Its snipers went back to the top of the mountain where Neil Roberts had lost his life and fought it out, nose to nose, with a determined enemy. Their reconnaissance guys got the drop on foreign fighters who were set to ambush American troops, and they also put guys in place to call in major air strikes that led to the eventual victory.

If you wanted to see combat fast, they were your best bet.

Yes, I was a new father with a very young wife. But what had all my years of work and training been about if not to avenge the deaths of Neil and all those ordinary Americans who went to work one morning and found themselves forced to decide between being burned alive or jumping from a smashed plate-glass window a hundred floors above the street? I can't tell you how many times the images of those tiny but obviously human figures free-falling helplessly from that burning tower played in my mind. And now, I was finally in a position to do something about it.

I worked my contacts, asked friends to put in a good word. Every member of the squadron participated in the selection of new members—another unique thing about Team ▇. We never knew in what order we were picked, who spoke for us or against us. One day the assignments simply appeared as if they'd been plucked from the Sorting Hat at Hogwarts.

I looked at the list and saw the name of the right squadron by my name. I still get goose bumps thinking about it.

I remember entering the "Team Room" for the first time and being in awe. It wasn't just because of the memorabilia all over the walls; it was because of the men, the "Shooters." I could tell they were a bit excited to have us. It's always exciting to get your new guys. That means there are new folks to take out the trash and clean up the place. It also means that the former new guys are being "promoted" out of the role of carrying the breaching ladders on patrol and/or the sledgehammer and/or the crowbarlike Hooligan tool or "Hooley." When the newest new guys show up, guess who gets those honors?

The first thing we did was sit down with the enlisted leadership. We met our Leading Petty Officer, Leo; our two Troop Chiefs, Ralph and Cole; and our Master Chief, Decker. They basically told us what to expect and how to act but that, because we'd just successfully completed selection training, there'd be no slowing down for us. We were expected to perform at the level of all the more experienced men. Then we got to ask questions. The first was, "What about grooming standards?"

Every other SEAL in Virginia Beach had to keep "Navy Standards" while stateside. Leo pointed to his beard with his index finger and thumb and, as cool as ever, said, "Let it goooo."

We'd arrived.

IN THE FIRST FEW DAYS, we were given our "cages" where we could keep all our gear and we moved our weapons to the squadron's spaces in the armory. The cages in the locker room were always a place of interest, sometimes fun, sometimes disgusting, always clever. The squadron had been known to prank each other and some of the senior guys were definitely masters. They were unbelievable in their creativity but even better at denial. I don't know if it was the training or what, but they could deny anything. If someone said, "You stole the cookies," they'd say, "No, I didn't." If someone said, "I see your hand in the jar!" they'd say, "This is not my hand!"

A common prank was the stink bomb. Guys would put area rugs down in their cages and tape down the sides to avoid slipping. Usually when they were in the shower, the perps would roll up, untape the rug, and slip one of those *MAD* magazine stink bombs under there—the kind that look like marbles but crack open when you step on them and then instantly fill the entire area with a stench that smells like you sold your ass to the devil. When the guy came back wrapped in his towel, he'd step into his cage and then it was on. Everyone in the locker room had to evacuate except the victim, who in the name of public decency had to put on some clothes while breathing in the fumes.

But stink bombs were a light warm-up. Some guys waited until the weekend so that they had two days to mess with a cage. That would give the perpetrator enough time to dye every single one of the victim's uniforms pink, dry them, and then hang them back up in proper order.

I've been pranked more than once in my career, in ways both funny and downright mean, but the prank that stands out the most hit me when no one was around to see it. The physical therapists at the command kept some industrial grade "liquid heat" lotion in the rehab room. They'd administer it to us on a limited basis to help us deal with injuries and recovery. One of my teammates got hold of the stuff and decided to hook some of us up with a good deal. He liberally applied it to the groin section of our PT shorts. I don't know how long this particular pair had been sitting neatly on my shelf, but I put them on and headed to the gym a few hundred meters across the compound. The funny thing about this vile concoction is that it really doesn't heat up until it gets wet. I was not wet yet.

It was a Saturday and the gym was empty. I decided to do a twenty-minute warm-up on the elliptical machine. About five minutes into it, I started to sweat a bit and "things" started to heat up, not warm up. I sensed that something was wrong but thought I could tough it out for the remainder of the workout. I was wrong. Seven minutes into my workout, I felt like there was a leprechaun standing under me with a blow torch aimed at my special parts. It burned so bad that I had to sprint back to the locker room, across the command. Halfway there, the heat was too intense to keep the shorts on. I was able to rip them off without disturbing my headphones and ran the rest of the way to the main building like Porky Pig: T-shirt and no pants, my crotch burning like a B-list porn star, with Demon Hunter blasting in my ears.

I finally got back to the cage area and headed to my locker. I wanted to grab my soap and towel so I could rush to the shower and wash the fire off. As I grabbed the bag that held my shower kit, dust flew up and I heard *boom* as a flash-crash grenade blew. God, these guys were good.

Pranking was a part of life in the squadron. Some sections of the locker room were better than others. My row was the worst. I was assigned to an area with the best prankers, guys who'd been around for a long time and honed their craft. They called it "The Gaza Strip" because stuff was blowing up all the time. One guy got so tired of getting hit and never catching anyone doing it that he finally figured he would commit a "Suicide Prank." This didn't mean that he hurt himself or anything; it would just be very obvious that he did it and then it would be open season on him.

He'd just finished work and was taking his gear off . . . BOOM! Everyone throughout the cage area started laughing and hollering and whistling. "What did you *do?*!" There were the obvious prankers doing most of the cajoling but no one admitted it. The laughter died down, the guys got undressed and got in the shower. The victim did not. He waited. Once all of the "usual suspects" were in the showers he grabbed a flash-crash grenade of his own, walked to the showers and announced, "Hello, gentlemen."

He pulled the pin and under-handed the grenade into the team shower. Then he turned and walked off. BOOOM!! A crash in a shower is several times louder than one in a locker room. I thought this was great revenge but he paid for it later: His locker was soon full of all the shredded paper in the squadron . . . with a few flash crashes under the bags beneath.

I was very happy to be a part of this group. At the time, morale was the highest I'd ever seen at any command. Even though there were arguments now and then, everyone got along. The camaraderie was incredible. The older guys really took care of the new guys and everyone worked hard together.

When we did our first CQB house run, I remember being in the middle of the train when the initial breach charge went off. Then the squadron was simply gone. The other recent selection training grads and I—all of us thinking we were hot shit at this—had to sprint to keep up. These guys were faster than I'd ever imagined anyone could be, but at the same time impeccably safe. The run was over before I knew it, and it was flawless—to me, anyway. The Safety Officers had nitpicky debrief points, but, come on. These guys were astounding. Once again, I would need to pick up my game.

Like the other new guys, I'd been in a kind of probationary period. Now that deployment was around the corner probation was over. It was time for . . . the Yard-In Party. (Cue *Jaws* theme.)

It's a tradition that, to be given your patch, you must drink a yard of beer without stopping. The yard is measured in a thirty-six-inch-long tubelike glass with a fat bulb at the bottom. I believe that a yard holds three beers, but there is a catch here, as always. The bulb at the bottom of the yard is filled with whiskey and the beer is ICE freaking cold. If your lips leave the glass, or if you throw up before you are done, better luck next time. It is preferred that you accomplish this feat in under one minute—while wearing a truly embarrassing hat with a big mat of hair and buffalo horns sticking out the side.

We were all so pumped up that we knew we'd knock it out on the first attempt, but two buddies and I decided that it would be smart to go to a bar before the Yard-In Party, which was being held at a buddy's house. The thought was: If we get a bit of a buzz and a bit of a base in our stomachs, we'll be good to go. I'm still not sure how good of an idea this was, but at least we were thinking outside the box.

So after a few beers at AJ Gator's, we went to the party. The entire squadron was there and we were lined up in alphabetical order. That was good for me because I could watch first and see how the low-alphabet guys handled it. We watched the "Beer Meister" fill the yard as the boss gave a speech. I shouldn't have watched: Good *Lord* there was a lot of whiskey. He must have put ten shots in there because it pretty much filled the bulb. Then he topped that with very cold Killian's. The first guy up gave a toast, and knocked it out in good time. When he finished, he looked like he was taking a standing eight count, but he didn't puke and he walked around getting handshakes and hugs.

The next dude, same result. This happened all the way up to me. I sure didn't want to be the first to have a spectacular fail. There was a famous story about a friend of mine named Lance who may have had the most spectacular Yard of all time. Lance had been through the BUD/S class immediately after mine, and had gotten through selection a year before I did. For some reason Lance went to get a big spaghetti dinner before his Yard-In, which is a horrible idea. Not surprisingly, when he was about three-quarters of the way done with his yard he threw up, and the bulb filled back up again—only not with beer or whiskey.

The first rule of yarding is that you can never take your mouth off the glass once you begin. Even in this "special" circumstance. Lance was a SEAL, so he refused to quit. He sucked all of that nastiness down again, got about three-quarters of the way. Same unfortunate result. Bulb filled once more. It was so bad, people all around were losing their own dinners.

It became known as "the good yard gone bad."

Trying to banish any thought of a "gone bad" disaster, I put on the big-ass "Buffalo" hat and waited for my yard to arrive. When it did, I raised the glass and gave a toast to The Tribe and put the yard to my mouth. It smelled and tasted like a huge glass of Jack Daniel's that someone had spilled some beer in. Normally the key to dealing with a bad smell is to breathe through your mouth; not gonna happen here. Time to chug it!

When you drink a yard, it's very important to mind the bulb at the bottom. The bulb will begin to fill with air very slowly as you tip it up and up. The issue is, once it gets too full, the air will rush in and push the liquid straight out of the glass at a high rate of speed. Did I mention that during a Yard-In you aren't allowed to spill a drop? If you do, disqualified, better luck next time. So it's imperative that the drinker lift the glass but also spin it at the same time. This avoids the problem.

So I worked this technique for a little over a minute and finished my yard. It was a tough drink but well worth it. I have a fuzzy memory of walking (or possibly stumbling) around getting handshakes and hugs. I was finally part of The Tribe.

We walked back into the living room and stood against the wall as the rest of the squadron watched. Our Command Master Chief said a few words that I doubt any of us remember, then gave us each our patch. I stared in awe at that thing for several minutes, feeling a sense of honor. That was one of the best days of my life. I was surrounded by all my best friends; we'd just finished nine years of the most difficult training imaginable. We were officially part of the team. And we were going to war.

CHAPTER TEN

Before my daughter was even a year old, I found myself kissing her goodbye thinking I might never see her again, and if that were true, how to her it would be as if I'd never even existed.

I don't mean to be overly dramatic, but that's the kind of thought that runs through your mind when you're flying off to face combat for the first time.

It was April 2005 and we were headed to Afghanistan. SEAL Team ▓ hadn't yet been sent to Iraq, or even been authorized to fight the Taliban in Afghanistan, if you can believe that. They were sending us over there to hunt high-value al-Qaeda targets. Some of the guys had already been there in previous deployments and explained that some parts of Afghanistan were like "going through a time warp to the tenth century. You need to see it to believe it."

We would definitely see it.

When Nicole dropped me off at the command, some of my team members were there already. We watched each other say our goodbyes and went inside. Guys were sitting around the Team Room having a beer, waiting for the buses to come get us. Most of our gear had already been loaded in huge metal shipping boxes and sent out a few weeks earlier. All each of us had with us was something like a North Face backpack with a sleeping bag, a ground pad, a few changes of clothes, a computer, and some other personal items.

We drained our beers, then boarded the bus for the short

ride to the big C-17 cargo plane that would fly us there. A C-17 is just this big open bay with benches on either side and about a half dozen of our huge shipping boxes lashed down tight (we hoped) in the middle.

Once the plane takes off, it's always funny because it becomes a race to see who can get their ground pads blown up first. You want to claim the best spot to lay it out (the ideal spots are on top of the boxes; the senior guys get dibs) so you can sleep your way to Germany. Not that any spot is going to be that comfortable. It's cold and loud as hell. We all wear ear protectors or just jam in earbuds and turn up the volume. Occasionally, we strap ourselves in with a big cargo strap as a protection against air turbulence. Then we take an Ambien. SEALs love Ambien—a very effective aid for falling asleep under any conditions, including on hard, cold, rocky ground when you know you'll be eating enemy fire for breakfast.

We got out at Ramstein Air Base long enough to grab a meal and refuel, then boarded again. After that, another race to dreamland, and bam, we were in Afghanistan.

It was actually refreshing, a solid fifteen hours of sleep before arrival at Bagram Airfield. It was the middle of the night, and we were wide awake after all our beauty rest. We broke down the big shipping containers and divvied up our stuff.

Then we split up for our different outstations. I was selected to go to the safe house in Jalalabad along with two other SEALs, an Explosive Ordnance Disposal (EOD) guy and a radio guy. We loaded up a C-130, which is a four-engine prop plane, and flew down to Jalalabad Airfield, which at the time was pretty rustic and not especially secure. The guys from the team we were replacing were waiting at the field. As we got off the bird, they got on. The situation was a little short on turnover protocol—unless you count some high fives over the roar of the engines that never turned off.

Toyota Hilux pickup trucks had been left behind, still running. We put our gear in the back, got in, and drove off into the city.

We'd been assigned an interpreter we called Larry, an Afghan who'd been fighting with the pro-government forces for years by then. Interpreters were always native speakers, contractors we hired. At first we let them carry guns because they'd all grown up fighting and we trusted them. But in later years of the war, not so much. They trailed behind us and were brought up when needed. Larry was my first experience working with a local. Since we didn't get a proper turnover, I wasn't sure what to think of this guy; he was the first Afghan I'd met. He was shorter than me and in average shape; dark features and dark brown eyes with no beard. Since it was my first trip there and I didn't know yet whom I could trust, I was very short and curt with him. I was even thinking I might need to blast the guy.

From that very first truck ride, whenever I drove in Afghanistan I kept a pistol in easy reach, either in my vest or under my leg. I put my rifle in the door in case I had to open the door and fall out. Your gun falls with you. You don't leave it in the truck.

It was a weird feeling suddenly being in the middle of Jalalabad, a major city in Afghanistan—a place where Osama bin Laden used to live. It was summer, hot and dusty, with the penetrating stink of trash and smoke saturating the air. The pothole-laden streets were lined with drab low-rise buildings, "bazaars" on each side of the street for most of the drive, and weird speed bumps every few hundred meters. After several encounters with those bumps and all of the deep potholes, we learned it was best to keep your speed up and hit them fast. After about ten minutes, we turned into a narrow alley and stopped at the gate of a huge courtyard fronting a comparatively unimpressive two-story structure that reminded me of one of those old no-tell motels.

My team leader, Adam, greeted us in the safe house. Adam was a master breacher. The door or barricade he couldn't batter or blast through hadn't been invented. He was one of the top performers in all of SEAL Team ▓ and had been awarded a Silver Star for his role in Operation Anaconda three years earlier. Even before the SEAL team that included Neil Roberts had attempted to insert on Takur Ghar, Adam had hiked through the snow for a number of days with a few other snipers and gotten the drop on some foreign al-Qaeda fighters as they were about to shoot down the first American helicopters to enter the valley. The terrorists had a huge anti-helicopter machine gun and were in perfect position. Adam and his team were better. Adam was a legend and I was thrilled to be with him on my first Team ▓ deployment.

He showed us around, let us pick our rooms. The safe house was a former motel with a walled courtyard. *And* armed guards. I ended up sharing a room with the EOD guy, Harp, because he and I had gone through selection together and had gotten to know each other well. He's one of the funniest guys I know, a master blaster, seriously, and just a cool dude. When I first met him I asked, "Where you from?"

He said, "Texas. How about you?"

I said, "Montana."

He said, "Montana, eh? . . . What part of Texas is that?"

Adam read us in on our mission, confirming what I'd already heard about hunting high-value al-Qaeda targets. Then we waited for the sun to come up and he took us on a neighborhood tour. Our alley had a nickname—Chocolate Alley. It was just off the main street. To either side of our safe house lived Afghan families. Another house nearby was where the case officers worked their sources and produced targets for us. It was also where the kitchen and cook were. At that time we had a lot more food than targets. By then, three and a half years after the American invasion, al-Qaeda fighters had mostly been killed or fled Afghanistan to regroup elsewhere.

Because we weren't yet cleared to take on the Taliban, we weren't going to be sent on any night raids against them, which meant we had to get used to living like normal people, awake during daylight hours. We'd wake up in the morning, get a workout, read the intel reports, wait for our meals. When we weren't eating or lifting, we'd sit around what we called the family room in the main building, which used to be the hotel lobby, and watch the seventy-inch flat screen we'd ordered from Bagram. That screen was way too big for the space, but it gave us an excuse to spend time collecting old DVDs. We watched every episode of *The Shield* more than once, and we all wanted to imitate Vic Mackey, the lethal badass cop who's the main character.

A lot of the time spent in these safe houses is dedicated to building them up, making them a better place to live. We had a certain amount of money budgeted. We brought in locals to build this really small pool. When I say small, I mean, bathtub-size—like four feet deep. We had treadmills and ordered weights and an elliptical. The Green Berets had a gym and we'd trade out with them. We also got hold of some mats so we could practice jujitsu.

It's odd to say, but to us, Jalalabad was a peaceful city. We had motorbikes we would drive around town. We'd go shopping in the bazaars, hit the shawarma and falafel stands.

It's not like we forgot our mission. We were always looking for sources, for people we could potentially run across the border to Pakistan to find out what was going on. While we were conducting interviews with former mujahideen, we were also trying to find locals to hire as security guards, electricians, interpreters. We had a huge backyard where we did the interviews. Lines formed down Chocolate Alley—dozens of locals hoping to work for the Americans. There wasn't a huge American presence at that time, so we didn't feel like occupiers. None of us dressed in uniforms. Our outfit was unconventional in more than its conduct of warfare, and we flaunted not having to abide by the strict dress codes that applied to all other US military personnel overseas. I guess we owed our sartorial liberation to SEAL founder Dick Marcinko, the ultimate rule breaker. But the more casual attire also served a purpose. It helped us blend in and be less intimidating when we drove or walked through the city. Every time we made our way up and down the alley, kids would come out and say, "Chocolate, chocolate," and we'd hand them chocolate. So *that's* why it was called Chocolate Alley. The kids loved us and we loved them back. The parents saw that and grew protective of us.

To further blend in, we hired people to drive us in these three-wheeled vehicles we called tuck-tucks. We'd dress up in local garb and tour Jalalabad, with no particular goal in mind. We'd drive out along the river, check out the dam, visit the bazaars. These days, if an American were to wander the city they might get their head cut off.

Back then it wasn't that bad. But there were still some bad guys out there. We were developing new technologies to track them—a lot of signal intelligence stuff I still can't talk about in detail. We'd fly in experts to work their magic. They'd get a bead on someone talking to people in Pakistan, trying to coordinate attacks on Americans. When we could be sure of the specific house where that guy lived, we'd hit it. Since Adam had only the three of us in the safe house, we'd fly a team of six from Bagram down to Jalalabad. Then we'd go.

The first mission I went on was a step on the learning curve. I grabbed my EOD guy, Harp, and I said, "Hey, man, what's the suicide bomber threat here? What's the IED [Improvised Explosive Device] threat?" He reassured me it wasn't that bad, but having seen the movies and watched the news, I was convinced suicide bombers were everywhere. We drove to the house we'd targeted a few hours after sundown. There isn't a lot to do in Afghanistan so the locals go to sleep early. They don't know what time it is or how old they are, but they do know it's time to get some shut-eye when the sun dips below the horizon. So we drove down Chocolate Alley, through a roundabout with a big globe in the center, made a right on the main street, drove a few blocks, and made a left, and then we stopped. This was an op in our own damn neighborhood. Adam led us on foot for a few more blocks and then pointed out the house. I put an explosive breach on the front gate. I was on edge, but when the breach blew the gate and we started to move, everything got so clear. I remember watching my boss, the team leader, and being amazed at how smooth he was, so unafraid, just walking around alertly, calmly taking care of business. I was thinking, *How can you be so cool?*

We blew the door and rolled in just like in CQB training. People were still sleeping. I was amazed that they could sleep through that stuff, or that they'd pretend to sleep through it. I would see that behavior over and over again, but this was a first. The kids were asleep, the wives were asleep. The targets are never alone in the house. If there are three adult males, there are nine wives and twenty children. It just multiplies. We went room to room and rolled up every adult male and then talked to them using the interpreter. In this culture the women are so subservient to the men that they just go sit in corners and the kids follow. There's some crying at first, but that stops once we give them glow sticks or candy. At that time the interpreters were still Afghan militia guys, so they carried guns, too. They actually rolled in with us and then they'd interrogate the suspects and tell us who the bad guys were. In this case the guy we were looking for was a big fat Saudi Arabian. Most of the time, when you run into an Arab in Afghanistan, he's not there for good reasons. I was all business as I was cuffing him, but then I noticed his grubby T-shirt well stuffed with belly fat. I couldn't help cracking up. It said in English—and I'm guessing he didn't even know what it meant—"It's not a beer belly, it's a fuel tank for a sex machine." Funny terrorist.

We hauled him out, drove him to the airfield, and put him on the plane to Bagram. Up there they had expert interrogators from different agencies and military branches who'd figure out this guy's reasons for being in Jalalabad and, hopefully, get some intelligence that could lead to other targets. He was probably low-level and would be deported with little fanfare. (I didn't know it then, but you had to be a pretty significant evildoer to merit waterboarding, let alone be shipped off to Guantanamo Bay.)

That was it for my first operation, but I was beginning to understand the proper attitude: You don't need to sweat everything. Just do it like you've practiced a million times and you're going to be just fine.

We carried out a half dozen more missions without firing a shot or being fired on.

Once we came close, though, and I learned an important lesson. We were sneaking up on a house at night using night vision when we saw some armed guys coming at us. I trained my gun on them. They were lit in my night vision by my flood light and laser—completely invisible to the naked eye. They had dots on them and they didn't even know it. We were getting ready to go hot when Adam said, "Hold on. I can de-conflict this. I don't think these are bad guys."

He was savvy enough to know that in Afghanistan, just because someone is armed doesn't mean he's a bad guy. There, guns are like cell phones. Everyone has one.

We kept our guns on the guys while we had a tense conversation in our broken Pashto, but it turned out they were Afghan cops on patrol.

If we'd killed them, which we could have, it would have been a huge incident, but because my team leader was so on top of it—*I'll take care of this*—he saved about five lives that night. I'll never forget watching how cool he was, and wanting to be just like him.

BY JUNE 2005, EVERYTHING WAS winding down in Jalalabad. Out at the airfield, they were doing some kind of buildup, creating a command center. They set up some tents and flew in some guys from SEAL Team Ten and SEAL Delivery Vehicle Team One. We were all excited. We heard rumblings that they wanted to put snipers up in the Korengal Valley in the rugged mountains near the Pakastani border. It was nicknamed the Valley of Death, and was, quite possibly, the most dangerous place in the world. The remote, forested mountains were loaded with a toxic mix of al-Qaeda and Taliban and allied warlords.

SEAL Team Ten wanted to go after one of the most significant threats there, a guy by the name of Ahmad Shah. He'd actually fought against the Taliban and al-Qaeda in 2001, but he'd since switched sides and was a key player in smuggling in foreign fighters to swell al-Qaeda ranks.

In emails and phone calls, our team leaders both from Jalalabad and Asadabad discussed with the SEAL Team Ten commander, a guy named Erik Kristensen, plans to go get Shah. Kristensen was a "task unit commander," which meant that he could propose missions to the overall "battle space owner"—an officer further up the command chain. My bosses, who were parallel to Kristensen, weren't optimistic about the timing. They told him, "We're not even sending in SEAL Team ▓ snipers. We think they have surface-to-air missiles."

There was a lot of back and forth about whether to go in or not. But Kristensen was an aggressive commander. You absolutely need guys like that, always willing to take it to the enemy. It's a risky business for sure, but so often, that's how wars are won.

Snipers were inserted up into the valley to scout things out. Oddly, these were the SEAL Delivery Vehicle guys, members of the submarine unit nobody wanted to be in. Four of their snipers—Michael Murphy, Danny Dietz, Matthew Axelson, and Marcus Luttrell—had drawn this tough mission.

Team Ten flew into Jalalabad Airfield to prepare for their incursion into the valley to take out Shah once the recon team had determined his whereabouts. We went out to see them at the airfield and had a nice little bullshitting session, catching up. These were guys I'd known from training or previous assignments, Jeff Taylor, Dan Healy, Jeff Lucas, and my friend Mike B. Healy and I had gone to sniper school together in 1998. He was a mountain of a man from New England who would only drink Sam Adams. The bushy beard he'd grown made him look bigger, but almost nicer, which wasn't possible. We talked about beer and how great it was going to be to get back home. No Sam Adams here. I hadn't seen Jeff Taylor since a birthday party at my mother-in-law's house in Virginia Beach a few months prior, but we picked up the conversation where it had left off: skydiving and base jumping. This guy was as good at extreme sports as he was fearless, and our wives were best friends. I kept hoping I'd go on the raid with them. My team said goodbye and rode back to our safe house.

Truth is, we were envious. They were about to see some significant action while we'd only been transporting obese Arabs to the airport. We hunted up our outstation chief and told him we wanted to go on the raid with them when the time came.

He said, "Hell, no. Take everybody from SEAL Team ▓ off those helicopters." There were none on there, but HQ wanted to be perfectly clear: SEAL Team ▓ would not be involved. He knew something bad was going to happen. We had the intelligence but SEAL Team Ten didn't listen.

Even as we'd been chatting in that tent at the airfield the four SEAL snipers were fighting for their lives. Some locals had spotted them in the valley and informed the Taliban. Fifty enemy fighters seized the high ground and began a devastating three-sided attack. The four SEALs, all wounded in the early minutes, nonetheless managed to elude quick defeat or capture by bounding down the steep slope with leaps of twenty to thirty feet at a time. Now they had cover, but their position among rocks deep in the ravine made it impossible to make a distress call. Dietz, the communications guy, scrambled for open ground, but as soon as he emerged from cover an enemy round shot through his hand, shattering his thumb. Murphy knew the only chance was for him to use his iridium satellite phone so he sprinted for an open place to make the call. The official Navy report reads:

Moving away from the protective mountain rocks, he knowingly exposed himself to increased enemy gunfire. . . . While continuing to be fired upon, Murphy made contact with the SOF Quick Reaction Force at Bagram Airfield and requested assistance. He calmly provided his unit's location and the size of the enemy force while requesting immediate support for his team. At one point he was shot in the back causing him to drop the transmitter. Murphy picked it back up, completed the call and continued firing at the enemy who was closing in. Severely wounded, Lt. Murphy returned to his cover position with his men and continued the battle.

We were hanging out in our tiny pool behind the safe house when a Ranger major—the overall commander for that area—came out and said, "Hey, your boys just got their asses handed to them."

He told us something had happened up in Korengal, and some MH-47 Chinook helicopters had taken off on a rescue mission. We sprinted to our motorcycles and raised dust getting back down to the airfield. When we got there, they told us that one of the helicopters had been shot down.

According to the Navy account, a Chinook with eight SEALs had set out with an escort of heavily armored Army attack helicopters that were there to, as the official account puts it, "neutralize the enemy and make it safer for the lightly-armored, personnel-transport helicopter to insert."

Knowing that every minute that passed decreased the chance that their brothers would survive, the men in the Chinook made the decision to leave behind the much heavier and slower attack helicopters. From the official account: "They knew the tremendous risk going into an active enemy area in daylight, without their attack support, and without the cover of night . . . but knowing that their warrior brothers were shot, surrounded, and severely wounded, the rescue team opted to directly enter the oncoming battle in hopes of landing on brutally hazardous terrain."

Before that could happen, the helicopter, which was carrying sixteen men—including the guys I'd just been chatting with: Jeff Taylor, Dan Healy, Jeff Lucas, and their boss, Erik Kristensen— was blasted out of the sky.

The other guy we'd been talking to in the tent, Mike B., had survived. There had been two rescue choppers with SEAL Team Ten operators on them. One—the lead helicopter, the one that went down—was called Turbine 33. The other was Turbine 34. Before they took off, Dan Healy, who'd been on Turbine 34, grabbed Mike B., who'd been on 33, and asked him to switch. Dan was an SDV guy and Mike was Team Ten. "Those are my guys on the ground," Dan told him. He wanted to be the first one to get to them. Mike agreed.

They had no idea they were making a decision that would determine who would die in the next few minutes.

When the surviving helicopter returned, we were waiting at the airfield in Jalalabad. The pilots were so shaken they landed at the wrong base across town. The guys had to run across the city to get back to the airfield. I saw them as they were coming in, one at a time: Greg Czar, Luke Newbold, then Mike, and with each face I thought, "The world's a better place because you're still in it."

"What the hell just happened?" I asked.

One said, "They're shooting missiles at us."

The official report said that a rocket-propelled grenade brought down Turbine 33. But the guys in the second helicopter told us they saw two missiles come out of the valley and turn. Rocket-propelled grenades don't turn. Heat-seeking missiles do. The first one hit Turbine 33. It wasn't like in the movies where it takes the hit and then tumbles down the mountain. They said it exploded on impact. The second missile missed Turbine 34. If it really was a surface-to-air missile and it missed, then someone was watching out for them, because those things are designed to shoot down jets.

With no rescue imminent, the four SEALs, pinned down in the ravine, were running out of ammunition. They'd held out for two hours and managed to kill a few dozen of their attackers. But finally their guns fell silent. Murphy, Axelson, and Dietz were dead. Luttrell miraculously survived a near miss from an RPG round, which blew him over a ridge and knocked him unconscious.

Again from the official account:

> Regaining consciousness some time later, Luttrell managed to escape—badly injured—and slowly crawl away down the side of a cliff. Dehydrated, with a bullet wound to one leg, shrapnel embedded in both legs, three vertebrae cracked; the situation for Luttrell was grim. Traveling seven miles on foot, he evaded the enemy for nearly a day. Local nationals came to his aid, carrying him to a nearby village . . .

Of course we knew none of that. All we knew was that we needed to get to the crash site, but we weren't going to fly there. At this point there were plenty of helicopters—Apaches, Chinooks, and other aircraft—coming in, but nobody was going to fly up to the valley with the possibility of anti-aircraft missile defenses. It was up to us to get there on the ground—which was arguably even more dangerous than by air.

This wasn't some command decision. We were sending people around to find a coalition of Special Forces guys—literally, going from hut to hut saying, "Hey, we need a couple volunteers. Here's the situation. A helicopter's been shot down and there are four snipers missing."

Every single Ranger we talked to hopped out of bed and said some variation of, "It should take us ten minutes to be ready but we're going to be out in five."

Within minutes we had Army Rangers, Air Force guys, Navy, EOD, Navy SEALs, Green Berets. We knew people were still working on other methods of rescue, and that at some point—nobody knew when—an airborne rescue might be launched. But we weren't about to sit around and wait for that. This was a five-alarm fire and we were the bucket brigade. We commandeered vehicles, Humvees, Hiluxes, whatever we could find, and then we drove. We drove north from Jalalabad, heading up the Korengal River road to a point we knew was directly on the other side of a mountain from the Korengal Valley. We drove up as far as we could and met up with our other SEALs from Asadabad. They had some donkeys, which we loaded with food and water and whatever shit we had on us. Then we started walking. Straight up. We started at about two thousand feet of elevation and had to walk up to ten thousand feet in less than a day, with temperatures well over a hundred degrees Fahrenheit.

The mountain was nothing like I was used to in Montana. It was a mix of dirt and rocks with little vegetation, and steep as hell. *Lone Survivor*, the movie version, prettified it. The mountains didn't look like that at all.

We labored up some ancient goat path that resembled an insanely steep flight of stairs that some lunatic had made, switching back, but always up, up, up.

That and the intense heat got to guys quick. Before long, one of the medics started handing back his gear because he couldn't carry it anymore. Guys were like, "What the fuck? We're not carrying this shit." Some were even ditching ammunition to lighten the load. As the day wore on, it got so bad that some of the donkeys refused to go any farther, and when we prodded them, they veered to the side and leaped over the nearest cliff. They sure as hell didn't want to be there anymore.

Everyone was so dehydrated that I knew we were going to lose people soon. We'd pull up by a bush or anything I could hang an IV bag on and I'd start sticking guys to keep them from going into heat stroke. Their veins had shriveled so small due to dehydration that it was a struggle to get the needle in. When I finally did it and squeezed the IV bag, I saw their body suck up the juice. I wasn't a medic but had learned how to do that in training. I must have given seven or eight IVs, but it wasn't enough, and we had to medevac some guys out. Only the little white pills someone was handing out kept us going.

About ten hours into the hike, we stopped for a break. I was sitting with two or three other SEALs, and it just hit me. I said, "Hey, did anybody call home before we got up here?"

They said, "Well, no, what do you mean?"

"Well, shit," I said. "All our wives in Virginia Beach are going to know a bunch of SEALs from Virginia Beach just died and they haven't heard from us."

I wasn't wrong to worry. Back home, Nicole was at our friend Karen's house. Karen was now a widow. Her husband, Jeff, was one of the SEALs who'd gone down on Turbine 33.

The somber men in the blue uniforms had come to the house and told her, so of course she was freaking out. Karen and Jeff had only been married a couple of months at this point. Nicole couldn't do much to console her—if you want to know what inconsolable really means, this is it—but she didn't want to go home because she didn't want those same somber men in uniform to be waiting when she arrived. She stayed there with Karen as long as she could. My daughter, who wasn't even one, was with her. Eventually the baby just had to go home.

Nicole made a long, horrible trip home at very slow speed, dread chasing every rotation of the tires. When our place came into view, the driveway was empty. No Navy officers waiting with terrible news. She breathed a huge sigh of guilty relief—guilty because she'd been spared and Karen hadn't. She got out of the car and walked into the house carrying our daughter on her hip. As she juggled the baby for better balance, a bib slipped out of the bag filled with baby shit. My wife didn't notice. She walked into the house. Closed the door behind her. Locked it. She'd escaped to this point, and could only pray a dead bolt could somehow keep the bad news out.

Still, she didn't feel safe. She just started pacing around the house, waiting for a knock on the door.

Meanwhile, my neighbor Ron had seen the bib drop in the yard. He decided to be a good neighbor, go out, pick up the bib, and bring it over to Nicole. The problem was, Ron worked with me. He was in his uniform.

He grabbed the bib and brought it to the front door. He rang the doorbell. Nicole looked out and saw a man in his blues. This was it. She set our daughter against a wall in the corner. The baby couldn't sit up by herself yet, and Nicole was thinking ahead: She didn't want to drop her when she fainted.

Then she walked to the door. She later said they were the hardest seven steps of her life. She . . . well, I'll let my neighbor Ron finish the story:

"The door opened and I said, 'You dropped this.' She punched me in the face and closed the door."

This is what was going on at home while I was up on that mountain, taking some of the hardest steps *I* ever had to take.

When we got to the top of the mountain we heard that the command had finally decided they could start flying guys in from Bagram to secure the crash site and recover the bodies. I never learned what made them reverse themselves. By this time we'd heard that Axelson was missing, possibly dead. The fate of the others was still uncertain. We turned around and headed back down the mountain to come up with a search plan.

It was night, and we began picking our way down in the dark. As we were descending we spotted a fire near the mouth of a cave. With our night vision we could see some men around the fire. Taliban, obviously. Probably the dudes who'd shot down Turbine 33. We called Bagram for an air strike, but nobody would authorize air support. They actually told us, "We're not saying there are women and children in those caves, but we can't prove that there aren't."

We'd just hiked ten thousand feet in a hundred degrees. We weren't about to let some jackasses sitting safe in the ops center beat us. We kept on them, and somehow persuaded them to engage. We called in A-10s. That was the first time I'd seen A-10 Warthogs get called in on guys. It was impressive. Those are big badass attack planes, a flying arsenal. They came in low, just tearing the sky apart, and opened fire right over our heads with their four-thousand-pound, seven-barrel Gatling guns.

We could hear the bullets going supersonic: We heard them hit before we heard them shoot. It was all backward, just insane. It sounds like a big dragon flying over you, screaming and spitting fire. Warthogs 7, Taliban 0.

When we got to the bottom we picked up our trucks and drove up to Asadabad to mount the search for the MIA snipers. By now, we'd been awake for two days.

The villagers who were aiding Luttrell did so because of their commitment to the Afghan code of Pashtunwali—the obligation to protect strangers who enter your home. Even when Taliban fighters came to the village demanding they hand over Luttrell, the villagers refused, despite knowing that the consequence could be death.

Ironically, one of the men who cared for Luttrell later said he was motivated by the same code that prompted Taliban leader Mullah Mohammed Omar to bring down a US invasion on his country rather than hand over Osama bin Laden.

While in hiding, Luttrell wrote a note that included his name, Social Security number, and some other minor information that let us know it was legit. By this point, we knew he was the lone survivor. An octogenarian village elder carried the note, stuffed inside his shirt, through Taliban-controlled territory to the nearest coalition military base. The Marines at the base brought the note and the old man to us.

The man looked like every other man who'd lived in these valleys for ten thousand years: traditional white "man-dress," dark suntan, wrinkled skin, a huge beard that men of his clan somehow manage to dye red, sandals, and a small white cap. He didn't have eyeliner on, so that was one indicator that he wasn't Taliban. He looked about two hundred years old.

The old guy told us the name of his village, but we needed to know exactly where Luttrell was, in which house, so we could go snatch him. When we showed him a detailed map of his village, his eyes just got this wide, blank look. His family had lived there five thousand years, but he couldn't recognize it on a map because he'd never seen a map. A map was an abstraction. We decided he might need to see the real thing. We sat him down in front of a computer and opened up some satellite images of his village. We might as well have showed him the face of Muhammad himself. This guy could not believe what he was looking at. He was so amazed at this technology that he got disoriented. Eventually, he settled down and showed us the house. A house anyway. We had to assume it was the right one.

The fastest way to do this would have been to fly in and fast-rope down on the house. But we hadn't been having good luck with helicopters lately. We said, "Hey, we're going to drive in there, and the old guy is going to walk us right to Luttrell's house. Then, we're going to get him and bring him back."

Simple plan, but we couldn't sell it.

All of us were like, "You're kidding me. We have an American hostage. We're going in."

Then they started saying the note was a fake because the T's in Luttrell weren't crossed, and it was all a setup for an ambush.

Really? How about the fact his Social Security number checked out?

The answer was still no. Normally, we would have done what they told us, but at this point we didn't really care because we had an American, a sniper, a SEAL, wounded in enemy territory and we had to go get him. The Ranger major who was in charge of our outpost made the final call. "We're taking him anyway."

I think the major eventually got banned from Afghanistan forever for that. But not that day. We put the old guy in one of the trucks and drove him toward the village.

It was probably the worst drive I've ever made. The roads were full of huge bumps and bigger potholes, and we knew Taliban were all over the hills. When we got to a spot in some hills across from the village, we got out and set off on foot. The sun was up at this point—our third day without sleep—and the heat was unbearable. We ran into some Marines who'd come out ahead of us. We were able to move faster than them because they were all wearing full flak jackets and helmets. All we had on were T-shirts and a couple of rounds of ammo. I remember thinking, "God, those Marines are hard-core."

Even more hard-core was the old man. He was practically flying up the mountain. It was all he'd known his entire life. The mountains were just part of who he was. Of course he wasn't carrying a weapon, and he hadn't been awake forever, like we'd been. Still, we were all impressed.

The terrain was almost as steep as the damn mountain, up and down, up and down. When we got to the final hill—one more climb and one more descent to go—one of my guys sat down.

"You know I can't go anymore," he said. "I've got to stop."

Climbing in a furnace on no sleep is a bitch. I could relate. But on the other side of the hill, Luttrell was waiting for us.

"Fine," I said. "We'll just tell Mrs. Luttrell, Marcus's mom, that we were this close to getting him but we couldn't because you got tired."

He said, "You know what, you're right," and he stood up and started walking.

I said, "Hey, do me a favor, bro. Tell me that exact same thing in about seven steps because I can't go any farther, either."

But we kept going and made it to the top of the hill. By then, the commanders decided to try to send a chopper in to pick him up, but they wanted us to keep going, mission redundancy, in case the chopper got engaged by enemy fire and had to veer away. Just as we were starting down we got word that the chopper had made it in, grabbed Luttrell, and flown out. Luttrell was safe. Great. But we still had to get out of the valley.

I looked at my buddy, and I said, "This is why SEAL training is so hard."

He said, "What do you mean?"

I said, "If we wanted to quit right now, where the fuck are we going to go?"

By the time we made it back to the truck, I may have been hallucinating, because on the way down I thought I saw some little Afghan kids. It was so hot I gave a little girl one of my water bottles. I watched in amazement as she poured the whole thing out on the ground—so she could play with the plastic bottle.

That couldn't have been real, right? But it was. Afghanistan's a time warp and we were sleepwalking in the fourteenth century.

We made the horrible drive all over again back to the base, then slept for twenty-five hours.

CHAPTER ELEVEN

n late 2005, we were home in Virginia Beach when we got word that the guys from Army Special Forces had been getting hit hard in western Iraq. For a full year, western Iraq had been a total shit storm. They had lost an entire troop—twenty-five to thirty-five guys—to death and injury. They'd taken casualties in intense close quarters gunfights, and from suicide bombers.

Iraq hadn't been part of our deal—I don't think an entire Team ▓▓ squadron had been there to that point. But now we were hearing people say, "We think we're going to go to Iraq this time."

We'd seen some shit on our deployment in Afghanistan, but Iraq, that was different. We'd heard about the IEDs blowing guys up everywhere and all the suicide bombings. Hell, we'd seen it on TV. Even as it sank in just how dangerous it would be, we felt this rising excitement, almost as if we were being called up from the minor leagues. We were going to the Show.

In January 2006, we flew in to Al Asad Air Base in far western Iraq, about seventy-five miles from the Syrian border. The base is a big, table-flat desert with rows of prefab buildings—big rectangular tin cans, basically. Right away we met with a whole range of Special Ops people who were there, and it quickly became clear that the reason for the high casualty rate was tactical.

America hadn't seen sustained, heavy combat since Vietnam,

157

and Vietnam-era tactics were still ingrained in many military units. In Iraq, a lot of our forces were just running straight into a house and getting the fight on. That was bad enough. Even worse: Al-Qaeda had studied our tactics. They'd leave a door open, and when they heard the choppers, a couple of terrorists with machine guns would be waiting inside to gun down the first four to six guys in.

It didn't make much sense, but I was learning how hard it can be to resist the power of "this is the way we've always done it." I've always believed that pairing old solutions with new problems is the worst way to run a team. Anyway, we started saying, "Why the fuck are we running into houses? Let's slow down. Let's change our tactics."

Our idea wasn't complicated. We'd land some distance away, far enough so that the people at the target couldn't hear the choppers. Then we'd walk our way in and either blow the doors or sneak into the house in total silence.

We set up quarters in a former abandoned building on the base—one that had been transformed into a frat house by the Army Special Forces boys; raw space, but plenty of it. Each team had its own room. As we did in Afghanistan, we set about homesteading, building up our man cave with big-ass screens and workout equipment. We linked up the various rooms with Xboxes so the gamers among us could play Halo. At times, there'd be sixteen of us sitting in front of screens, using controllers to command monsters to kill each other. The guys who didn't like video games could catch up on the latest *Shield* episodes, work out, or play cornhole, that game where you try to toss beanbags into a small hole.

Unlike during my first deployment in Afghanistan, we were now on the strike teams, so our day began just as the sun was going down. We'd wake up, get briefed on the latest intel and possible targets, drink some coffee, and go to chow. It was always fun driving the truck with the team down to the Army chow hall, enjoying the contrast between all the standard-issue military guys and our bearded, T-shirt-and-blue-jean-wearing rabble. The food was good, and we were always joking around and high spirited. We were on a mission we believed in, doing something very few in the world could do as well as we could. And we had absolute faith in and love for everyone on our team. When we called each other brothers, we meant it.

There were two new guys on our team whom I wound up forming a deep bond with. Jonny was a guy I'd actually met before in, of all places, the enlisted club at Fallon Air Station in Nevada, just south of Reno. I was still in SEAL Team Two at the time, training with Scott Neil, another friend who'd go on to do twenty years as a SEAL, retire, then, after surviving scores of combat missions, die a block from his house riding his motor-cycle. Anyway, Scott and I were having a beer when this kid came walking in and told us, "I just finished Hell Week."

Scott and I laughed in his face. He was telling his lies to the wrong guys. If he'd just finished Hell Week he'd be in Coronado, not Fallon fucking Nevada. "You're so full of shit, dude," I said. Scott suggested that Jonny's penalty for spreading his bull should be to buy us some beers.

Jonny wasn't lying, though. He'd been a rescue swimmer—an awesome job that involved jumping out of helicopters into rag-ing seas in the most dire circumstances—and Fallon was where he'd trained with his air crew. Given a few days of leave after Hell Week, he'd flown up to see his friends in the helicopter squadron. Once we decided Jonny was for real, we bought *him* some beers and had a great time.

His full name was Jonny Savio, and he looked like a typical Italian boy from the New Jersey neighborhood. His Jersey accent had faded, but he still said "mozzarella" like he was from Sicily. He was good-looking, dark-haired, perfect hairline, with very little space between two aggressive eyebrows. He dressed sharp and wore sharp shoes. The ladies always seemed to appreciate that. He was single, but unlike most of the single guys he always took care of himself and his money. He was squared away in every respect. His gear, his house, his car—always immaculate. He knew wine, was an excellent cook and a better friend. In the years ahead, we'd become close. If I was out of town and someone was giving my wife a hard time, I could call him and he'd fix it. If my sister was lonely, he'd take her to a movie.

He wasn't the super physical type, never a top one-percenter, like the freaks who ran sub-five-minute miles. But as far as tactics, he was top-notch, knew everything down to a science.

Jonny checked into SEAL Team Two about seven months after we'd met, and we became good buddies there. He entered selection training about a year after I did, and ended up being No. 1 in his selection class. My squadron had first pick in the new operator draft that round, and we snapped him up.

I was glad to have him with me on my first deployment to Iraq.

The other new guy I wasn't so sure I was glad about. Not that Andy wasn't a great guy. He was English, a transfer from the British Special Boat Service. He was another "No. 1 in his class" type, just a tip-top, awesome operator. But he had a rep-utation among the Brits for having a war cloud following him. Everywhere he went he got into some huge battle.

He'd participated in the 2003 invasion of Iraq. His sixty-strong squadron was assigned to drive six hundred miles to the Tigris River in lightly armored Land Rovers and accept the surrender of Iraq's one-thousand-strong 5th Division. I know that looks like a misprint, but coalition intelligence had concluded that the 5th was demoralized and simply looking for someone to surrender to.

When Andy and his guys arrived at their objective, the 5th Division, instead of greeting the coalition forces with a white flag, opened a heavy barrage of artillery and automatic weap-ons fire and even anti-aircraft weapons. The whole surrender story had been a ruse, one our intelligence had unfortunately fallen for. Andy and his mates had been lured into a trap. Vastly outnumbered and outgunned, they had no option but to re-treat. Just as that grim reality sank in, so did the Land Rovers. Eight of their eleven vehicles bogged down in the soft black sand. The men set ninety-second-delay charges on each of the now-useless vehicles, and all piled into the three still-drivable Rovers as the charges detonated around them, at least creating a diversion.

One of the men later told London's Sunday *Times*, "The enemy fire was devastating and relentless and remarkably impressive. Looking around at the guys dodging bullets and tracers reminded me of the film *The Matrix*."

The fleeing coalition forces hung over the sides of the over-crowded Land Rovers firing rifles and grenade launchers, wanting only to give a good account of themselves until they were killed, but somehow they made it to the cover of a dry riverbed where waiting Chinooks evacuated them.

So maybe it wasn't really Andy's fault. Bad intelligence had nearly gotten them all killed. I had to think we'd made some strides in that area since the beginning of the war.

We had people working around the clock—a day shift and a night shift—in a room with big screens everywhere trying to figure out who the hell was doing what. They'd identify a house that aroused suspicion, put a drone above it, and keep watch for days or even weeks. All activity was duly logged: A truck showed up, this many people got out, they stayed this long, made this many calls, discussed this.

It was a huge intelligence process that didn't really involve us until they had identified someone significant in the al-Qaeda-assisted insurgency and located him in a specific house.

At our briefings, the intel people would say: Here's a house where we think there's a bad guy. Here's his picture. Here's a list of his relatives and the aliases he uses. Here's what we think he's doing, and here's his big spiderweb network that could lead to the No. 1 target, Abu Musab al-Zarqawi.

Zarqawi was a forty-year-old Jordanian who'd sworn alle-giance to Osama bin Laden and led a particularly brutal leg of the Iraqi insurgency, specializing in hostage beheadings and suicide bombings, and turning the Iraqi conflict into a civil war between his Sunni sect of Islam and the Shias, who'd long been oppressed under the fallen regime of Saddam Hussein. A few months before we arrived, Zarqawi had masterminded the coordinated bombing of three Jordanian hotels frequented by Western diplomats, killing 60 and wounding 115. With bin Laden gone to ground, Zarqawi had become the most wanted seemingly obtainable prize, with a $25 million price on his head.

In this deployment, we were working up the lower reaches of the terrorist pyramid that would lead, ultimately, to Zarqawi. (The search eventually led to a safe house in an isolated village about thirty-five miles north of Baghdad, where, on June 7, 2006—six months after we arrived—two five-hundred-pound smart bombs put Zarqawi permanently out of the conversation.)

After laying everything out at our wake-up briefing at sunset, the intel crew chief would say, "Here's what we think. There's the probability, do you want this target?"

The answer was almost always, "Yes."

Then we'd start putting our game faces on. Everybody made sure their gear was good to go; batteries were changed out and everything was confirmed clean. The guns and night vision equipment, I mean. (Our clothes were filthy. Some guys—okay, a lot of guys—rarely washed out their operational cammies. We were superstitious about it. They'd gotten us through a lot of tight spots, so why rinse away good juju? As a result, we smelled like shit.)

While we got ready, the leadership would huddle with the pilots and come up with a plan, then we all came together for a twenty-minute brief with the commanders and laid it all out down to which of our combat dogs we were taking. Then we put on our gear and walked from our room to the helicopters, which were right outside, not more than fifty meters from our door. And we'd launch.

The first few missions weren't much different from the houses we'd rolled in on in Afghanistan. We were still learning how to interrogate. We'd never had any classes or formal instruction. The first time we conducted an interrogation we brought the suspects into the kitchen of the house we'd entered. We'd grabbed this twenty-two-year-old guy and had him on the ground. Four of us stood around yelling at him in English, and he was yelling back in Arabic. There was no interpreter, and one of our goddamn dogs was going crazy, barking and snarling at him. The dog got so excited he actually bit my boss on his leg. My boss stopped yelling at the guy, turned around, pointed at the dog handler, who pulled the dog away. The poor Iraqi kid was staring up like, "Oh, my God, these guys are so crazy. They let their own dogs bite them." We got nothing out of him.

As we gained more experience we honed our assault tactics. The old way emphasized speed: Hit the house fast, move through the house fast. Doing that meant leaving your night vision up— meaning, not using it—and using the high-intensity white light at the end of your gun so you could see everything clearly and move more rapidly. The problem was, the bad guys could see that light, too. We started thinking, *Well, shit, let's just keep our night vision down. We'll use our lasers so no one else can see. We'll be slower, yeah, but more methodical, and, most important, invisible.* It would give us a huge advantage.

Imagine shining a flashlight in a very dark room. Now imagine nobody can see it except you. That's what you see through night vision. If you shine it at the ceiling it will light up the whole room. Every one of your buddies can see what's being lit up, but none of the bad guys can see shit.

We went out every night and gradually learned that war was really good training. It wasn't as scary as the news makes it look and sound, and there aren't bogey men with suicide vests around every corner. Not that we got complacent, we just got realistic and began to fine-tune our tactics. The only guys really "going hot" were our snipers, especially one named Greg. This was my first time working with him, but it wouldn't be the last. He saved more lives and ended more than anyone I'd ever heard of. I'm not sure, exactly, how you "confirm" a kill. No one I worked with ever did. But Greg has hundreds of "non-confirmed," though you'll never hear that from him.

When you go to SEAL Team ▮, you specialize. You can be a sniper or an assaulter. Most of us were qualified to do either. "Sniper" is a qualification. If you go to the school and graduate, you're a sniper. It's the same as being a "breacher." If you go the school and graduate, you're a breacher. Ditto being a communicator, jumpmaster, range safety officer, and so on. You can think of these designations as being like merit badges—ones a SEAL earns but doesn't necessarily use on every mission. Most assaulters are qualified as snipers but perform assaulter duties: They find a way to penetrate a house and assault. The snipers—many of whom are simultaneously qualified as breachers and jumpmasters—go up to the high ground and protect the assaulters. Ironically, given my ambition when I joined the Navy to become a sniper, I found that I preferred being on the assault team. When I told people that and they asked why, I'd jokingly reply, "Well, snipers kill more people, but assaulters kill more *famous* people."

We hadn't killed anyone especially famous yet, but Greg was piling up the kills. While he shot, we worked on tactics. One night it changed for us all.

INTELLIGENCE CAME UP WITH THREE major compounds filled with terrorists all in the same area. We decided it was a perfect time to try out our new ideas. It would be a huge joint operation. In the briefing we said: "We're going to do an offset. We're going to land five clicks away, all of us, and we're going to walk in because they won't hear us, and we can all sneak into the target compounds." Everyone agreed.

We landed at our remote spot in the pitch dark and began our hike. At first it was just sand, open desert. As we got closer, we could hear dogs barking. We didn't worry about that because dogs bark on every target and never give us away. I'm convinced dogs don't ever stop barking in the Middle East. As we got closer, the ground grew swampy, and we began to see some trees and even a few small vineyards. At about five hundred meters out, we could see the outlines of our compound. This was a set point, our last chance to get ready for the assault. I reached up and blindly changed the batteries in my night vision to be sure they weren't going to quit in the middle of a gunfight. Fresh batteries, check. I was ready to go.

Batabatabata! Choppers zoomed overhead. It was fucking Army Special Forces coming in on little birds. They'd refused to walk in. They wanted to land on the X. The Brits did the same thing, only they came in a Chinook, which is way worse, louder than shit.

Our guys were all cursing. Everybody and their fucking cousin knew we were there, and we had to hustle now. The snipers and ladder carriers sprinted to the nearest roofline to get up high. As soon as they got up there I heard some shots. Suddenly everybody was blasting. We moved on our objective—each unit had one of the compounds—going in and going dark, using the new tactic.

My team got to the main entrance on "building 1-1," our target. Because there was a gunfight all around us, we decided to put a charge on the primary entrance, the front door. Our breacher made his way up with my team leader holding security. The breacher placed the charge and moved to a safe distance and blew the door. *Boom!* We quietly entered and found ourselves in a long hallway. The charge had filled the house with dust while Andy, Jonny, two other guys, and I made our way forward in our usual CQB formation, only moving more methodically because you don't sprint with the night vision down. I was the fourth man back. The infrared torches at the ends of our guns lit up the space. A guy with an AK-47 pointed right at us popped out of a doorway just like in one of those amusement park houses of horror. We were standing there looking at him, and he was looking right back at us, but he couldn't see us. It was like we were ghosts. Before we could shoot, he disappeared back behind the door. Andy and another guy, a big tough guy, pushed through the door, and I heard the distinctive *brraaatt* of the big guy's gun. Blasted him. We were all a little awed by the moment. This big, seriously tough guy had never killed anybody before, and now he'd just shot a guy in the face.

I would learn that in a gunfight the combination of adrenaline, muscle memory, and super-human focus leaves no psychic space for fear. I wasn't shutting it out. There was just no room for it. When we returned from a mission and let down a bit, a thought would sweep over me: *Wow, I almost died!* Then I might feel that chest-clutching, stomach-churning hand of fear reaching in. But my only emotion in the actual moment was . . . curiosity.

We knew Andy had been in more gunfights than goddamn Jesse James, so when we came to that body in the room, we said, "Andy, go check that guy." Andy walked over to the crumpled figure and shined a white light on him. The guy's face was split wide like a melon dropped on a cement floor.

All Andy said was, "Oh, he's fucked, mate."

Okay, so we were officially in combat. We finished clearing the house. Jonny and I heard the snipers going hot outside. The two of us left the building and saw a sniper, a guy we called Dirty, up on top of one of the buildings looking down at us. That was good. His job was to cover us as we made our move. Jonny was ahead of me in a little alley between two of the buildings. We needed to move around the corner and had to assume there were enemy fighters on the other side. Jonny started moving forward. I knew by the angle he'd taken that I needed to split to the other side of the alley so I could cover in front of him, and he could cover in front of me, our fields of fire crossing at a point ahead of and between us. No words, no hand signals, just years of practice.

We'd done it hundreds of times in training, and it had worked—with paper targets.

We were both moving now. Then two bad guys popped up with guns and—*braaapp*—we both blasted them. It was instantaneous and simultaneous. Both gunmen dropped, lifeless weight. We'd both killed our first guys at the same instant.

"Shit, Jonny," I said. "I just killed that guy." I pointed my invisible floodlight at the body. It wasn't like you see in the movies. Guys don't crash through windows or fly through the air when you shoot them. They just collapse on themselves in awkward positions. My invisible light was showing me this now: crumpled terrorist with an AK-47 by his head.

I was still looking when Jonny said, "I just killed my first guy, too."

"What do we do now?"

"Well, now we do one of those bounding things," he said.

Obviously, there were bad guys in the building up ahead, and we needed to move back to get more guys so we could take it down. Bounding meant a staggered retreat. We went back and grabbed some guys and cleared that building. There was one guy inside the house who had a nasty-looking leg wound. He'd managed to dispose of his weapon before we got to him so he was unarmed, but he was obviously a bad guy. We put a tourniquet on him and prepared him to be moved to one of our helicopters and then a hospital. I doubt al-Qaeda would do the same for us.

When we came back out, there was gunfire everywhere. I could hear the bullets cracking above our heads. I was thinking, "Man, these guys are lousy shots." What I came to understand was that most of the enemy truly believed that Allah would guide their bullets. So why bother to aim? Their faith is probably a key reason I'm still in one piece.

But even poorly aimed fire was a threat, especially so much of it. Our snipers were all shooting toward a nearby mosque where the mujahideen had fled to make a last stand. I saw someone running for the mosque door and fired a round just as he was going in, but I couldn't see if I hit him. We didn't know what weapons they had in there, and we didn't want to find out. Instantly, we thought of the Rangers who'd come in with us.

Rangers are our big blocking force. Typically, they would

defend our perimeter as we went in after high-value targets. When the time for fighting with precision is over and you need to fuck people up, you turn to the Rangers, who have black belts in fucking people up. We had one Ranger who was about 6'6" and he carried the Carl Gustav, a Swedish-made shoulder-fired rocket launcher, like a bazooka. Another Ranger, who was about 5'5", followed him everywhere. His job was to carry the backpack filled with the 84-millimeter rockets that the Carl Gustav fires. This poor son of a bitch, I don't think he even carried a gun. For every step his giant of a partner took, he had to take two, lugging those goddamn heavy rockets. Who says the Army has no sense of humor?

So yeah, the bad guys were in a mosque, but they were shooting at us. This was early in the war, and the rules of engagement were flexible. If you're taking fire, you're taking fire. So permission to engage, engage. *Fire that Gustav.*

The big Ranger loaded the son of a bitch up and launched one right into the mosque. We told him to hit it again. He reloaded and—*whoommph*—another rocket goes to meeting. The mosque was dead silent at this point, a black cloud drifting from the door. We were about to go clear it when the little short dude said, "Can we fire one more?" One less rocket to carry? Sure, why not? So we launched one more.

When we got in there, it looked like Jason Voorhees from *Friday the 13th* had beaten us to it. Bodies were flung everywhere, sliced and diced. It was pretty bad. But the thing that haunted me a little wasn't so much the gruesome sight—rather, it was the sound, a sound like water pouring out of a spigot. It was blood flowing from a severed arm.

When we got back to the base we did a debrief. I told the story of Jonny's and my cross fire in the alley, and the sniper, Dirty, related how he'd engaged those guys from the rooftop. Then the bosses said, "Okay, what happened in the mosque?"

I said, "Well, we cleared it with the Rangers. I'm going to let this Ranger debrief it."

Most of the Rangers were young kids, and they never say anything in briefings. Now I was putting the kid on the spot. He stood up, and kept standing up, until he reached his towering 6'6".

"Well," he said. "We made entry. The No. 1 man was Carl Gustav."

That was my first real gunfight and we all learned a lot: Walk in, don't fly, because that's what stirs up the hornet's nest. Stay blacked out as you go in; don't shine your white light, it could get you shot up.

Maybe the most surprising thing I learned was, it's exciting. I'd been training for so long to get into fights, and now we were in it, and it wasn't as bad as I'd feared. I was able to keep my shit together and make decisions that improved my position. My buddies and I were almost overqualified to fight these assholes. We were good at it.

And I had my first kill. I don't want to compare it to my first buck, and yet there was some similarity. I'd envied the guys who'd already killed an enemy fighter and bragged about it. Now I was part of the club. I felt no remorse. Zero. These guys would have sooner slit my throat than look at me. They lived a life dedicated to destroying Western culture and everything it stood for. They were part of a network whose biggest celebrations came when they managed to bring down a tourist hotel and kill men, women, and children who were doing nothing more threatening than trying to decide between the hot or cold buffet. They'd created a cult of death.

Enjoy paradise, gentlemen.

CHAPTER TWELVE

By 2006, I had a house, a mortgage, a wife, and my kids. For the next six years, I also spent an average of 325 days a year away from home, either training or fighting. It was a life that all SEAL Team ▓ wives were used to, and they were really good at supporting each other. But it was also a life that I knew my wife, on a tough day, could sum up in a single sentence: "He was never here."

I don't mean to say she didn't appreciate those forty days a year when I was around—twenty on leave and twenty working twelve-hour days but home by 5:00 p.m.—or the roughly $75,000 pay that came our way, or the housing allowance that helped pay the mortgage. And I don't mean to suggest that she didn't support the work I did but couldn't talk much about. I just want to acknowledge the very large sacrifices made by my wife and children, and all the families of my fellow SEALs. For most Americans in 2006, the wars in Iraq and Afghanistan had receded to faint background noise on the evening news, while for our families it was a constant roar of absence, and the ever-present threat of a more permanent vacancy.

For me, far longer than I or anyone could have imagined, the sound of war was the thumping of helicopters, the chatter of automatic weapons fire, and the voice of a SEAL sniper in my ear alerting me to some mujahideen in the next room waiting to blow my head off.

And in the fall of 2006 in Afghanistan, one almost did.

We were operating out of Camp Chapman, near Khost in eastern Afghanistan, the place where three years later a man American Intelligence thought was working as a double agent for our side would kill seven contractors and agents with a suicide car bomb. After the briefs that provided our targets, we'd drive out in Humvees with Army Rangers riding shot-gun, Carl Gustav at the ready, just in case precision didn't get it done.

One night our target was a large compound—nothing unusual by Afghan standards, but hard for Americans to picture. Think part crossword puzzle, part Ewok village. Inside high outer walls was a maze of structures intersecting randomly in a pat-tern that, from above, would look like the layout of a crossword puzzle. The meandering arms of the crossword were a series of rooms surrounded by a wall. At the heart of the compound was a two-story windowless structure. Hallways wound around, seemingly pointlessly, like a maze. I knew right away it would be a nightmare to clear.

One guy on this mission with me was my friend Lance—still renowned for his infamous "good yard gone bad" patching cer-emony. Lance's misadventures hadn't stopped there.

Lance was an amazing guy. We nicknamed him the Cobra because he was wound tight and seemed always about to strike. He also had this quality we called "the Lance factor," a tendency for harrowing near-misses in which he'd almost die, but emerge without a scratch. His death-defying incidents became so com-mon that we almost expected them. Seemed like someone was always saying to him, "Jesus Christ, Lance, how did *that* just happen?"

In Iraq in 2005, Lance had been taking down a house filled with terrorists during a night raid when he fell into a swim-ming pool. Iraq was the last place you'd think you'd have to worry about swimming pool hazards. But it was a serious situation. His gear was so heavy, it was dragging him under.

He told me he was holding his breath trying to swim out—a miserable training exercise come to life—when he saw a live, sparking power line hanging down about to touch the water. As he was wondering whether he was going to drown or get electrocuted, his vision narrowed to a tunnel. Just before blacking out he looked up, and at the end of the tunnel looking down at him was his buddy with this half-perplexed, half-horrified expression that said, *"WTF are you doing in a swimming pool?"*

Lance told me the worst part was thinking that the last thing he'd see in life was his buddy looking down and pointing at him, almost laughing, saying, "Oh . . . my . . . God!"

Lance couldn't remember swimming out, but he did, alive and unhurt, of course.

Everyone loved Lance, myself included. He was meticulous about everything: perfect locker, perfect uniforms, perfect tactics . . . just unlucky.

Another time, we were skydiving in Arizona and Lance was serving as jumpmaster—emcee of the proceedings. It was his responsibility to set a drogue chute for a pair jumping in tandem. One was a tandem instructor—it happened to be the super sniper Greg—and the other was a guy doing a tandem jump for the first time. Two guys hooked together in tandem fall faster than single jumpers. The function of the small drogue chute is to act as an air brake, slowing them down enough so that everyone can stay together. Lance's job was to hold the drogue as the tandem pair jumped clear, set it, and let it go, then jump himself.

But Lance jumped too soon, tumbling into the still unfurling drogue chute and getting tangled in its cord. Now they were all screwed. If Greg pulled the main chute, it would wrap around Lance and all three would plunge to their deaths. As his altimeter spun crazily, Lance struggled to free himself. At the last moment, he worked his way out of the tangle, pulled his chute, and jerked clear, allowing Greg to pull *his* chute, thus saving the life of one of the highest performing snipers in American history.

When they touched ground safely, the first-time tandem jumper began to dance around and celebrate his first jump until he saw two ghost-white faces beside him. The entire time he'd been blissfully oblivious to the fact that he was seconds away from death.

So with Lance beside me in this maze of a compound, I maybe should have expected some near miss. We were halfway through clearing one of the houses when multiple shooters opened fire. At Lance, of course. Now we were in a gunfight in this maze. It took us a while, but we killed the two guys shooting at us. Still, one room remained uncleared. It was at the end of a long hallway, breaking off at an angle. There was no door, just an entryway partially blocked by a fence. The entryway was in the corner, so most of the room could not be seen from where we were, and might be harboring more bad guys.

We stepped over the bodies of the fallen gunmen and moved ahead. Some guys peeled off to go down another hall, and I found myself in the number one man position. It was now my job to come around that fence into the room first.

Angles were what I was thinking about as I prepared to enter the room. I could already see the corner in front of me was clear. I'd need to slowly "cut the pie" from left to right and clear as much of the rest of the room as I could from the hallway. In that situation, you can only cover 170 of the 180 degrees of the room. That last ten degrees, the sliver between the entrance and the far wall, is blind. Too bad. Nothing you can do about that. At some point you just have to commit, take a sliver of risk. And the enemy knows this.

Some bad guys knew to hide in that ten-degree blind spot, waiting for us to step in. That possibility is a real pucker factor, and a lot of guys have been killed that way.

When I felt the squeeze from my two man, I stepped in. Immediately I heard *pffft-pffft-pffft*—three shots from a silencer-suppressed gun. With a startling thunk an insurgent fell out of the wall and hit the floor, still clutching an AK-47. He was bald, shirtless with white pants, and very recently deceased. It was a surreal moment. My brain scrambled to put the pieces together and soon I had the whole picture. This guy, still in his pajamas, had been wakened by the gunfight. He'd scrambled out of bed into the hidey hole he'd predug into the wall—precisely in the blind spot. No accident. As I said, these guys studied our tactics. He was going to ambush the first guy in. That would be me. I instinctively looked up to the roof of the two-story structure. It was Greg. Of course it was. He was standing up there with his gun slung over his shoulder, staring at me like some kind of war god. We used to call him Hoff—after attractive Hollywood actor David Hasselhoff—because he was so annoyingly good-looking. He clicked his push to talk and I heard him in my earpiece saying dryly, "Yeah, you're all clear, Rob."

That's when it began to sink in. Not that he saved my life; he'd saved my life plenty of times. What impressed me was that at a distance of thirty meters, in the dark, he could tell who I was by the way I walked and by the gear I was wearing. It really sank in: *Wow, we really do know each other. We really do have each other's back.*

Not that SEALs are always perfect under fire. I've talked about how fast we move, and sometimes guys start slowing down a bit. We had a guy we had to fire just because he began to show the slightest hesitancy. We needed guys who, when it's time to commit, commit. This was war.

It can happen over the course of a couple of missions. Someone will say, "Hey, I noticed this guy and he kind of vanished." We might bring it up in one of our periodic performance evaluations—nothing too formal, we just get together and talk about how we're doing. Someone will say to the guy, "Hey, what's going through your mind?"

The decision is usually mutual. Guys will return to conventional SEAL teams or become instructors on one of the coasts. Sometimes they'll leave the Navy altogether.

There's not a lot of blame or anger. Usually, guys know it's time. We had a team leader who just sort of disappeared on targets. We didn't know if it was fear or what. We went over his head, talked to his boss, and said, "We want to make you aware of it."

The boss pulled that guy aside and he didn't deny it. He said, "Yeah, I'm kind of at the end of my career and this isn't for me anymore," and he stepped down and we got a new team leader. That sort of thing happens but it isn't common. Most guys want to get in there and mix it up.

ONE OF THOSE MIX-IT-UP TYPES was Nate. Nate was among the most aggressive guys I've ever worked with, just an excellent SEAL, but he'd been on a couple of deployments and by this 2006 stint in Khost, had yet to shoot anybody. Just as we'd teased Andy the Brit for having a war cloud following him around, we kidded Nate for being trapped in a peace cloud. There was no reason for it, just happenstance, but it got under his skin. Nate wanted to join the club.

One night that fall—it was actually Halloween—Nate, Lance, and I were taking down a house. We were short-handed, so we decided to compromise on our usual tactics and take it down with just us three. Not ideal, but not all that unusual. We were often short manpower. Nate was the point man. When he entered, one of the targets lunged at him and they got in a fistfight. That woke up two other guys. With the night vision down, I could see them rolling over and grabbing their AKs. I don't know what got into me, but before they could get their guns on us I yelled, "Trick or treat, motherfuckers!" and blasted both of them. It was the one and only action movie line of my career. Nate, who had this guy in a headlock, looked up and said, "God dammit, Rob."

"What?" I said.

"You always shoot people," he said. "I never get to shoot anybody. What the hell?"

I said, "Well, I don't know, throw that guy in the middle of the room and shoot him."

The terrorist's eyes went wide. He looked at me, and he said, "No, no, sir, this is bad idea."

I said, "Who's talking to you, dude?"

I was messing with him—obviously we weren't going to do that. We pulled him in for interrogation. We said, "Hey, we know this truck pulled in here at this time, because our assets were watching the house. Who owned the truck?"

The guy was clever. He pointed at one of the dead guys and said, "It's his truck."

"Good answer," I said.

We put a hood on his head and left the building so we could extract. Lance led us out and as he was walking through the yard a big, scruffy dog charged him without barking. He was fast. We heard over the radio, "Oh, Jesus Christ, Lance!" *Bap Bap*. It was Greg. He saw the whole thing and saved Lance from getting chewed on and, being Lance, probably getting rabies. Who goes to war and gets attacked by a house pet?

A YEAR LATER, WE WERE on a deployment together in Iraq. Nate still hadn't killed anybody. We were out on a mission in central Iraq and the mujahideen were now sleeping outside in the palm groves under the trees because they knew their safe houses were no longer safe. This was one of many ways our dogs were useful; if the bad guys were out there, the dogs sniffed it out instantly.

On this particular mission, we were out with Toby the dog, and his handler, Jimmy. Jimmy, like all the dog handlers, had special training and constantly worked with Toby to improve his work skills and their communication. It was a busy job—the dogs never stopped needing to be taken care of. Some guys loved it, and some didn't. If they didn't have enough volunteer handlers, they'd assign a new guy. We wanted to bring dogs whenever we could, so the dogs joined us about 90 percent of the time. The dogs would listen to *all* of us in a combat situation, not just their handlers, but you had to get their attention, either by using a laser pointer or calling the handler to bring the dog up. The dogs always listened to their handler first, the shooters second. They were incredible at going after military-age men and as a rule didn't bite kids—though they could and did on some occasions. We'd always have a 'terp (interpreter) yell at the house, "Everybody out! We'll send a dog in." That mostly worked: noncombatants came out. But I've seen women come out, leaving babies in a house about to be cleared by dogs. You just had to shake your head. If the dogs bit the women, we'd bandage them up and give the family some money.

On this night, Jimmy gave Toby his instruction and Toby, a lean and mean Belgian Malinois, took off down the path as we followed. All of a sudden, he darted to the right. We called him "the fur missile" because of the way he just launched himself after targets. He just blasted off into the trees and immediately had this guy's arm in his mouth. The guy was yelling, trying to stand up and aim his AK-47 at this snarling predator, but Toby was vibrating with rage, hopping around, irrevocably clamped on the arm in his mouth. The two of them, man and dog, were locked in this snarling, screaming dance, and the guy began firing his gun. Bullets were flying everywhere. Nate was carrying an SR25, which is a big sniper rifle, much louder than the regular guns we had, and it wasn't suppressed. Just as it looked like the bad guy might be getting a bead on poor Toby we heard Nate's gun go off. *Boom!* The guy's head split open. The guy dropped and Toby, his life saved, stopped barking. For a moment, there was this heavy silence, and then Nate said calmly, "I'll be damned." He'd finally gotten his first kill.

There'd be many more that deployment. All that time we'd been learning and adapting to a tough, seasoned al-Qaeda enemy. They'd react to us, and we'd react to their reaction. We evolved and became the most lethal and stealthy team in modern history. And we were about to reach our peak.

CHAPTER THIRTEEN

It was always a little strange to come home from war and go right back into the routine of our training exercises. That's where I found myself in the spring of 2007, having a perfectly miserable day packing tandem rig parachutes. Tandems are huge and packing them involves stuffing a four-hundred-square-foot canopy into a bag about the size of my computer. And because this was SEAL training, they made it extra-special fun by making us pack them, then unpack them, then repack them, and then jump them. Then pack them, unpack them, repack them, jump them. It just sucked, and I was in the final steps, cinching the fucking thing down, when the pull-up cord snapped, and it all popped back out. I had to start all over. Again. Life could not get any worse.

Just then I got a text from Nicole that said, "Call me." I called her and asked, "What's wrong?"

She said, "I'm pregnant."

Okay, so maybe life couldn't get any worse, but it could get vastly more expensive and immensely more stressful, and just catch you completely unprepared for another baby. It would all turn out to be one of the *best* insanely expensive and stress-inducing things to happen to me, but first I had to go back to war.

The summer of 2007 was the moment the war in Iraq shifted: Up until this point, we'd been in a stalemate with no clear strategy. Gen. David Petraeus, the top American commander in Iraq, would eventually get credit for turning the tide by bringing about "The Anbar Awakening." The Sunni Muslims, a power in the Anbar Province of western Iraq, had been hostile to the cause of unifying the country around the American-supported government led by their Shiite rivals, and they'd mostly sided with al-Qaeda fighters who were Sunnis.

Petraeus got credit for engineering a Sunni change of heart and persuading them to turn on their al-Qaeda co-religionists. In fact, this was a *partial* truth: The Sunnis were aiding us now, but it wasn't because of their love for humanity and a new belief in freedom for all. It was *partially* because of the famous "surge"—an increase of about thirty-five thousand in American troop levels. Enough al-Qaeda members were being killed that the rest of the Sunnis—many of whom had become both disdainful and fearful of al-Qaeda—felt they could now stand up to them. We killed more al-Qaeda fighters in these few months than at any time in SEAL team history. With us killing enough terrorists, the Sunnis "awoke." We helped win the war, if this type of war can be won.

By May of 2007 our numbers were growing. More SEALs were in the pipeline to begin with because they'd increased the number of people going through BUD/S. They moved Hell Week from the fifth week to the third, thinking that if guys were less broken at the start more would make it. Hell Week still sucks, because that's the whole point of Hell Week, and I think 80 percent still fail to get through to graduation. But higher numbers *in* mean higher numbers *out*, and more conventional SEALs means more who may be elite material. By increasing our personnel count, the thinking went, we could increase the time all of us had at home. That didn't happen. More guys were simply thrown into the action. It also meant we were pulling some guys right out of training to go to war. Even though there was no time for the usual selection period, some of these "newer guys" would turn out to be among the best warriors America has ever produced.

My father, Tom, and my siblings and me (far left) in Missoula, Montana, in the summer of 1981.
Courtesy of the author

Here I am as a high school senior in the spring of 1994. I'm wearing my letter jacket from Butte Central Catholic High School.
Courtesy of the author

My dad and I took down this Boone and Crockett records book ram on November 2, 2001. From an early age, hunting with Dad was both a bonding experience and a lesson in making every shot count.
Courtesy of the author

Here I'm demonstrating the "Slide for Life" during the third phase of BUD/S in December 1996. One of our snipers used this technique in rescuing Captain Richard Phillips, who'd been taken hostage by Somali pirates. *Courtesy of the US Navy*

SEAL trainees holding a log in water. The hard-nosed instructors never lacked for ways to test our resolve. *Courtesy of the US Navy. Photo by Chief Special Warfare Officer (SEAL) Darren McBurnett.*

SEAL trainees with ankles tied together in pool. What we were asked to do was always meant to prepare us for the possibility of the worst in combat. *Courtesy of the US Navy. Photo by Chief Special Warfare Officer (SEAL) Darren McBurnett.*

In BUD/S, students run hundreds of miles with these inflatable boats on their heads. During Hell Week, classes don't go anywhere without them. Some guys get bald spots that remain for months. *Courtesy of the US Navy. Photo by Chief Special Warfare Officer (SEAL) Darren McBurnett.*

Saturday, less than twenty-four hours after finishing Hell Week. My dad is wearing his Leadville 100 belt buckle, showing that he finished the 100-mile ultramarathon. I felt as though I'd just done something even harder, though; yes, running both those gauntlets is about strength of will.
Courtesy of the author

Graduating SEAL training
Courtesy of the author

April 10, 2002. Here my SEAL Team Four Delta Platoon mates help me "celebrate" my birthday at Blackwater USA, Moyock, Virginia. What can I say—SEALs have a unique sense of humor.
Courtesy of the author

Before my first deployment at SEAL Team Two, I went to Sniper School in Camp Atterbury, Indiana. An operator from SEAL Team Four, on the left, and I just passed the first of ten stalking tests. Notice how much "natural vegetation" is on our ghillie suits. It's particularly important to blend into what's behind you. *Courtesy of the US Navy. Photographer unknown.*

Parachuting solo like this was usually fun. When we jumped tandem, it got more complicated—and sometimes deadly. *Courtesy of the US Navy. Photo by Chief Special Warfare Officer (SEAL) Darren McBurnett.*

Neil Roberts
Courtesy of the US Navy/
Getty Images

Close quarters battle
Courtesy of the US Navy.
Photo by Chief Special
Warfare Officer (SEAL)
Darren McBurnett.

Captain Phillips returning home *Photo by Darren McCollester/Getty Images*

Aerial shot of the bin Laden compound *Photo by Digital Globe via Getty Images*

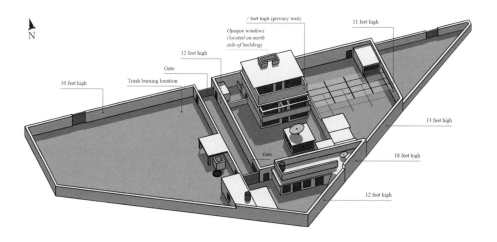

N

7 feet high (privacy wall)

Opaque windows
(located on north
side of building)

11 feet high

12 feet high

Gate

Trash burning location

10 feet high

13 feet high

Gate

18 feet high

12 feet high

Diagram of the bin Laden compound *Courtesy of the US Department of Defense*

Crowds celebrate in front of the White House after President Obama announced that bin Laden had been shot. *Photo by Brooks Kraft LLC/Corbis via Getty Images*

The day I donated my shirt to the 9/11 museum *Photo by Jin S. Lee, 9/11 Memorial Museum*

I think of this particular period I spent in Iraq as "The Deployment That Never Was" because most of our squadron was sent to southern Afghanistan while one skeleton crew of SEALs headed to Iraq more or less under the radar. It was my immediate commander who made the request. This guy was smart. He knew his team wanted to kill bad guys, and being a small unit away from all our top brass in Afghanistan would free us up to do what came naturally by now without too much over-thinking. The troop commander's name was Rich, and even though he was merely a lieutenant commander, he'd be the highest-ranked SEAL in Iraq. He was one of the best leaders I've ever known. His motto, which I've stolen from him, is, "Nobody ever worked for me. They worked *with* me."

Our deployment started out in western Iraq's Anbar Province at the Al Asad Air Base, the same base as my previous Iraq deployment in 2005. We quickly succeeded in hunting down and capturing or killing the relatively few al-Qaeda targets in our immediate neighborhood in far western Iraq, and found ourselves flying east to Ramadi and Fallujah for our nightly targets. These flights were long, inefficient, and uncomfortable, so we made the decision to pack up our portion of the base and head east.

Within the course of two cycles of darkness—our daytime—the task force packed up all of its gear, including personal items, guns, explosives, computers, and everything needed to run a war, into large CONEX boxes, which were lifted via helicopter. We were operational again in forty-eight hours.

We installed ourselves in a former mansion on the banks of the Tigris River. The living was not as plush as it had been in Al Asad, where we'd built out our space to suit us and had the routine down to a science. Army Rangers had occupied the old mansion for some time. They were more about Spartan living than we were. Compared to our built-out digs at Al Asad—with its seventy-inch plasma TVs, networked Xboxes, refrigerators, and coffee stations—the new quarters seemed a little primitive to us. But we figured we'd be moving east soon anyway—toward Baghdad, where the most serious fighting was going on.

As it turned out, we never lacked for targets. We went out pretty much every night after the daily brief in the JOC (Joint Operations Center) in a neighboring mansion. Though only about a hundred yards away, the JOC seemed much farther as the temperature consistently teased 120 degrees, even after sunset. We didn't dare drink any coffee until we got into air-conditioned spaces, and we knew enough to soak up that refrigerated air. There wouldn't be any where we were headed.

We'd recently learned a valuable lesson the hard way: Al-Qaeda knew some of our special operations tactics for breaching. As I've said, the breacher is the guy who gets the assault team inside a target no matter what. He'll break windows, chainsaw through walls, pick locks, whatever is necessary. The most common method of entry for a breacher, though, is blowing open the front door with explosives. If the team judges that explosive entry is required, the breacher is the first one to the door. This is often the case when timing or terrain forces a team to land right next to the house or on the X. Al-Qaeda knew this, too. They'd wait a few seconds after they heard the helicopters, then shoot through the door with deadly effect, taking out the breacher and any other guys with him. Contrary to what Hollywood represents, bullets go through doors. Many good guys were killed while placing charges.

So a more clever approach was called for.

At one brief, we were handed targets that required us to hit three separate, adjacent houses simultaneously with three of our teams working together. This was a time-sensitive target: The guys we wanted were there at the moment but might not be in a few hours. We could potentially take out an entire cell with one operation if we acted fast. The fastest way was to land on the X, which left me more than a little concerned. These houses outside Fallujah were filled with al-Qaeda. They'd definitely hear us and be ready at the door. I needed to come up with a system that would minimize my time there. So I built a seven-foot strip of C-6 plastic explosive that could be rolled like a Fruit Roll-Up, only less delicious. The material opposite the explosive is extremely sticky, so as the bomb is unrolled down the door, it adheres to it. That could be done in an instant. I saved even more time by pre-attaching the blasting cap to the explosive. Don't try this at home. It's definitely a risk to run around with a charge already "capped in." But getting shot is no good, either, so I took the risk.

Now all I had to do once the bomb was placed was attach the cap to a twenty-foot-reel of "shock tube"—a kind of fuse that rolled out from a wheel like fishing line. As we prepared to launch, I stowed my gear in two M60 pouches that I rigged on my right hip.

A few hours after the sun went down we took off in three Black Hawks. The other shooters with me were Cole, Delicious, and Mack. Needless to say we all had nicknames. Mine was NSRO (pronounced nizzro) for Navy Seal Rob O'Neill. My boss liked yelling, "What up, my nizzro?!" Mack was a college rugby player and a total badass. He was missing a front tooth and had dark hair down to his shoulders along with a big black beard. He looked like an awesome, tough bum but was as sharp as a tack and a tactical wizard. Delicious was the best-looking guy we had and a physical freak of nature. Perfect physique, tan skin, and pearly whites. I'm pretty sure he could bench press a Buick and climb buildings in his free time.

As for Cole, he was the most aggressive SEAL I ever worked with. "Fearless" is a word that is thrown around too often, but perfect to describe him. Again, brilliant tactician and a very physical guy. Great-looking, too. Starting to see a pattern here? Tall, dark, and handsome, Delicious and Cole could be on posters. Mack? Only if he fixes that tooth!

Our team leader, Cruz, had one of the driest wits ever. He was a massive Polish-American with huge, long arms, dark features, and a great black beard. He and his family all spoke fluent Polish, and his brothers were all as huge as he was. Two of Cruz's brothers actually made it to SEAL Team ▇, and I worked with them. They were meticulous and probably the most loyal men I ever met. They all had the same nickname, "Cruz," based on their last name. I first met this particular Cruz at SEAL Team Two. He immediately saw action in Sarajevo and Kosovo and was known off the bat as an operator. He made the leap to SEAL Team ▇ at the first opportunity and quickly moved up to Team Leader for D Team, my team. He was a thinker, a natural leader, almost impossible to beat in a race on land or sea, and as strong as anyone I'd ever seen. Despite his size and strength, he prevailed in arguments using cool logic rather than intimidation, and was always careful to hear all sides. His side was usually right, though.

Cruz was famous for getting every legitimate penny out of the government when we'd fill out our "Travel Claims." Each man is responsible for getting his own reimbursement but none of us knew the rules. Cruz knew *everything,* from house-to-airport miles to allowable percentages of clothing costs. Once, he took the time to explain to the entire squadron some of the intricacies. It was enormously complex, and we were a tough audience. We'd just returned from war and nobody gave a fuck. I waited until Cruz was finished, then said, "Oh, one more thing, guys, before you all go home to see your kids for the first time in months: You may pass a pay phone on the way home. Stop and check for a quarter. You can *keep* that shit!!"

Everyone laughed, Cruz the loudest of all, and we all went home.

Anyway, on the short flight in the Black Hawk to hit the three adjacent houses outside Fallujah, I was going over the breaching drill in my head to make sure it was flawless. I wasn't scared, exactly. I'd call my mood serious and concerned. I didn't want to have any snafus in front of that door. I was listening to chatter over our radios: updates on the target and the status of the people there. Nobody had left. They were quiet, and there were a few sleepers on some of the roofs. That was concerning but not alarming. Given the intense heat, people often sleep on their roofs. Still, they *could* be snipers, and they could even have a belt-fed machine gun.

I heard the pilot say "Two minutes" in my earpiece. I hung my legs out the right-side door of the helo and began focusing on what was going on to my left—the direction of travel. I was looking at rooftops and fields, trying to see if we'd spooked anybody yet. Nothing. The pilot kept our altitude at about a hundred feet as we sped forward. "One minute." This is when the heart starts to pound. There are few things more exciting than landing on the X. Ernest Hemingway once wrote, "Certainly there is no hunting like the hunting of man and those who have hunted armed men long enough and liked it, never really care for anything else thereafter." I didn't happen to be one of those doomed to never find other forms of excitement, but I can understand exactly what he meant. Even though taking out bad guys is very dangerous, it's a kick-ass rush. Time to do some serious Navy SEAL shit.

In my first combat experiences I'd been strangely detached, as if I were observing from above. It was like, "Oh, that's what a bullet sounds like when it misses your head by inches," or, "Okay, so that's what a direct hit does to a man's forehead." I don't know why I didn't feel fear then—there was a time later when I did. But in those early days I found myself craving the moment when bullets would fly at us. Before this Iraq deployment, I'd say that 70 percent of the missions we went on were "dry holes"—offering little resistance and no targets of great significance.

When gunfights broke out, you knew you'd found the enemy and that the night wasn't going to be a waste of time. I've got a video of some of the fights we were in and when the guns start firing you can literally hear me saying, "Fuck, yeah!" Like, "It's on, let's fight."

"Thirty seconds."

I could see our target now and I traced the route I'd take to the front door of "building 1-1," the primary target. My gun was up, night vision down, invisible laser on. I was lighting up the front door for myself so that I could take a shot if a head and gun popped out. Nothing. We hit the deck and I sprinted toward the door. I had three of my guys—Cole, Delicious, and Mack—with me for security. Delicious and Mack would stand back and hold the corners while Cole came up with me to "cover the crack"—meaning hold his gun on the part of the door that might pop open while I placed the charge. We got to the door, which was a standard, heavy wooden door with the knob on the left. That meant the hinges were inside on the right. I was going to put the charge on the hinge side. I was attaching seven feet of C-6. It was gonna open. I made sure to stand off to the right side as I placed the charge. I could sense Cole beside and behind me with his gun reassuringly fixed on the crack. If the bad guys had shot through the door in the three seconds it took me to unroll the sticky strip, the bullets might have missed by a few inches. *Might* have missed. I was maximizing my chances, but it was still no sure thing. As I bolted away, unrolling the shock tube as I went, Cole was right behind me. We ran about twenty-five feet from the door, and I clacked it off. BOOM!

A charge like this is big and loud, even at a "safe" distance—so loud that a lot of guys suffer from cumulative traumatic brain injury later in life. It's a load-pushing charge that destroys everything in front of it. This was no exception.

The guys who'd come in on the other helicopters hadn't even set off their charges yet, so I guess my system had worked. Now there was a ragged hole where the door had been. We charged into the house. I was the number two man, right behind Delicious. The room opened up into a small living room with another room off to the left and a stairwell to the right. Straight ahead was an open door to a kitchen. Delicious went right, and I went left. I cleared my corner first, and as I swept my weapon back to the right, I saw a body crumpled on the floor beside an AK-47.

My eye followed the wide blood trail that led from the body up the wall to a red impact smear near the ceiling. Clearly, the insurgent had been standing at the door about to fire when my seven-foot-long charge beat him to the punch.

As I looked more closely at the very dead body, a cold shock ran through me. The insurgent was no him. It was a woman. A woman waiting to kill me with an AK-47. She was an enemy combatant, yes, but she was also a woman. I remember thinking, *I hope God forgives me.*

I would think of this many times and never feel completely right about it, but I had no time just then to indulge in guilt. Delicious had cleared his room and returned. Together, we moved past the woman's body and through the door to the kitchen. The kitchen was clear, but there was another door at the far end leading to a bedroom. Since the door opened into the corner of the room, I could "pie" it—stand just outside the door and sweep the room slice by slice. When I was 50 percent through, my invisible laser exposed another insurgent pointing an AK-47 toward the entrance, waiting for us to come in so he could unload his weapon. Behind him were three small children. Unfortunately for him, I could see in the dark, and he couldn't. *Pop! Pop!* I was able to take two good head shots, and he went down. I finished my clearance to the best of my ability and then we entered.

The three children were fine, but frightened, obviously. That was the last room on that floor, and the rest of the team had finished clearing the second story. Now the house was clear, two insurgents had been killed in action, and three children were physically okay. We could hear gunfire at some distance outside. The two other teams were getting it on.

While my guys searched the house for weapons, explosives, and intelligence, I took the three kids into the kitchen and brought in my interpreter. This was difficult. The kids were standing there staring up at us, and they were the ages of my kids and my buddies' kids. It really sucks that children are involved in this, and there are always kids in these houses. *Always.* The children told us that most of the folks nearby were family, but that there were strangers in town. This was their father's house; that was the man I'd shot in the bedroom. They'd been sleeping in there when the helicopters woke them. Their father had sent his wife, their mother, to the door with an AK-47 to martyr herself and possibly take one of us with her. Now these kids were orphans.

They didn't even know at this point that their father was dead—they'd only heard two suppressed shots, which might not have said "gunfire" to an innocent ear. Nor did they know that their mother had been blown up at the front door. But I did. I asked them where their nearest family was. They said their aunt lived in a house across the small field out the back door. I told the kids to grab their shoes. I shouldered my gun so I wouldn't scare them and walked them about thirty meters to the aunt's house. Here I was in the middle of a gunfight, and I actually rang the damn doorbell.

It was probably the single most reckless thing I'd ever done. But it was a very terrible feeling to know that I'd killed these children's parents—essentially, right in front of them. I wanted to make sure the kids were taken care of and not any more frightened than they already were. They'd had nothing to do with any of this, and after all, we were the *good* guys. The ability to save the lives of noncombatants was one of the most important skills SEAL Team ▓ offered. When intel pinpoints a terrorist safe house, the leadership can just order up a guided bomb and blow the place apart. Since, as I've said, you can always multiply the number of fighters in a safe house by wives, kids, and cousins, the collateral damage in a strike like that can be something like twenty-plus to one. If you drop a payload on a house, you risk killing twenty innocent people for every one terrorist. By contrast, we were precise enough to hit our target without killing innocent people. That's why we were given latitude—at least, back then. We'd proven we could do exactly what the command needed.

I put the kids in front of the door and backed into the shadows. A woman came to the door and spoke for a second before bringing them in. They crossed the threshold, then, and I'll never forget this, they turned and waved.

When I got back to the original target, the gunfight was on-going all around us. My team had found AK-47s, grenades, and some homemade explosives. We were in the heart of al-Qaeda country, and this was proof of who lived here. So was the heavy armed resistance. We walked in patrol order through the compound to the secondary target. The team leader there, Street, met us at the main entrance and gave us the dump on what was happening. They'd cleared the building, killed two of the enemy, and arrested two more, who were currently being interrogated by the Tactical Questioning Team. The remainder of his team was searching all the nooks and crannies where al-Qaeda liked to hide weapons and intelligence.

As Street was talking, he was interrupted. *Bap! Bap!* We heard the unmistakable blat of an automatic weapon. Two rooms away from us, part of the search team had uncovered a fighting-age male in a hiding hole in the wall. He was armed and attempted—but failed—to get some shots off when the team moved the false wall he was standing behind. That first "bap" was the last thing this guy ever heard.

We rolled up all of the men and left all of the women and children behind. We told the women not to leave their houses until the sun was up. We explained that our aircraft would remain in the area, and we didn't want them to be mistaken for reinforcements. That could be bad.

In all, that night we killed seven al-Qaeda fighters and took nine more off the battlefield. It wasn't even an unusually eventful evening. We were getting in fights every single night, and it got to the point that if we only killed five al-Qaeda, we considered it a slow night.

We remained in our humble abode in Ramadi for about ten days. As we honed our tactics and technique, we became so good at entering targets silently that we started playing a game we called "counting coup" in honor of Native American warriors of the past.

To demonstrate their courage and stealth, Native Americans would creep up to their sleeping enemy and touch him, even take items off his person without waking him. So we started doing that, too. We'd sneak up on a house full of bad guys and enter as quietly as we could, forgoing explosives for the silent removal of windows, picking of locks, or whatever other clever ways we could think of that would make minimal noise. When we found a sleeping enemy, we'd stand over him and slowly remove his blanket. Then we'd run a finger lightly down his chest to check for a suicide vest. Some guys slept in them. If the bad guy had a vest on, it was time to shoot before he had a chance to "clack himself off." If he didn't have a vest, it was time to wake him up. This was the fun part. I'd put one finger over his lips and quietly whisper, "Shhh, shhh, shhh, shhh." It was always interesting to see how these "feared enemies of America," these holy warriors, reacted. Without exception, they turned into complete cowards and cried like schoolchildren who'd just crapped their pants on the playground. And usually, they *did* crap their pants. But who can blame them? They'd awoken to their worst nightmare. American justice.

On these visits, we'd leave our interpreters outside until the houses were clear; it was too dangerous to bring them in with us. I remember talking with intelligence folks and analysts about this. They questioned how we could communicate with our captives.

"You don't speak Arabic," they'd say.

"Yeah," I'd respond, "but everybody speaks 'gun.' "

ONCE AGAIN, AS WE KNOCKED off one target after another, the al-Qaeda population seriously thinned. Commander Rich was asked if we wanted to be moved from Ramadi, which was slowing down, to Baghdad, where we'd be working directly for an Army Special Forces commander. The Army commander was the same rank as Rich, but this was his territory, so he'd be in charge. Most SEAL officers would have respectfully turned down the opportunity. Certainly, there were times in the past when SEAL commanders refused to work underneath other units. Believe it or not, SEALs can be a touch arrogant sometimes.

No, it's true.

Rich, however, didn't need arrogance because he was so deeply self-confident. He felt he could work *with* anyone. Rich understood what this collaboration could accomplish for his men and, more important, for the overall mission. So when the question was posed, he didn't bat an eye. We were lucky to be invited into the belly of the beast. The tide was beginning to turn, and we were helping to turn it.

Our small task force packed up once again for a flight to Baghdad International Airport, or BIAP. It was impressive, getting off the helos and looking at the hardware arrayed in front of us. We were used to fighting in remote outposts, but here we were in the heart of American military might. Arrayed before us were cargo planes, jets, attack planes, and bombers. Abrams tanks stood sentry near the perimeter walls. Talk about muscle; I'm glad we have those things, and the bad guys don't.

Also available were smaller armored personnel carriers, the Strykers, primarily used to drive badass infantry or Rangers into the fight. And then there were the Pandurs. Pandurs were even lighter, smaller, and more maneuverable. Army Special Forces loved using those for missions into the city, but I had my reservations. By this point, lots of Americans serving in Iraq had been killed and maimed by Improvised Explosive Devices (IEDs), and I didn't care to be one of them. I felt better flying or walking, but our counterparts claimed that this was the way to go. We'd find out that they were right.

Meanwhile, we were more than reassured by all the helicopters on hand: Chinooks, Black Hawks, Kiowas, and several Little Birds. Little Birds were the coolest because they were small, fast, and maneuverable, and best of all, had benches on the *outside* of the fuselage. Shooters would literally ride outside the bubble of the cockpit, next to the pilot, hooked in by a small lanyard. No matter the mission—"dry-hole" or straight-up Wild West shoot-out—a guy always felt cool riding on a Little Bird. Every time I took off on one, I'd say to myself, *Yep, chicks dig this.*

We grabbed our gear and had an escort show us to our new living quarters. They were located inside a huge warehouse-type structure that had been sectioned off to create long hallways dividing large living areas. Army Special Forces had been here awhile, and they were pretty much set up for success. Their homesteading instincts were as well developed as ours—in fact, the Army Special Forces closely resembled us in the way they fought and played. They had individual bedrooms, living rooms with stadium seating and flat-screen TVs, snack bars, and a coffee mess. Besides all that, they were flat-out cool. We were, after all, SEAL Team ▒, but I did catch myself thinking a few times, *Wow, that's fucking Army Special Forces.*

We were starting from scratch again. All we had was space. Our bedrooms had six beds in open-bay format, and that was about it. No desks, no couches, and no TVs. We didn't even have sheets or pillows. This would need to change.

We had a two-step process in mind: 1) find someone with abundance; 2) commandeer. Sometimes this meant sweet-talk or using the "cool-guy" factor. If you find a group of support folks who rarely leave the wire, or *never* leave the wire, they may agree to hook up some operators just to feel like part of the team. Of course, this can backfire. Some of these folks have been around actual cool guys for so long that they think it has rubbed off on them. Those are the ones you steal from.

Don't feel bad for them. There is actually a name for these folks coined by someone funnier than I: Fobbit. It's a blend of two words, FOB and Hobbit. How that breaks down is simple. FOB is the acronym for Forward Operating Base. Hobbits are a fictional race famous for sloth and the accumulation of creature comforts. Put the two together: Fobbit. Fobbits are known for going to the personnel exchange, or "PX," and buying up all of the good stuff before the men and women who actually fight can get any. We're talking about tobacco, coffee creamer, video games, snacks, electronics, and magazines. Fobbits don't work out, they eat all the high-calorie junk food and drink up all of the soda and Rip Its. Since they don't have to fight actual enemies, they put all their strategic effort into being first in the chow line or soaking up all the hot water in the showers. Then they call home and talk about being in "The Shit." They love to use words like "Down Range" and "War-Fighter."

Lame, those Fobbits. Don't feel bad that we stole from them.

If the Fobbits fail you, find the construction guys. Most of my time over there, this meant going to the Navy's Construction Battalion or Seabees. Seabees kick ass. They are generally some of the hardest working folks in the US military. They make it work for you, even if they don't have the supplies. And they do it outside the wire and fight people, too. Plus, they have beer. Not in a war zone, of course, that would be illegal. Just sayin'.

In this particular case, the Seabees had minimal guys and supplies and were overworked on other projects, but they happily gave us access to their salvage yard. It consisted of cut-up 2 x 4s and 4 x 4s, miscellaneous hand-me-down office furniture, and other handy items. I even found a practically new French assault rifle amid the clutter: never been fired and only dropped once.

So we grabbed what we could out of the yard and started building. Having no carpentry skills myself, I helped with picking out good materials and bringing them to the measuring and cutting station. It turned out that good carpentry skills didn't matter. "Can-do" attitude coupled with a little bit of bullshitting trumped that. The best at this tactic was Cole. He was one of the six men in our room and he convinced us that we had nothing to worry about. As long as we cut him the material and found him some tools, he'd take care of us.

Cole only had one speed, full throttle. I would and did trust him with my life. In fact, if my hands were freezing I'd let him pee on them—Cole was the fellow BUD/S trainee whom I'd asked for that special favor all those years ago during Hell Week. On top of being a fearless, aggressive SEAL, he had a funny quirk. He was always eleven minutes late for everything. On his very first training assignment with our squadron, we were driving through town to the site of the exercise with only five minutes to spare when he said, "Oh, look, a Boot Barn, let's stop and look for boots." I looked at him cock-eyed and said, "You've got to be shitting me. We're almost late and you want to . . . no. We can stop for a can of Copenhagen but we're not shopping for boots."

From then on, I tried to get everyone to call him Boots, but nobody liked it. Whenever he was eleven minutes late for something and the boss would ask where the hell he was, I'd say, "Shopping for Boots." Still nothing. It frustrated the hell out of me that nobody could see that this was the perfect nickname.

Until this deployment. On one of the missions near Ramadi, I was on a rooftop in a gunfight, and I saw him run into a house by himself, which he shouldn't have done. A massive gunfight ensued. From what I could hear, there were at least three shooters, which meant he was outnumbered. I kept a bead on the exit, but when the shooting stopped, he came out alone. I said, "What the hell just happened in that room?"

He said, "Oh, I had to go in there and deliver the boots."

Now it stuck.

Boots may have been habitually late, but he couldn't be faulted for his work ethic. He worked on his construction projects around the clock. And his products were hilarious. He built a desk that would have made Shaquille O'Neal look like an undernourished grade-schooler and matched it with a chair that might have been stolen from Verne Troyer. A guy would put his computer on the desk and sit in the chair. Even if his hands could reach, and most couldn't, it didn't matter because he couldn't see the screen.

We complained to Boots about this so he remedied it. I came into the room and saw a bizarre contraption—a rickety old office swivel chair mated with the bottom of a lawn chair. To make it high enough to reach the huge desk, he'd added a nailed-together mess of 4 x 4s as a base, upon which the swivel chair/lawn chair combo appeared to be precariously balanced.

I walked over to inspect it and maybe tell Boots that it was unsafe. To make my point, I attempted to pull the chair off the 4 x 4s but, sure enough, it was thoroughly connected. It was one big, glorious, ridiculous chair. It smelled like a Dumpster and barely fit through the door. But at least we could see over the top of the desk.

We lived like this for a while, stoically; we'd become accustomed to not having Xbox and didn't have time for movies. There was a very nice gym full of everything we loved: CrossFit, heavy bags and pads, free weights, plenty of cardio machines, and lots of room to stretch or utilize the foam rollers. There was also a big latte, espresso, and cappuccino coffeemaker in the Tactical Operations Center (TOC) and a great chow hall. The other stuff we could do without. We were here to hunt.

CHAPTER FOURTEEN

When people think of SEALs and Army Special Forces, they probably imagine a fierce rivalry. Well, they wouldn't be wrong. As I said, a lot of SEAL commanders would have balked at an assignment in which we were, nominally at least, reporting to their commander. But from the start we were glad to be working with them, and we benefited from their expertise in the most exciting (and fun) style of attack, which they were doing daily while crushing the enemy.

On one such adventure, they hit a convoy of bad guys that included too many vehicles for them to handle. Two of the cars got away. Fortunately, we had several assets in the sky, and the Air Force was able to watch and follow the vehicles to their safe house. Both vehicles parked, and five insurgents went into one of three adjacent houses.

Back at the Baghdad Airport, we were in the operations center monitoring the houses as the higher-ups decided what to do. The bosses were discussing the possibilities: Should we send in an assault team? Army Special Forces had killed all of the other insurgents so it might well make sense to interrogate someone to find out more about their cell. Should we "go kinetic," which means drop some bombs on the house? That would certainly kill all of them, but we'd get no further intelligence.

As the conversation went on, someone suggested a third option: "Send in TF Blue," which was us—Task Force Blue, as in Navy Blue. The idea was batted around for a bit when finally an officer from the Special Air Service (SAS) announced, "Yeah, send in TF Blue. It's just like going kinetic. Only you can tell them to bring one out alive!" He was semi-joking. But the commander actually said to us, "Hey, you guys have been killing everybody. Try to bring one back alive so we can interrogate him."

The intel folks in the Joint Operations Center (JOC) kept eyes on the target while we planned the hit. The house was quiet: lights off and no sign of activity. So we said, "You know what? It's been a long deployment. Forget hiking in. Let's just fly in and land right in front. We'll clear the whole place in ten minutes and leave. The night will be over and we can come back and hang out with our weird furniture."

We chose a landing spot a hundred meters from the front door. It was dangerous because we knew they were bad guys, that they were armed, and that they were spooked. But even if they came out shooting, we thought we could get the drop on them. Our plan was complacent, overconfident. When things go so right for so long, you stop thinking about ways things can go wrong. This is how success can kill.

We took off in three Black Hawks and beelined for the houses. We were only in the air for a short while when the call came from the pilots: "Ten minutes."

The doors were open, and I was on the left side of the rear helicopter, Dash Three, with my legs hanging out of the open door. This was always my favorite part, high on adrenaline and the wind whipping my face. I went through my checklist: double check NOD—Night Optical Device—and weapon . . . look forward to watch for movement.

"Two minutes . . . one minute."

"Thirty seconds." We all had the houses in our gun sights now. Sure enough, the bad guys had heard us coming and were running outside. They opened fire, and we returned it from the air. We were in a gunfight before we'd even touched the ground.

The helos all hit the deck at the same time, and the teams jumped out. Because of the cover of darkness and our night vision capability, we were able to quickly eliminate three of the fighters while the other two split and ran into separate, adjacent structures.

A small team inspected the bodies while Echo Team went to the house on the right and my guys, Delta Team, went to the house on the left; each contained one bad guy. My team covered the entrances and the windows and did what we called a "de-escalation of force." Instead of rushing in with guns blazing, we took up positions outside and "called out" the terrorist.

Just like in the cop shows on TV, we shouted the few phrases we knew in Arabic, "We know you are in there. Come out and no one else needs to get hurt!" Nothing.

Time to let loose the hounds. Seriously. We had Toby the dog with us, and he was one tough son of a bitch. Literally. "If you don't come out of the house," we shouted, "we're sending in a dog and he *will* bite you! Come out!!" Nothing.

We gave Toby the signal, and he tore inside, unarmed with anything but his teeth and protected only by a working vest that had no bulletproofing, just a handle on the back in case his handler needed to pull him away. He raced around in the darkened rooms, using only his keen sense of smell. A few seconds later, he began to bark emphatically. We've worked out a complex way of communicating with these highly trained animals: If the dog is barking, we think he has found something. If the dog is barking, and there is a grown man screaming, we *know* he has found something. Not complex, actually.

We had dogs on pretty much every mission. They were absolutely fearless and added an essential dimension to our capabilities. They'd enter a house near the back of the "train" with their handler and would come up when called. If there was a sensitive situation—barricaded people, or someone not coming out, or we just simply weren't sure and had a funny feeling—we'd send the dog in. Sometimes the dogs had cameras and sometimes they didn't but we could see the images real-time when they did. We also used the dogs to chase down "Squirters." Those are folks who're trying to run. The Squirters would either get run down by the dogs and crushed, or they'd find a hiding spot, and the dogs would locate them and tear them up. The dogs would charge heavily armed men without hesitation. The enemy was terrified of them. They thought of dogs as mangy scavengers, the lowest of the low, so to them these fierce and magnificent creatures must have seemed like some other kind of animal entirely. Whenever they could, they'd try to shoot them down.

We lost quite a few dogs in combat, and mourned them as we would one of our brothers. In front of the SEAL Team ▓ headquarters in Virginia, there's a huge, trident-shaped piece of steel from the World Trade Center and a large black wall with the names of the fallen. If you stand with your back to the wall, looking forward, a few feet ahead and to the right, there's a smaller wall with the names of our fallen dogs. That's where they walked: forward and to the right.

When we weren't on missions, the dogs would hang out with us wherever we were bedded down—kind of like pets, with a difference. When they don't have their gear on, you can mess around with them, play ball with them—they like their ball more than treats. They'll sit there and watch TV with you. But you can never forget they're dogs of war. If they sit on the same level as you on the couch, you have to push them off. If they sit next to you and put a paw on your leg, that's not to say *I love you*, but *I'm dominant*. You have to be careful. If you let them feel dominant, they might attack. Some are better than others. Some are friendly, and some are just straight-up dicks. Only one was like that actually, but he was a complete psycho.

Toby, though, was a great dog. Confident that he was on to something, we cleared the rest of the house and worked our way toward the last room, where the barking was coming from. It happened to be a bathroom. In the middle of the room, there was a small, bathtub-looking basin. It was built into the floor and was serving as the drain right below a showerhead. Toby was scratching violently at it and barking right at the drain. We thought that was quite odd so we backed Toby off, and two of my guys, Boots and Mack, stood on either side of the tub with their guns pointing at it. Keeping as low and away as they could, they squatted down and each grabbed an edge of the basin and started to lift. As they did, bullets exploded out of the tub and flew inches from their faces. They dropped the basin as if it had suddenly become a writhing viper and returned fire as they backed away.

They got off about six shots each. The bathtub, never again to hold water, ceased all resistance. Breaking the unique silence that follows the cacophony of a gunfight, one of the guys said, "Holy shit, we're actively engaged in a gunfight with a bathtub!!"

We gathered our emotions for a second, as we all contemplated how close we'd come to an unnecessary death. Then with one of us covering the crack, we gingerly lifted the tub out of the floor. Beneath it was a dug-out cavity and lying dead in it was the insurgent. Beside him was a machine gun and a stack of grenades. He'd dug that fighting position with the intent of martyring himself in a fight just like this. Fortunately, he hadn't managed to martyr us along with him. Sometimes, it's better to be lucky than good.

We knew we shouldn't have landed right next to the houses, but we'd done it anyway. Maybe next time we'd remember a lesson that came very close to being written in blood: Complacency kills.

The guys in the other house were able to grab the last insurgent without firing a shot. They could have justifiably shot the a-hole because he was armed, but they showed restraint. After all, the bosses had asked nicely.

We loaded up the weapons and incriminating documents and brought the prisoner back to Baghdad Airport. Here you go. Time for breakfast.

*   *   *

THE MAIN DIFFERENCE BETWEEN RAMADI and this new gig was mobility. We had it in spades.

We could use the Little Birds when we needed and also had that fleet of armored vehicles, including Pandurs. They were lightly armored, highly maneuverable, small, fast, and relatively quiet. We were able to load an assault team plus a sniper and an interpreter in each and could quietly drive anywhere in Baghdad. While I was never a fan of driving in Baghdad, Army Special Forces had proven that for chasing bad guys in congested neighborhoods, Pandurs were the way to go. On the downside, they'd also proven to be death traps when hit by IEDs. In tactical situations, one needs to ask, "Is the squeeze worth the juice?" Sometimes it is, and you roll the dice.

One such day, we were targeting a terrorist whom we believed to be a high-value target (HVT). He wasn't *that* high-value, but he was one to go get if he popped up. And he just had. It was the middle of the day, our night, so we shook ourselves awake and ran to the ready room to put on our gear. We boarded the Pandurs and headed out the main gate toward the house. We brought four Strykers full of Army Rangers for some extra security.

We knew where the house was, and we were on our way. We surrounded the place and carefully cleared it, rounding up the men inside for interrogation. The target wasn't there. We left the guys we'd rounded up in mid-interrogation and went after the elusive HVT.

The new house we thought he'd fled to was only a few blocks away, so we decided to go on foot. The Pandurs and Strykers could catch up with us a few minutes later. We split our patrol into two lines, one on each side of the street. This way one side could cover the other. Patrolling in Baghdad was dangerous in 2007, especially when the sun was up.

We quickly made it down the street and around the corner

to the house. We surrounded it and had the interpreter shout commands through a bullhorn. He told the inhabitants of the house that we were coalition forces and everyone should come out. They all did, mostly women and children, plus two military-age males. We separated them, and had our guys start to interrogate as the rest of the team began to clear the building. This was tense as always because bad guys didn't always come out when asked politely. Some wanted to fight and die.

The house proved to be empty, but as we were working through it, the HVT popped up again. This time he was three blocks away. It was uncanny how he was keeping a step ahead of us. Guys were taking this personally, and it only made them more determined to get him. We hopped back in the Pandurs and raced toward the new target. On the way there, the HVT disappeared again. A few minutes later he popped back up in a house about five blocks away. This time he stayed up; he didn't disappear. *Let's get him!*

We all jumped in our Pandurs and rolled again at top speed. All of the operators were excited. We were getting closer by the second, and this time, he wasn't getting away. As we turned the corner about two blocks out, we could see the target building. We were almost there. And then we saw a bridge between the target and us.

"All stop, all stop, all stop!" our troop commander, Rich, shouted over the radio. "Turn around, we're going home."

The guys in my vehicle were visibly angry at this point. They'd been hustling all day in 120-degree heat through a very dangerous neighborhood chasing a guy they really wanted to grab, or kill. Tempers were flaring. "Why the hell are we turning around?!" Boots said to me, "He's right fucking there!! . . . Let's go crush him!"

"He's right there across that bridge, bro," I said. "It could be wired. This is a good call."

"I don't give a shit if it's wired, let's nail that guy!" he said.

It didn't matter what we said in my Pandur, the call was made, and we turned around. We drove back to Baghdad Airport with a little bit of bitching going on. Most of the guys wanted to take the HVT down, bridge or no bridge, but they were fueled too much by emotion. The HVT could have been bait, intentionally luring us over a booby-trapped bridge. The commander had made the right decision. Eventually the guys would agree, just not right now. They all needed time to cool off.

A week later I brought this up with three of my guys. We'd done several missions since the HVT, and I wanted to drive something home. I said, "Does anybody remember the name of that HVT we went after who was across the bridge?"

They all said no. I said, "Do you remember the names of your kids?"

I could see it sinking in.

The point I was making was that you can't fall in love with a target. You need to take a second, even if that's all you have, to make sure you don't make crucial decisions based on emotions. This is true not just in SEAL life but everyday life: Your first loss is your best loss, and it's okay to take it.

We never found out if the bridge was rigged, but the odds were definitely against us based on the HVT's actions. What we do know is that nobody on our team got hurt. In the big view, missing one HVT was insignificant compared to the wins we'd been accumulating. In fact, we and Army Special Forces had been putting such a hurting on the Sunni terrorists that they were moving out. It was time for us to do the same. We were headed a hundred miles north of Baghdad to Baqubah.

OUR ENABLERS IN OUR NEW home were so efficient they were scary. Four tents, each the size of a large Ryder truck, materialized within hours in the middle of the desert in 130-degree heat. Then the enablers produced Pelican hard cases full of wires, screens, keyboards, and antennas and went to work. Soon after, we had an operations center up and running that included

Internet access, both secure and unsecure, as well as the phones and communications we'd need to track terrorists. It was like a pop-up command post—impressive save for the fact that we only had one Porta John for the lot of us.

Actually, they'd skimped on a few other amenities in our tent quarters. All we had were cots, sleeping bags, and ponchos. We hung the ponchos so we could get some limited separation and cranked up the air-conditioning—I recommend it for all camping trips—and that worked surprisingly well, thank God. The Seabees brought in massive A/C units and installed them. When the units break, it's a nightmare—a waking nightmare because sleep is impossible. Also, we had great showers everywhere but here. We went thirty days with no showers. The A/C was our only relief.

You can't put up shelves in a tent, so we strung up 550 parachute cord to hang gear from. The tents were tan on the outside and white on the inside. I'm not sure if there's a science to those colors, but it sucked for us. We worked at night and tried our best to sleep during the day, but the sun is dazzlingly bright during the Iraqi summer. We were fortunate, most of the time, to have access to Ambien; our medical folks were cool and understood the deal.

While we got situated, our intel folks coordinated info on targets. The first target would be the best one. There was a group of Improvised Explosive Device (IED) makers on a small peninsula. We loved targeting IED makers because those roadside bombs were responsible for the vast majority of American casualties in the war. When we killed the producers, we knew we were saving American and coalition lives.

This group had chosen their hideout wisely. The peninsula was so small that it was practically impossible to penetrate without being noticed. In fact, no Americans had ever been there. There were too many women and children present to call in an air strike. The size made it too risky to fly into; the chances of being shot out of the sky were great. And because there was only one road in, it was littered with IEDs. A convoy would get blown up for sure. Result: Al-Qaeda had been able to run its operations there, totally unchecked, since 2003. They felt safe. We knew they were complacent.

Our plan was simple: Don't fly in, don't drive in. Hell, we were SEALs. We'd swim in.

It was perfect. The enemy believed they'd hear any Americans invading by air or land. The idea that we'd swim in would have never occurred to them. They'd totally forgotten to build a moat and stock it with crocodiles.

There were a total of nineteen terrorists in ten houses on our hit list. We weren't sure how many would be there, so we brought the whole crew: seventeen SEALs, two of our dogs, and a few enablers. We'd all get wet together.

We loaded up our helos and made the short flight to our point of insertion. We walked a bit until the dry land turned into swamp. It wasn't too bad; mostly swampy mud with a few points of deep water where we'd swim. Of course, I wasn't the one carrying the poles and ladders—we always made the newest guys do that. For them it sucked. The dogs hopped through most of the mucky stuff. In the deeper water, we needed to lift them up—they had handles on top of their vests so you could carry them like a very squirmy briefcase. Our guns were packed in "shoot-through" bags. The guns fit in them snugly, with a built-in rubber glove so you could reach the trigger and "shoot through" it if you had to.

We made it across in two hours and hit dry land again. The peninsula was pretty small, about the size of a couple of football fields, but packed with houses, huts, and narrow roads. It was obvious from first look why we'd have never been able to land there, and fast-roping would have provided the enemy with too much time to shoot as the helicopters hovered. But we were there now. It was 1:00 a.m. local time.

We made our way to the primary target buildings. They were side by side. The one on the right was three stories tall. The one on the left, my team's target, was two stories. Our plan was to surround both and get the snipers up high for security. Then we were going to enter both structures simultaneously and silently so that we could get the drop on the enemy. That plan didn't last very long. A sentry on top of the structure to the right saw us. He didn't know who we were for sure, but he knew we shouldn't be there. He started shooting his AK-47 right down on top of us. My guys and I were in a narrow alley just below him, in between the two buildings.

He missed us all somehow—I'm guessing because Allah was busy elsewhere—and we were all able to scramble to cover. Nobody could get a clear shot off, and we were disciplined enough not to randomly fire in his direction. You want to aim at what you shoot at and hit what you aim at. Plus, if we didn't fire back, it could confuse the enemy. This guy was on a balcony and would fire quickly and blindly and then retreat back a few steps. That's why we'd been able to get adequate cover.

Greg, who was a lifesaver for us but the angel of death for al-Qaeda, did what Greg does: He saved the day. Luckily, when the shooting started, our snipers already had their ladders out and were preparing to climb. The sound of an AK-47 simply made our snipers do their ladder setting faster. Greg was able to get to the roof first, three stories up, and get an angle on the terrorist. The bad guy had his back to Greg, but his wife was standing right next to him. Greg's problem was that the spot he'd climbed to was a small entryway into the house and there was a light on right above him. The illumination was bad news, so he crept over and started to unscrew the lightbulb. He turned the bulb off just in time because as it became dark again, the woman turned around and headed back for the entryway. She walked right up to Greg, stopped for a second face-to-face with him, then went inside. Greg had his night vision on so he was looking right at her the whole time. She never noticed.

The sentry with the AK-47 took his last shots down at the alley and then bolted for the inside of the house to get more ammo. Just like the woman, he wound up face-to-face in the dark with

Greg, only this time Greg didn't just get out of the way; he put two bullets from a suppressed .45 into the guy's head.

"Rooftop, building 1-1 clear." Damn he was cool.

Because the fighters in our building had certainly heard the ruckus outside of their windows, my team decided that we needed to enter immediately while we still had some surprise advantage. We left cover and ran to the main entry of the building on the left, which was just around the corner at the exit of the alley. I found myself in the one-man position and stopped at the front door to see if it was open. It was. I waited less than a second until I got the squeeze from Mack, the two man.

I went left, he went right. Right away we encountered two terrorists on their feet with AK-47s. One was off to my left in a bedroom with a woman standing next to him. I could see them through the open door. The other was coming out of a bedroom farther down the hall off to the right. He had some kids next to him. This is why we didn't want to just bomb the place.

As soon as I recognized the threat, I took two shots just to the left of the woman, hitting the armed man in the head. I could hear Mack taking his shots at about the same time. Both terrorists fell dead.

We now had four of our shooters in the house, and we began to clear. I went to the bedroom on the left where I'd just shot the bad guy, and I now had Boots behind me. Mack cleared up to the bedroom where his guy had come from and entered with Delicious. Our last two shooters from D Team entered behind us and made their way to the stairs, which were at the far end of the main room.

Our room was cleared quickly, we searched the dead guy for a body bomb, which he didn't have, and grabbed the woman. We walked her out of the room and placed her in the far bedroom with the rest of the women and children. The two men killed were the only military-age males in the house. One of our shooters stayed behind to watch the women and children while the other five of us went up the stairs. We could hear gunfire coming from the other building. E and F Teams were eliminating terrorists they were encountering as well as those trying to escape outside.

As we made our way up the stairs, we slowed our pace. It was still dark in the house so we might still have an advantage. If there were more fighters upstairs, we didn't want to announce that we were coming.

The stairs went up to a halfway point, and then you had to turn left to get up the other half. I was the third man going up. When the one man turned to get up the second part of the stairs, he noticed something that made the hair on his neck stand up: There was a hole in the wall right at the back of his head. He pointed his gun at it and turned on his white light to illuminate it. There was nobody there so we ran up the stairs and secured it all, then checked out the hole in the wall. On the other side in a closet was a mattress—a fine sniper's nest. Had there been a shooter in place, the point man would have taken several 7.62 mm rounds to the back of the head.

With the main building secure, we rounded up the women and children and handed them off to an enabler. The fighting in the buildings that E and F Teams were taking down was still noisy but our snipers had cleared the roof so we were good to make a move.

By the time we got to the next target, building 1-3, all the terrorists were definitely awake. We entered slowly so we could get all of the angles through the doors and windows. If we could avoid getting into another gunfight, the slowdown would be well worth it.

I found myself in the one-man position again, and as I began to clear the first room through the main door of the house, I spotted an armed man waiting for us. I dumped him with two shots to the head and finished my pan. Night vision and invisible lasers are such a great advantage. I entered as far as the crumpled body and stayed there, allowing the train to move into the interior. All five guys from D Team began to methodically clear. They ran into one more al-Qaeda operative in the room farther down the hallway and Boots shot him. The team finished clearing the floor and moved to the second floor. I was in the rear of the train, waiting to be needed and watching the guys go up the stairs. Delicious was the point man. He went to the top of the stairs, carefully panning the areas he could without entering the space. *Pop! Pop!* He'd found another gunman and sent him to hell.

As we moved on to our next target, Nate was still up high on building 1-2. He'd been watching us shoot our way through the compound, and he was tired of watching. "Fuck this up-high shit," he said over the radio, "I'm rolling with D Team." He ran downstairs and out the door. He made his way to the back of our train and went to the next building with us.

Cruz was in front this time, and he slowly made his way to the main entry that was near the right side of the building as we faced it. Nate went over to the left where there was a good place for him to climb just above a large window. I walked with him to cover his movement. Nate slung his sniper rifle and climbed to the roof. He reached for his .45, aimed at the large window, and shot three times. Out of my sight, there was a man with an AK-47 hiding behind a table, waiting for the entry team to come in so he could ambush them. Nate saw him at the last second and gave the guy three to the chest. Again, darkness was our friend.

Cruz and the others cleared this structure quickly since the one dead guy was the only person in there, and, as it turned out, the last terrorist on the peninsula.

In our after-action assessment, my boss and I were going through the list we'd made and started counting. With two dogs and seventeen SEALs, we'd killed all nineteen of the terrorists without hurting one woman or child, or taking any casualties.

The next day, the locals who'd been terrorized by this al-Qaeda cell for four years realized that all their oppressors were dead. We could see their reaction because we had aircraft circling overhead, watching in case any more bad guys showed up to bury the dead. No more bad guys, just a big celebration. The party got so big, with all these jubilant people drinking juice and dancing in the street, that a newspaper in Baghdad sent a reporter up there. He asked, "Who did this? Who came last night?"

The women responded: "Ninjas, and they came with lions."

That was the headline the next day in Baghdad.

CHAPTER FIFTEEN

Back from war, back to training. Again with parachutes.

Even though I'd yet to parachute to an objective on a live mission, the ability to insert a SEAL Team ▪ troop on any given X by high-altitude jump is a potent weapon and those skills need to remain sharp. Which is why, on a jump trip to Arizona, we stretched our luck trying to get in one last jump before being shut down by weather. Lance was the jumpmaster—Lance of the "Lance Factor," so I should have known something "interesting" was about to happen—and I was the lead jumper. As the first one out of the plane, my job was to get out below and in front and lead everyone to the target in our stack formation.

I never jump a HAHO with goggles because they always fog up, so I go barefaced. Normally, that's not a problem.

On this jump, we could see a storm below us, billowing black clouds lighting up like flickering lanterns with angry bolts. We should have backed off, but we were determined to get in one more jump. Lance gave the word and I leaped—right into a hailstorm. I shut my eyes and fell for six seconds with hail hitting me in the face at 150 miles per hour. You may not appreciate this, but six seconds is an eternity when you're being blasted in the face by dagger-sharp ice pellets at high velocity. When I calculated that I was in position, I pulled my chute and, as I did, tasted the blood streaming down my face into my mouth. From that point, I led the stack into the landing zone.

After we all got down, I ran into one of my bosses, and the first thing he said was, "Jesus, man, you look like you were wearing a beehive for a helmet."

It wasn't Lance's fault—we *all* made the call to do another jump. It was just his typical luck that he was the jumpmaster when shit went sideways. As everyone was having fun at the expense of my pulverized face, Lance came up and said, "I think I know why you're bleeding. It's because you were hitting the raindrops on the pointy end."

The next day, we went back up. I was lead again and Greg the sniper brought up the rear. Sometimes we'd put our experienced jumpers in the back to manage the stack. They could see how everyone looked and tell the lead jumper what was up. Everybody pulled, and we got into formation. The air park where we would land was fifteen kilometers away. Visibility was good, and I could see the park as soon as we assembled—which made it easy to judge my angles. Everything was fine, or we *thought* it was, until Greg came on the radio from the back of the stack and said, "Hey, Jumper No. 12, you've got a line over, and you need to cut. Cut away."

"A line over" means the parachute is open but one of the cords going from the chute to the harness has wrapped over the top of the chute. That's an obvious malfunction for the guy behind him to see, and that jumper could see it, too. Or he *should* have been able to see it. The jumper turned out to be one of our Air Force PJs (para-rescue guys)—an absolute wizard at any kind of medical needs from ibuprofen to field surgery. Cutting a parachute at high speed is no big deal—it's muscle memory—you just chop it. But at low speed, under canopy as we were now, you have time to think about it, which isn't a good thing. Because the Air Force guy was thinking, *If I cut this one, I'm down to my reserve, and if my reserve doesn't open, I'm dead.* It didn't take a medical guy to realize that.

We were at thirteen thousand feet, and his chute was still doing its job up there, so he looked up at the canopy and said, "No, it's fine, it's good."

Greg said, "Yeah, it's good now but we're going to get to lower altitude and it's going to get worse. You don't want that thing collapsing at a thousand feet. By the time you get your reserve open you're dead." I was up front, but I was hitting my risers, twisting them so I could turn around and see this guy. Everyone behind me was doing the same. We could see the guy's face get this kind of puckered, frowny expression. He was thinking about it. And then he said in a high-pitched little helium kind of voice, almost like a little kid, "Oh, ooookaaay."

He chopped his cords and—*boom!*—just as fast as you can imagine, it flew off, yanking the static cord on the reserve and—*boom!*—the reserve was up and perfect. He was still right on heading, and had maintained his position in the stack. He hadn't missed a step. His voice boomed over the radio: "I'm back, motherfuckers."

So now everything was good again, we were back in formation with a couple of kilometers to go. As we were flying we heard, "Hey, you guys got an aircraft moving from west to east."

I looked down expecting to see a crop duster. You'll see those quite a bit, and you can avoid those. But this was no crop duster. A commercial passenger jet was coming straight at us like a sky shark hurtling toward prey. It zipped past me, and it was silent. I knew it was US Airways not because I read the side of the aircraft, but because I could see the insignia on the wings pinned to the pilot's uniform. They were that close. I could see passengers in the porthole windows.

Theoretically, in that situation you could cut away your main chute and try to drop out of the plane's way before deploying your reserve. But it happened so fast that no one did anything. We just watched this giant aircraft zoom past us. Then we heard some rumbling over the radios and somebody said, "Jesus Christ, what happens when we go through his jet wash?"

All of a sudden, we were in the spin cycle of a giant washing machine, just getting hammered by the jet's wake, and we were all thinking the same thing: *We almost got hit by a fucking plane!* If it had hit any one of us, the whole plane would have been wrapped up in a 360-square-foot canopy. All that silk and rope would have gotten sucked into the engine, and the plane would have gone down. Appreciating how close we'd come to a major disaster certainly made the rest of our descent less frolicsome, that's for sure.

The thing is, it never should have been the close call that it was. We'd submitted what's called a Notice to Airmen to all airports in the region, major and minor, the day before. It says that during a particular time frame there shouldn't be any aircraft in the area because there are going to be twenty guys under canopy there. Obviously, somebody either didn't give a shit or paid insufficient attention.

Maybe we ought to do something about that.

IN LATE WINTER 2008, WE were getting ready for another deployment to Afghanistan within weeks, and I was an instructor in yet another jump-training course in Arizona. Lance was there, too—yes, the Lance who almost got electrocuted in a swimming pool in Iraq, got tangled in a tandem drogue chute, and jumped into the middle of a hailstorm. When he said he was going to take the most dangerous jump course, instructors were saying, "Hey, Lance, this is a bad idea. With your luck, something's going to bite you, man. You can't do this course."

They were serious. It is a dangerous course. I hated it. It's fucking scary.

In the middle of the jumps, I got called to go on a mission to rescue some hostages in Colombia. By the time I flew from Arizona to Virginia Beach, I was too late: The plane had already left for Barranquilla. We had just two other guys who were home, so instead of flying back to Arizona, we figured we'd work out and then go out to Suffolk and get some jumps in. We finished a jump and were packing up the chutes when my boss, Street, who was there with us said, "We've got to get back now because Lance just died."

It's like an electric shock goes through you. You never forget where you were when you heard one of your brothers has died. We'd lost Tom Valentine, a wonderful guy with a wife and small children, less than a month earlier in another jump-training accident. His body was found on a golf course green where well-heeled golfers were enjoying the safety and security Tom had helped to provide. His guys loved him as did everyone else. He was one of the best. One of the guys jumping with him that day told me that in Tom's last seconds he reported his chute malfunction—it's called a "horseshoe"—to the rest of the jumpers in the stack. His last words were, "I love you, guys."

A week before that, Mike Koch and Nate Hardy had both been killed in the same room while clearing a terrorist compound in Iraq. Two months before that, Mark Carter, one of those amazing SEALs who survived being a Smurf during Hell Week at BUD/S and was nicknamed Badger after the 5'5" dude took down a 6'5" monster in a wrestling match, died on another Iraq mission. He stepped on an IED while holding external security on a house in a very dangerous city.

And now Lance. We later learned that he'd been jumping when the same thing happened to him that had happened to me a year earlier. Only I'd initially pulled the chute at a high altitude of 13,000 feet instead of the usual 5,500—giving me time to fight against the g-forces and reach the release. Lance had only pulled at 5,500, and couldn't release the reserve in time. He hit the ground at a hundred miles per hour.

Guess what everyone said: "Jesus, we need to fix this."

You *think*? We should have fixed it a year earlier.

Before we'd started losing so many guys, the command had us fill out these "What I want if I die" sheets. Because we hadn't suffered any losses yet, we just had fun with those sheets, mocking the idea. One guy said, "If I die, I want Nitro, our one-legged guy who got his leg blown off on top of Takur Ghar during Operation Anaconda, to perform 'Tiny Dancer' a cappella."

Everyone treated those forms as jokes until we started losing guys for real.

When Lance filled *his* out, he said he wanted to be buried in this cemetery in Pennsylvania, and he wanted a Camaro to pull up to the gravesite playing music from his favorite band, Iced Earth, at top volume while we all stood around drinking Natural Light. His mom would put the first shovelful of dirt on his coffin, then we'd all follow. After that, his instructions read, he wanted all of us to go to a titty bar right down the street.

So that's what happened. We drove one of his Camaros out to the cemetery, playing Iced Earth as loud as we could. We all drank beer and told "Lance stories" to his mom. To be honest, it was kind of fun. It was horrible because we'd lost Lance and everyone loved him, but it was neat to imagine him being happy that we'd pulled off his "if I die" wishes.

Then we all went to the titty bar. We didn't bring his mom.

CHAPTER SIXTEEN

Within days of Lance's funeral, I flew in to a former Russian military base in Asadabad, an unimpressive little city in a bowl surrounded by rocky mountains. It was interesting occupying what had been a Russian military facility—a reminder not to let happen to us in Afghanistan what had happened to them, i.e., have our asses handed to us.

Being at a remote outstation, I had more interaction with the locals, and for the first time really got a feel for what an entirely different perspective they had. You can sit back in America and watch the war in Afghanistan and think: *If we just give them democracy they'll overcome the problems holding them back.* But it's not that easy. Many Afghans—especially in remote regions outside major cities—don't think like we do. For instance, it's not uncommon to find people who believe in dragons—*literally*. We'd intercept phone calls and listen to two Afghans talk to each other about some event upsetting the dragon that spits a gem in the sky every morning to light the sun. That rumble of thunder? It's the dragon expressing his displeasure. One time, we heard a guy saying that the only way to kill the dragon was with a German-made B-52, which doesn't exist, by the way.

I began to realize that when we *thought* we were communicating with these rural Afghans, we were often saying something that didn't fit their worldview. We had a cook, named Idris, who lived in town and came to the base each day to prepare our meals. I used to chat him up and got to know him pretty well, but one day something he said irritated me, and I made a contrast between the slow pace of technological change in Afghanistan and the strides my country had achieved in only two hundred years. I mentioned America's putting a man on the moon. His response was, "Mr. Rob, you're so stupid. You can't put a man on the moon." He held his thumb and forefinger an inch apart. "It's just this big!"

At this point in the war, we were working with an Afghani team—an elite, well-trained, and well-paid corps of fighters the United States had pretty much hand-picked.

With some exceptions, the regular Afghan military was a joke, but these guys were legitimately good, though I worried that they'd eventually be a pain in our ass because their loyalty is family first, then tribe, then money. So when we leave and our money leaves, the pay cut they're looking at compared to what the Taliban will pay them . . . Let's just say that whoever they work for, they're good enough and better enough than the regular army to be the ones running the store.

There wasn't much going on in Asadabad then. We had a tough time getting missions. The ones we did get tended to fall through. This was the first deployment where I was the team leader. I'd worked my way up through the ascending ranks to chief petty officer—which was a huge deal in the Navy. Being a "chief" made me eligible for leadership roles on the team level. In this case, that brought with it the responsibility for working with a guy there, named Tom, who had a tough Cold War style, huge smarts, and experience. He had a deep understanding of the landscape: the tribes, the villages, the valleys. He really got it. He wanted to kill the enemy. I loved it.

Eventually, our intel guys gave us a worthy target, none other than Zabit Jalil, the guy who'd orchestrated the "lone survivor" ambush on a SEAL recon team, killing three of four, then shooting down a rescue helicopter with eight SEALs, two pilots, and six air crewmen aboard.

His voice kept popping up on the Pakistan side of the border near the Sirkanay District. We knew our rules of engagement made it tough to deal with the Pakistani border; the enemy would attack on the Afghan side then slip back into Pakistan where they knew we couldn't chase them.

Unless . . .

There were two acronyms that we could work with: TIC and PID. They meant "Troops in Contact" and "Positive Identification." If we were in a fight with an enemy force (Troops in Contact) and they tried slipping back into Pakistan, as long as we could maintain visual confirmation that it was the same group we'd been fighting (Positive Identification), our rules of engagement allowed us to pursue them up to ten kilometers beyond the border.

We decided to do a bait-and-switch operation. We'd fly in at night with a few of my guys and a small force from the Afghan anti-terror team and hike up to the top of the mountain before the sun came up. From there we'd have a clear view of the border. Our hope was Jalil's people would see us and attack—not realizing Americans, and their bombers, would be involved. Once they'd engaged, we'd call in artillery and hopefully air support and pursue them as they retreated.

We assembled our men and made sure we all had enough gear to sustain us for twenty-four to forty-eight hours. Because we were a small team and would be hiking in rigorous terrain, we split up some of the essentials. I carried extra batteries for the big radio, Tony carried the radio, Jesse had the Med Pack, and someone else carried the water purifier; not that we'd find any water worth purifying up there, but there was a river at the bottom of the mountain and you never know where you may end up.

As team leader, I would serve as Ground Force Commander, which meant I would be directing the action. The commander is usually an officer, but there were none on this mission. I had with me Tom and Seth from the US Army; with the assistance of their interpreter, they could intercept enemy transmissions and help us anticipate their movements and intentions. We also brought about forty Afghans along. We prepared everything, and half our force, which included my team, loaded onto a CH-47 for the fifteen-minute flight southeast to the border of Pakistan. Once we inserted, the helicopter would go pick up the other half of our force and return with them.

I grew concerned as I listened on the helo's Internal Communications System and heard the pilot explain to the aircrew what he was seeing and what he couldn't see. Because the 47 is bigger than a school bus and mostly metal, the pilot doesn't see what the rear of his helicopter is doing. He listens to the enlisted aircrew in the back as they give him measurements. Even though I could tell that the pilot was calm, it was obvious that the peak he intended to land us on had a smaller landing area than he'd anticipated, with bigger and more abundant trees than he'd hoped. Given the tight squeeze, the pilot decided the only way to land was to back the huge helicopter in and parallel park. He'd need to trust the guys in the back as they "walked" him (and us) in. I listened as they gave him measurements and adjustments, then finally, "10, 8, 5, 4, 3, 2, 1" and I felt the back two tires rest on the peak. I unplugged my headset and jumped off the ramp onto the small clearing. We set up a hasty perimeter until the big helo took off again.

Once the bird lifted off and the backwash from its rotors died down, I led my crew a few hundred meters away where we waited for about forty-five minutes until the helicopter returned. Once it did and the rest of the troops disembarked, we all linked up, and I led the march up to our predetermined positions on the border. These were impressive mountains. They reminded me of Glacier National Park in Montana or the Grand Tetons in Wyoming. Just ridiculously steep. I led us up because I was the most experienced of all of us. My two other SEALs had yet to be in combat; it was their first trip overseas, and I wasn't willing to let any of the Afghans lead the way. This was a unique operation, and I wanted to make sure we got to where we'd planned.

In the middle of the hike, we dropped off twenty-five of the Afghans to set up a "fallback" position for us in case we needed to fight down the hill quickly. They had mortars to provide us some indirect fire as well. I didn't really trust the Afghans to be accurate, but I didn't want to bring all of them up with us to the peak; if we showed too much force the enemy might not want to fight. That left about fifteen Afghans, my team of four Americans, and one interpreter to complete the hike. At the peak, I split us into two flanks, each consisting of seven or so Afghans with my team in the middle. I had about 150 meters between my position and each flank.

From here the plan was simple: We'd wait to see if we were spotted. We didn't want to make it obvious that there were any Americans in the group; that would both discourage an attack and limit its duration. The enemy knew that with Americans came bombers and gunships and they are devastating. Because of that, we limited the number of aircraft observing us. Having aircraft aloft is great for numerous reasons: They can watch the surrounding areas and report on enemy and friendly movement; they can be a force multiplier by dropping bombs and shooting missiles and guns; and they can pluck friendly troops from danger by picking them up and giving them a ride. But they also tend to get too close when teams like mine are trying to be sneaky, and they make a lot of noise that alerts the locals. So we had one aircraft watch us as we patrolled to our spot on the border, but then it departed after thirty minutes. After that, we were alone. We set up two positions at the highest points and put ground pads behind some cover. We were on the mountain peak above the timberline, so it was barren. If Taliban fighters were here, they'd soon see us. So we waited.

AS SOON AS THE SUN came up, we began to see activity on the Pakistan side of the border. Since we were on the high ground and above the tree line, we could see for several miles on both sides of the border and down three valleys. It was a really good spot to observe. We noticed six armed men walking in and around a small fenced-in area with a few tents. It was about half of a mile away from us on the Pakistan side, obviously some sort of checkpoint. In this part of the world, however, that doesn't say much. We knew we were right in the middle of a Taliban and al-Qaeda supply line so the chances of this point being friendly Pakistani military were slim to none. Regardless, it was obvious that they could see us, too, at least some of us, and they were discussing what to do.

After thirty minutes of deliberating, four of the armed men began to walk in the direction of our flank position on the right. It didn't concern me too much: We had an elevated position and they were outnumbered. Also, we'd be able to watch their movements as they walked the eight hundred meters that separated us. As they got closer, I noticed they were wearing similar uniforms. They weren't military but wore some sort of militia-type garb. We simply remained still and kept our weapons trained on them. Once they were about two hundred meters from the right flank, they began to yell at us in a few different languages; English wasn't one of them. I asked the interpreter next to me what was being said and was told that the men were yelling for the senior officer to come down for tea. I had the interpreter tell our senior Afghan officer to go down to the uniformed men and bring five of his guys with him. He was to tell the men that he was part of an Afghan force that was patrolling the area. If the armed men asked if there were Americans here, he was to say, "No."

The six Afghans went down the two hundred meters and had a discussion for about forty-five minutes. They drank tea. Then they came back up to our position. I was informed that the armed men claimed to be a part of the "Frontier Corps": a militia composed of Pakistanis paid and armed by the United States to help guard the Afghan/Pakistan border. It was a complete waste of money, and these guys couldn't be trusted. This part of the world was lawless, and it didn't matter how much money was given away, the border remained unguarded. Giving these people guns was an even worse idea.

My senior Afghan guy told me more of what had been discussed at tea. The Frontier Corps leader told him that they were fearful of the Taliban, who were everywhere around here. He said that if they showed up and attacked, we should help them. Conversely, if they attacked us, they would help.

It was complete crap, and I knew it. There was no way the Pakistani military would station a few guys out here on their own. These teatime hosts could be working for a few disparate entities, one of which was certainly the Taliban. I was betting that these guys were, in fact, a Taliban checkpoint and that things were about to get exciting. Reassuringly, we still had superior position and numbers. I had Tony make radio contact with the Tactical Operations Center at Bagram Airfield, informing them that all was quiet. I was happy we could still talk to them whenever we wanted.

The morning went on and we continued to watch the checkpoint. At about 10:00 a.m., we saw two trucks driving up the mountain toward it. There were guys in the cab and in the back. There was a chance that they were simply bringing supplies and relieving the guys who'd spent the night, but I didn't think so. They dismounted the vehicles and the trucks departed. Then the trucks came back—three of them this time and more guys. Then more.

The tide had shifted—now there were several hundred obviously hostile troops just a few hundred meters away. I began weighing the options: Stay on the top of the mountain with four Americans and fifteen Afghan militiamen and shoot it out, potentially, with a few hundred Taliban and al-Qaeda fighters. Or back my force out quietly, regroup with the troops and mortars behind us, and call for a daylight extract. Even though we'd be giving up the high ground, I liked this second choice because it looked as if the new group of men were still setting up and weren't prepared for us to leave. If we fell back quickly and called for the extract soon, the sound of the approaching helicopters might keep their heads down. Plus, if we could get about a mile away from the checkpoint, we'd be out of their range due to distance and terrain features. I radioed down the hill, gave them a quick summary of the situation, and told them we were on our way.

I got a quick head count and made sure all the men were briefed on the situation. I led the patrol out because I'd led it up and knew the quickest way back. We'd been hurriedly walking for about ten minutes toward our fallback position when I heard the Afghan boss, whom I'd never heard try to speak English, start yelling, "Bad guys, bad guys."

He pointed up the mountain, and we could see enemy troops splitting up. I remember how fast they were running and all of a sudden we started taking fire. We dove for what little cover we could find. I scrambled toward a small rock barely big enough to cover me. Bullets were cracking and zipping all around. We hadn't quite gotten back to the friendly position but were close. I needed to figure out coordinates for these enemy shooters and call in an air strike. Then we could call for the extract. For that, I needed the radio.

I looked for Tony but couldn't see him. As we'd made our way down the mountain, I'd split up the SEALs to keep a better eye on our Afghans in case shit went south. Now I was wishing I'd kept Tony closer. I could talk to him on our headsets, but this situation had gotten chaotic, and I wanted to be right next to him to avoid any confusion. I hadn't thought the enemy would hit us so soon or so accurately.

Up the hill, I could see the guys who wanted to kill us executing "shoot and maneuver" positions. A base of five or six guys would lie down and lay down continual machine gun fire to force us to keep our heads down. As they were shooting, another contingent would advance along our flank, spreading the battlefield in an attempt to surround us. It was working, too.

Once the maneuvering group had covered a sufficient distance, they would lie down and begin to fire. The base would then get up and become the maneuver. There were also rocket-propelled grenade (RPG) teams doing the same thing: base and maneuver. One team would fire a few RPGs while the other moved to surround us. That was a very effective way to keep our heads down since RPGs are loud and scary, and it's extremely hard to tell from where the next one is coming. All of these teams were a few hundred meters behind us to the east, and they were spreading out on the mountain to our north and south. The situation wasn't good.

And then it got worse. The high-pitched scream and thundering crash of incoming mortar fire announced an unexpected escalation of the forces arrayed against us. The trajectory suggested they were coming from mortar teams inside the checkpoint that we'd been observing all morning. I hadn't seen any mortars there, but they could have been hidden, or maybe one of those trucks had delivered them. Either way, they were hitting close enough to prompt the "pucker factor." The enemy was organized and motivated, and I was pretty sure they still assumed they were ambushing a small Afghan army force and didn't anticipate any air power. That meant they'd do this all day until we were dead. I needed to find Tony, but he was nowhere to be seen.

Still pressed against my little bit of cover, I inched my head above the rock and scanned our portion of the battlefield. I could hear bullets zip just above my head while airbursts from the rocket-propelled grenades went off all around. Slightly above me, the Afghan boss who'd just spoken his first words of English started crawling on his hands and knees up the hill, trying to regain some high ground when an RPG exploded into his backpack and blew him right out of it. His hat went flying and he fell back down the hill, tumbling violently on the rocks below him. I'd seen lots of people die before, and it looked a lot like this. I thought, *Okay, this is getting serious. We just lost our first guy.* I was shocked when he sat back up and looked around. He dusted himself off, and for some reason we locked eyes, stared at each other for what seemed like a long time. Then he yelled his second phrase ever in English. He put his thumb up and shouted, "Okay, USA!"

He ran back to his machine gun that had been left behind in the blast. I was relieved he was alive, and happy he could return some fire. I thought that would be the most impressive thing I'd see all day. I was wrong again.

I lay there watching the unthinkable unfold above me. I needed support. I needed bombs. I needed to find the radio. I needed Tony. I finally spotted him, squatting behind some small rocks and a few trees about 150 meters distant. He was hunkered down and returning fire but was not talking into his headset. It was probably the right call on his part—for two reasons. One, we'd yet to devise a plan, and he had no one to tell him the way to go. Two, he'd never been in combat and was probably more than a little hesitant to call for air strikes on the border post, inside a country we weren't at war with. I needed to get to his position to tell him where we needed to bomb and also to reassure him that in our current situation it was within our rules of engagement to drop on Pakistan. The only problem—well, *one* of my problems—was that I had to run across an open field in the middle of the day with a lot of people shooting all kinds of shit at me.

I remembered back to one of the first classes I'd had in initial SEAL land warfare training: There are three "lines of gear" that a shooter wears into the field. The first line is clothes and whatever is on the belt: blowout med kit, cash, knife, whatever is in your pockets. The second line is the gear attached to the shoulder harness we call a web: magazines, water, grenades, and radio. The third line is the rucksack. In it is food, extra water, sleeping bag, ground pad, and anything that is extra or nonessential. The thinking behind this way of packing is that a shooter can ditch lines of gear in a certain order if the situation is dire enough, making himself faster. The third line of gear is dropped first because it has the fewest essential items in it. I'd never heard of anyone doing it, but I did read the manual.

The enemy fire was getting more intense, from about seven different positions plus airbursts from mortars and RPGs all around. It was time to get it on. Or get it over with. I threw my backpack on the ground and started running to Tony. I remember thinking as I was running, *I'll be damned, I'm lighter and faster, the manual was right!*

When I got to Tony, I dove on top of him and said, "Okay, remember that checkpoint? That's where these mortars are coming from. Their command is up there, hit that with whatever the pilot wants. Shooter's choice, make it go away."

"Sorry boss," Tony shouted back. "We have nothing. No fighters, no bombers, no helicopters."

"When are they gonna get here?"

"No one seems to know."

We were screaming to be heard above the ongoing firefight. I could see the enemy maneuvering up a steep hill to the east, making their way toward both our flanks. Others were pushing right at us. They had us pinned down so they could move pretty much wherever they wanted. We were returning fire, but with our heads down and from an inferior position, it was ineffective. One of the worst feelings in the world is having someone shoot effectively at you while your bullets have no chance of reaching them. I didn't care for it.

While I was assessing our rather grim situation, one of our guys yelled, "Hey, Rob, air support would be better now rather than later."

I was like, "Dude, I'm trying."

Finally, Tony got in contact with some of the Forward Operating Bases in the area that had artillery and they were sending rounds out. They refused to fire on the checkpoint in Pakistan but they'd fire at some of the positions above us on the mountain. The rounds came in but were pretty much worthless. By the time we relayed where we wanted them, the fighters had moved. The artillery ended up simply being more random explosions, as if we didn't have enough of those.

The enemy force continued pushing toward us and was now so close that I could hear them yelling. It was mostly Pashtu, but I remember hearing Arabic, too. That meant al-Qaeda for sure. Where were those damn jets?

ONE GROUP GOT SO CLOSE I remember looking at the guy shooting at us. He had a belt-fed machine gun and he was white, with a big red beard. He looked a lot like me. I remember thinking how odd that was: He *could* have been from these parts, the illegitimate son of a Soviet soldier, but it was also possible that he was Chechen. They'd been seen here before, mainly when the war started, but were still around and still ruthless. Either way, he was shooting pretty much right at me while yelling "Allahu Akbar" (God is greater) over and over. I'm still not sure which was more annoying, the screaming or the shooting. All that was separating me from the impact of his bullets were the few rocks I was behind.

Directly behind me were my two Army guys, Seth and Tom, and their interpreter. They managed to crawl up to tell me what they knew. They'd intercepted enemy radio traffic and our interpreter had translated. It turned out that someone simply known as "Commander" had been giving calls to the fighters on their handheld radios. All that told me was that these guys were somewhat organized, and that their boss was on the mountain; potentially Zabit Jalil, the guy I wanted.

The enemy kept on maneuvering and shooting, and the RPGs and mortars were getting closer and closer. It was serious now and that white dude wouldn't shut up as he kept shooting right at us, "Allahu Akbar! Allahu Akbar! Allahu Akbar!" The bullets were cracking against my rock and zipping all around and everything seemed to be exploding near us. The airbursts were the worst: exploding directly above us, spitting shrapnel everywhere. It all churned together in a sickening whirl. Time didn't stop so much as repeat itself. I kept wanting to lift my head to see if my legs were still there, then remembering that if I lifted my head I'd get it blown off; yelling at Tony to ask if we had any jets yet; and listening to some guy who obviously had a big problem with me shoot his machine gun and remind me that "God is great!"

This went on forever, or by my watch, just over an hour. An hour in a gunfight, when you're surrounded, is a very *long* hour. The enemy was doing a good job of continuing a forcing fire that made us keep our heads down. I didn't get a single shot off for the full sixty minutes. Tony spent the entire time on the radio trying to coordinate howitzer fire and air support from nearby bases. Our third SEAL had maneuvered to a good position on a small hill off to the right of us and was able to get off some shots from time to time. Some of our Afghans were shooting sporadically with their belt-fed machine guns, which helped slow the enemy advance. I was simply aware that my 5.56 mm 4-16 wouldn't reach the enemy effectively, and I didn't want to waste ammo. I didn't know how long this fight would last, and I only had four magazines. I needed each bullet to count. I kept thinking about the speed and the noise and the chaos and the permanence. The word that hit was permanence. *This is fucking for real.* I wondered what it was going to feel like to catch a bullet in the forehead. *Will it hurt? Will I even feel it? God, I wish it was dark, when will it be dark? Shit, it's noon. This is going to be a long day. If I last that long.*

The enemy was trying to force us into a valley to the south, to our right. I could see that more fighters were setting up on the southern top end of that valley in ambush for when we were forced that way. We were lying there, I was on top of Tony, and I was engaging in a personal pep talk. "We're not going in that valley. You need to get help here because we're going to pick the hill we die on, not them."

As I was spitting out those words, two tracers flew in between my gun and my ear. I saw the flash, I heard the snaps, and it sounded like really fast, really nasty bugs zipping by. I stopped thinking about tactics and started thinking about my family. I had a conversation with myself: *You're about to get shot in the face now, you better get ready. It's going to happen, it's going to happen, it's going to happen.*

"Rob!" It was Tony. "I got Bones 22 on station ready to drop!!"

To be honest, with so many call signs, I didn't know who or what Bones 22 was, but I didn't care. My radio guy had just told me he was ready to drop, so that meant bombs and bombs would be good.

"Tell him to drop whatever he thinks he needs on that checkpoint!"

"I can't, Rob, the batteries in my radio just died!"

"Well, fucking change them!"

"I can't, you have the extra batteries!"

"Okay, the batteries are in my rucksack . . . Oh, fuck!"

That would be the backpack that I thought would be so efficient to drop. It was now in the middle of a wide-open field behind some very-ineffective-as-a-shield little rocks. We needed those batteries, and I needed to get them now. But first I needed to gather myself. Instinctively, I reached in my pocket and grabbed my can of Copenhagen. I put one in my lower lip, and put the can back in my pocket while taking my gun off my shoulder and handing it to Tony. I needed to be as fast as possible and the gun would just be extra weight. I wouldn't have time to shoot anyway. I'd run, open the backpack, get the batteries, and run back, or I'd get shot somewhere in between.

"I'll be right back."

I got up and ran about 150 meters to my rucksack, feeling a little like Forrest Gump. I knew my guys would try to cover me with as much fire as they could manage from their pinned-down positions. The problem was, it wasn't enough. The enemy fire became particularly intense just as I broke for the batteries, and I could still hear my newest acquaintance screaming, "Allahu

Akbar." During that sprint that seemed to take forever, I was thinking that once I got to the bag, I'd find cover, open the bag, get the batteries, take a deep breath, and run back. It seemed like a sweet plan until I actually got to the backpack. The nearby cover was useless, virtually nonexistent. There were bullets hitting the bag and I thought, "Screw this!"

I opened the bag right where it was and reached in for the two square batteries. Naturally, they were at the bottom. I grabbed them, turned around, and ran as fast as I could, another 150 meters, listening to cracks and snaps in the air, the occasional explosion, and one guy yelling at me. At first, it seemed like the goal just kept receding before me, but somehow I crossed the distance and jumped back behind my last position in front of Seth and Tom and tossed the batteries to Tony. "You're opening them, motherfucker!"

I grabbed my rifle back as Tony pulled the batteries from their plastic wrapping. I rolled over and reached back into my pocket for my Copenhagen. When I put some in my lip, I heard from behind, "Hey, Rob! Did you just put in a new dip in the middle of all this shit?" It was Seth.

"No, bro. I just freshened up my old one!"

Tony managed to get the new batteries into the radio and instantly got Bones 22 on the net. By this point, an unarmed surveillance aircraft had also shown up, and we learned from it that the enemy was moving mortars and ammunition back and forth between the checkpoint right on the border with Pakistan and their positions on the mountain. The pilot, Tony, and I agreed that meant the rules of engagement allowed us to air-drop four GPS-guided bombs on the checkpoint, even though that meant impacting the Pakistani side of the border. Bones 22 dropped all four; three were two thousand pounds that would airburst in a triangle just above the checkpoint. The fourth was a five-hundred-pound bomb that would smack down right in the middle. It was going to be awesome.

Tony let me know, "Bombs away, two minutes out!"

"Two minutes???" I shouted, "What, did he drop them from the fucking Space Shuttle??? We need them now!"

It was then that I found out that Bones 22 was a B-1 bomber that flew at about fifty thousand feet. I guess these things take time.

While we waited, the enemy fire was at its highest pitch. And so was the screaming, "Allahu Akbar!" Man, I was getting sick of that guy, and he'd moved closer. But I knew my moment was coming. I'd been having trouble returning fire with this guy because he had a bigger gun and a more advantageous position. But I knew something that he didn't: The tables were about to turn; I simply kept my head down and waited. I was sort of on my back so I could look up the mountain and observe the area where the checkpoint was. It was only about a thousand meters from us, so a loud day was about to get louder. But a bad day was about to get awesome.

It was barely audible at first, but the sound of sizzling got louder and louder. It was the sound of four bombs falling from the heavens at terminal velocity. *ZzzzzzzzzBABOOM!*

The fireball was brilliant, and I felt the shock wave of 6,500 pounds of ordnance exploding right on top of our enemy's stronghold. It felt like fucking victory. Just boom. Then all the shooting stopped. Everyone inside that checkpoint was surely gone as if they'd never existed. Every other fighter now faced the fact that this wasn't just a small Afghan force they'd been attacking; there were Americans here, too. Extremely *angry* Americans.

It shocked them all at first, none more than the man shooting at me. He immediately stopped shooting and yelling and got up on his knees to look over his left shoulder toward the impact site. He was about seventy-five yards in front of me. "Allahu Akbar, motherfucker!" I yelled as I shot him in the head several times. He fell dead. Finally, I could take a knee and really survey the battlefield.

I could see most of the enemy positions, and the fighters had all started to head in the opposite direction. They were still taking potshots but they wanted to get back to the Pakistan side of the border. The mortars had definitely stopped, and that told me that the first strike had been successful. But I still considered all the fighters threats and maintained our situation as "Troops in Contact."

Most of the enemy was trying to get into a valley directly in front of us, just about three hundred meters behind the position of the white guy I'd just shot. It seemed like the easiest place to take cover from the aircraft while trying to get back to the checkpoint and their vehicles. The others who'd been setting up an ambush to our south were now moving northeast, trying to get to the same place. Most probably didn't realize that there would be nothing left when they returned.

As I watched this, I worked with Tony and figured out the coordinates for four more strikes walking right up the valley to our front. We coordinated the movement of the B-1 and Bones 22 dropped again. Two minutes later, four separate explosions walked in from west to east all the way up the hill. These impacts weren't quite "danger close" but they were close enough that we could feel them. These four large blasts lit up the entire valley, and when the initial smoke cleared, I could see enemy fighters running around on fire.

Now the enemy was in full panic mode as they frantically ran toward the top of the mountain. They were continually in our view and that of the aircraft flying overhead. Because they were moving farther from us, we began to use what the pilots could see. Since I was the Ground Force Commander I'd be ultimately responsible for what was happening on the ground.

I was informed that a new jet had just arrived. His call sign was "Dude 12," and I got excited. Dude was an F-15, and those bad boys were usually flown by cocky young stud pilots, just the type who'd want to drop bombs on Pakistan. I was also informed that the insurgents had reached the Pakistan side and had stopped running. They were actually attempting to set up more positions, thinking they were safe. They weren't.

"Tony," I said, "clear Dude to drop on that position. They are ID'd as the same fighters, and I still consider us in contact."

Tony did just that, and Dude went at them. I would have loved to have been a fly on the wall inside that cockpit listening to the clever shit that pilot was saying as he flew in to drop on the "troops in the open." They were in Pakistan, and they were now lollygagging, sure they were safe. Once again, I knew something they didn't. Dude dropped four five-hundred-pound bombs and hit the men directly. For those not killed in the blast, the race was on again. All they could do was run as fast as they could farther into Pakistan.

At this point, we trusted the pilots to follow them with cameras mounted on the aircraft. We couldn't see any more fighters but we remained on the radio and followed the progress. Several minutes later, *Boom! Boom! Boom! Boom!* Those blasts turned out to be four more GPS-guided bombs dropped by Dude about two kilometers inside Pakistan. It was brilliant. I remember thinking, *I'm totally gonna hear about this the next time I see my boss.*

The former battlefield was now relatively safe. There were still munitions on the ground and God knows how many unexploded RPGs, but we finally had attack helicopters overhead and we were coordinating our extract. There were three helicopters coming for us—one CH-47 and two H-60 Black Hawks. Most of the Afghans and some of their advisers would fit on the 47, the rest in one of the Black Hawks. My small team of Americans would fly out on a single Black Hawk. I'd leave last.

The first two helos landed and loaded and took off. The third bird, my Black Hawk, came in last. I loaded up Tony and Jesse, Tom and Seth and their 'terp. Then I got on. I'd been on helicopters nearly every night on every deployment, but this one seemed cooler. I was sitting on the floor with my legs out of the starboard side. We were flying south to northwest, and I wanted to observe the battlefield. It was abused and smoky but the scenery was breathtaking. Flying down the steep cliffs, the trees and Konar River seemed so beautiful. And oh, yeah, I was still alive.

Just then it hit me: I'd been in the most intense gunfight of my life, which had stretched an hour or more, and I'd only used up one and a half magazines—a total of forty-five bullets.

WHEN WE LANDED AT THE Forward Operating Base (FOB) everyone met us outside. I ran into Tom, the guy in charge, and he seemed pleased. He knew what had gone down. With a wide grin he asked me if I wanted a glass of Jack Daniel's. I said yes, and we went inside.

He pointed out as we drank, "You know, we're not at war with Pakistan."

"We were today," I replied.

"What do you think?" Tom asked.

"Well, first of all, I'm very happy to be alive, and that all my men are, too. I think that some of our Afghans have minor injuries. It's a shame that it required a full hour to get any jets while we took overwhelming fire. I guess I'm either getting a Silver Star or going to Leavenworth. What do you think?"

"I think you're right."

A Silver Star, the third highest military award for gallantry in combat—below only the Distinguished Service Cross (or Navy Cross) and the Medal of Honor—is what they give you when, by acting in ways that are most likely going to get you killed, you end up snatching victory from the jaws of defeat. It's very hard to come by. I figured this was the unlikely option, but not impossible.

Leavenworth—the prison you get sent to when you take the fight across the border of a country that is masquerading as America's ally—was a greater possibility.

In the end, both sides investigated. Pakistan claimed that the battle started as an unprovoked attack on a Frontier Corps unit and Pakistan military checkpoint and that they, along with a local tribe, tried to defend themselves but were overwhelmed by American airpower, resulting in the death of eleven Pakistani soldiers.

The United States sent two generals my way, and we told them the truth. They interviewed Tony, Jesse, and me and told us that they had footage of the fight from the beginning—footage that they hadn't shown the Pakistanis. It was clear that we'd been attacked from Pakistan, and that the supplies for the fighters had been brought in from there. We were well within our rules of engagement, and that would be the end of it. They eventually showed the Pakistanis the footage, and it's available now on the Internet. I didn't go to Leavenworth after all. They decided to give me the medal instead.

We never did get the final count on enemy killed, just reports from paid local informants. Though Pakistan reckoned its losses at eleven soldiers killed, and had its typical "Death to America" funerals all over the news, I heard numbers of up to a hundred killed. We'll probably never know.

I *did* continue to pursue information on Zabit Jalil, wondering if we'd finally served justice. The only report I got was that he'd been wounded in the bombing. He had a big hole in his chest and had a butt cheek blown off.

When I heard that I said, "So what you're sayin' is that I *did* drop a bomb on his ass."

It took some time to adjust to being alive and out of mortal danger. It's really like entering a different dimension. One of the first normal thoughts I had was that I needed to call home. They hadn't heard from me for three days, and I knew that my dad, especially, always assumed I was in the middle of whatever shit was happening. Of course, this time he was right. I called and told them I'd been in a fight and everything was fine. I wouldn't get into the details until I got back. Even then my mom wouldn't want to hear about it. She'd rather I not add details to her nightmares.

I flew my family down for my Silver Star ceremony. I figured it was at least as big a deal as my SEAL graduation, and they ought to be part of it.

Even before I joined the Navy, my mother would worry about me getting hurt—just doing the stuff that guys do in Montana. That's when I'd say, "Mom, stop worrying. I'm here to do something special. Don't even worry about me." She worried even more when I began going on deployments, even before 9/11, and I'd say, "Mother, stop. Don't worry about me. I'm here to do something special. Chill out." Then 9/11 happened and I'd try to calm her down. "Not a lot going on, but don't worry. I'm here to do something special."

Then she came to my Silver Star ceremony, and she heard them read the citation. She freaked because it was the first time she'd heard the details, and they were worse than her worst imaginings. I couldn't really say it was no big deal this time, so instead I said, "Mom, I swear to you, I'll never get another Silver Star again. That's the last time."

CHAPTER SEVENTEEN

On Wednesday, April 8, 2009, the captain of the merchant ship *Maersk Alabama*, Richard Phillips, was taken hostage by four Somali pirates just off the coast of east Africa. During this ordeal, Phillips was forced onto a small lifeboat where he waited to be delivered to his fate. The pirates attempted to drive the small, covered craft to the lawless land of Somalia where they could try extorting a ransom from the United States or sell the American to al-Shabaab, an al-Qaeda-linked terrorist group.

As Phillips sat in the cramped and overheated hell of the small enclosed boat expecting to die at any moment, US Navy warships steamed toward the scene even though they lacked the specialized personnel to attempt a rescue. The ships blocked the pirates' route of sail, sent helicopters to hover just above it to make navigation more difficult, and even watched helplessly as the abducted captain tried to escape by jumping into the Indian Ocean. He was hauled back in by the pirates.

The pirates knew that getting back to shore was almost impossible, but they also knew that they could negotiate with the captain's life. The Navy knew it could keep them from shore, but the more time that expired, the more danger the American faced. The situation was at a standstill when the pirates' boat ran out of fuel. After a tense negotiation, the destroyer USS *Bainbridge* began towing the lifeboat through the water. Both sides were getting anxious as worldwide media watched.

Back home, we all knew of the situation as soon as it started. We also knew that politics were going to be a huge factor in how this ultimately would be resolved. Either way, we started planning, excited at the prospect of such a high-profile mission. Though we trained for just this eventuality all the time and were the best in the world at it, Team ▓ had never completed an entire hostage rescue at sea. Some SEALs had jumped in before, but they were always turned away when it was time to pull the trigger. This time would be different.

We began brainstorming all the possibilities. We planned and planned. You'd think we'd have thought of everything in twenty-five years of planning, but we'd never thought of a fully enclosed lifeboat being towed by a Navy cruiser. The lifeboat was about twenty-eight feet long, covered, with only one door in the back and a hatch in the front. How the fuck were we going to get this guy out?

As days passed without resolution, we continued to plan, waiting to get the "green light." By late Thursday, it was becoming pretty obvious that negotiations on the *Bainbridge* were going nowhere. We all had a feeling this was coming quick.

Friday, April 10, happened to be my birthday. It was also my four-year-old daughter's Easter party at her preschool. I had agreed to take her and was excited to celebrate with her. The plan was for the children to sit at their tables as the adults went through the buffet line and served them their brunch. We were both enjoying the quality time together, and I was especially aware that there weren't enough days like this.

I was in the middle of the buffet line, reaching for cupcakes and whatever other stuff preschoolers like to eat, when my pager went off with a top secret code. This was it. We were going to attempt a rescue.

I had to call my wife, "Hey, it's me. I have to leave right now, so I need you to come right away."

She already knew. SEAL wives are smarter than we are, and they have a better intelligence network. She was already on her way. She knew I had one hour to get to work. Then we'd be taking off in our two C-17 transport airplanes, carrying two speedboats. Time was of the essence, and we all knew it, including the wives.

Once Nicole arrived and took control of my daughter, I kissed everyone and left. Off to war. It was going to be a twenty-minute drive to the command and I'd already been waiting at the school for ten. I still had a few minutes to spare, and I had a plan for using them. There's a 7-Eleven right outside the base where we were stationed, so I figured I'd stop there, get as much cash as I could out of the ATM, and grab a log of Copenhagen and a carton of cigarettes. My thinking was that we were going to jump out in the middle of the ocean, and I didn't know for sure where we might end up. It could well be somewhere we didn't intend, somewhere not especially friendly to American SEALs. If that happened, I might be able to buy my way to freedom or barter with tobacco. Or I'd just end up somewhere on my birthday with a bunch of cash and tobacco. I could live with that, too.

As always, the battle plan didn't go as envisioned. I went to pay for my stuff, and there was a guy in a hard hat already at the register, obviously not too eager to get back to work digging out sewer lines or whatever. *You* know the type of guy I'm talking about. Have you ever been at a traffic light and one car in front of you hesitates just long enough for the light to turn red? That's the guy. Or maybe on the way home from work one day you stop at the grocery to pick up a handful of items for dinner, and the person ahead of you in the fourteen-items-or-less line has thirty items and is writing a check? That's him, too.

So there he was in my 7-Eleven conspicuously taking his sweet time. He was a big, jovial guy wanting to chat up anyone who looked his way. I noticed one of the things he was buying: a *USA Today* with a Captain Phillips headline. Very patriotically, but very *slowly*, he slammed it down and said, "Man, I sure wish someone would do something about this."

I said, "Hey, buddy, pay for your shit, and we will."

To his credit, he instantly recognized where this particular 7-Eleven was located and what that implied. He kind of staggered out of the way as he collected his change, and I quickly purchased my items. I was out of the store, back in my car, and pulling up to work within minutes. Things were buzzing in the parking lot as I parked and jogged to the side entrance.

I ran up the stairs to the second deck and went directly to the Team Room. The roster was on the wall, just like when we trained, so I signed it and logged the time. I'd made it with plenty of time to spare but still needed to hurry. There was a lot to do, and we knew the time would move quickly.

Downstairs the team leaders and senior operators were talking tactics and finalizing jump order—who was jumping when, and who was in which boat on which plane. We all knew this stuff already, but a triple check couldn't hurt. While this was going on, the junior assault team members were loading everyone's bags into predesignated box-trucks. Every member of the squadron had four bags that were loaded and labeled prior to this specific mission. We took maintenance of these bags seriously. Each bag is stored in each operator's cage, labeled for the environment—water jump, land jump, desert, jungle, high altitude, diving, whatever. Next to that is a laminated inventory of what's inside and a dry-erase marker. That bag might be sitting there for a long time. If you want to train with a piece of gear from the bag, when you take it out you mark it off, so you know it's no longer in the bag. After you're done with the gear, you clean it and put it back in the bag, always being careful to mark it off, so you know the item has been returned.

We would hand carry the first bag we were taking on this mission—the "Jump bag"—onto the aircraft. It contained all the gear that was necessary to jump out of the plane and swim to the boat. The second bag was labeled: "Underway, Counter

Terrorism." It was loaded into the hull of a designated boat and would be inside it when the boat parachuted down. This bag contained all of the equipment needed to conduct a hostage rescue—body armor, a rifle, helmet, night vision, and the like. Once the team jumped into the ocean and climbed aboard the speedboat, we'd put on all the gear and be ready to roll. The third bag was a "Forward Staging Base" bag, and it could be loaded into the boat and remain inside or be staged at a forward base by the aircrew if the boats were too heavy. This contained forty-eight hours of comfort items in the event the team was in place at a base or ship either before or after the mission. It had a shower kit, flip-flops, and extra socks and a uniform. The fourth bag was a "Follow-On" bag that would remain at the command in each shooter's cage. It contained extra war-fighting items in case more missions appeared as the team was forward. If needed, someone else would fly it into theater.

We loaded all the gear and drove to the airfield. We stowed the assaulters' gear in the boats and grabbed our Jump bags. We counted the parachutes. Twice. It was time to go. We were "wheels up" at exactly the target time we'd been aiming at for years.

The long flight to the Indian Ocean exposed something we call a "training scar"—a flaw that goes unnoticed no matter how realistically we train for a mission but that becomes obvious during the real deal. Whoever designed the C-17 mustn't have figured we'd fly for sixteen straight hours with so many people on board—either that or they had a warped sense of humor and decided it would be hilarious to install only one shitter on the plane. With fifty people sharing, it didn't take long for that thing to fill up. We had to use whatever we could find. MREs (Meals, Ready to Eat) come in these really thick plastic bags, so guys started using those, and then throwing them in one huge common bag. It was nasty.

When we weren't engineering personal waste disposal solutions, we were planning the mission. The decision was made for us to jump as planned, and then ride our boats to a flat-topped amphibious assault ship, the USS *Boxer*, which normally supports helicopter missions and amphibious landing craft. We hadn't been given execute authority yet so we'd utilize the big Navy ship as a forward staging base. We originally intended to jump all four boats, and all the shooters. The backstage people, the enablers who'd flown in with us, were going to turn around with the two planes and land in Djibouti. But we started thinking that we might need all these people down there—the radio guys and tech people—to help get things set up. We'd brought enough tandem parachutes to take them with us on the jump. This new scheme complicated a few things, though: People who hadn't planned on leaving the aircraft now had to, which meant the boats would be over capacity. That meant we needed to take some of our gear out. First to go were a lot of our comfort items, since they were "nonessential."

The other not-so-minor complication was that a lot of support personnel were about to make their very first skydive. Not everyone was happy to be going for a jump on such short notice. When I told one of the guys, "Change of plans, you're jumping now," he said, "No, no, I'm going to Djibouti."

"Negative," I said. "You're jumping. We're going to hook you up to this guy." I introduced him to Boots, who would be his tandem master. Boots was especially jovial and excited about the mission. His passenger wasn't. He whined the whole time about how he'd never wanted to jump in his life and certainly didn't today. I tried to motivate him, expounding on how warm the weather was and how clear and beautiful the water was going to be. A damn tropical vacation! He kept complaining, "I didn't join the Navy to be a SEAL. I'm not a SEAL, and I can't jump!"

I said, "Well, you're half right. You're jumping!"

When we were about an hour out from the drop, we all dressed out. I gave jumpmaster inspections to jumpers and tandems and had another jumpmaster check me out. When the time came, the ramp dropped for the first time, and I could see the beautiful Indian Ocean and a large gray rectangle: the USS *Boxer*. We moved to the skin of the plane because it was almost time for the boats to jump, and they came out really fast. Each plane would release both of its boats and the three crew members for each boat would follow for a total of six jumpers. As the green light came on, the boats were gone. The six boat guys followed.

After that, both planes did a wide "racetrack," or a big circle in the sky to ensure that the boats had all landed, and that all of the boat guys were accounted for. Down on the ocean's surface, the boat guys began de-rigging the boats and we prepared for our jump. I was on the edge of the ramp looking down at the ocean. I could see the USS *Boxer* but not the four boats. It was critical that I find them, as I would lead the entire stack from both planes to them. If we missed the boats and landed too far away, the boats would have to come pick us all up one by one and that could severely throw our schedule off. The chances of our losing a guy forever became real, too. No pressure.

While I was standing at the edge of the ramp, I took a look back at the line of jumpers behind me. Everyone was pumped. My eyes locked with those of the tandem passenger who was afraid of jumping. In a last ditch effort, I gave him a thumbs-up and a smile. He just shook his head in fear. Then Boots's head popped out from behind his with a grin from ear to ear. He gave me a thumbs-up and let out a "Yeah, buddy!" His passenger turned to see what was going on and Boots said, "Don't look at me, bro . . . I don't know what half this shit does anyway!"

The poor guy's eyes popped wider than they were already.

I got the signal from the primary jumpmaster, and I left the ramp. One thousand, two thousand, look thousand, pull thousand. We were in the air with 102 jumpers and 96 canopies: obviously six of our parachutes were tandems.

With every one of those following me, I searched the water below for our four boats but could see nothing. I took a hard left turn to show the others who I was, and one by one they followed. I only had a few minutes to find our landing zone, and all I could see were the huge whale sharks skimming below the surface of the clear water. Very cool, but I didn't have time to check them out. I was busy trying to find the speedboats, which turned out to be conveniently located in the middle of the sun's reflection off the Indian Ocean. This was another training scar—in practice, the boats always drove around the landing zone in such a way that big circular wakes formed, creating a beautiful bull's-eye. But now we were actually doing it and . . . nothing. I was thinking, *Shit, I'm leading a hundred people and I have no idea where I'm going.*

I decided my best course was to transect the area at right angles, hoping whatever was obscuring my view would resolve somewhere along the way. I led the stack on a downwind leg, then turned right on a crosswind leg. We maintained this course for a few hundred meters, then turned right again at about five hundred feet above the water. There they were, all four boats, off to our left.

Each guy knew which boat to land next to. I was aiming for the second boat and landed right beside it. On a big jellyfish. Perfect. Luckily, I had enough clothes on that I barely got stung. We all climbed in our boats and took a head count. We were good and started driving toward the *Boxer*. My pager had gone off fifteen hours and forty-six minutes earlier. Not bad for the first time.

The *Boxer* craned our boats aboard, and we instantly found a place to plan. We didn't have a big enough space for everyone, so the junior guys got busy finding a staging area for all of our gear and a place to clean up. They also secured us some berthing.

When we boarded, the *Boxer* was about five hundred miles out from the *Bainbridge*. It's too risky to skydive at night—if a guy got separated from the stack we'd never be able to find him. So the idea had been to station the *Boxer* well over the horizon, have our guys do a day jump, then sail into the theater, arriving after dark. That's exactly what we did.

When we arrived, our plan called for a small group of shooters to leave the ship and go to the *Bainbridge* where they could set up. My buddy Jonny was one of them. As he was leaving, he looked up at me and said, "Hey, Nizzro, this shit's ending one way, you know that, right?"

"I know," I said. "We didn't come here to fucking talk them out of it."

As the snipers waited on the *Bainbridge* for a clean shot and orders to execute, other SEALs would replace the team that had been delivering supplies to the captain and the pirates. The *Bainbridge*'s crew had been doing that up to this point, but now our guys would do it, dressed like the ship's crew. Guys who knew how to end a situation quickly would get close to the pirates without tipping them off.

Meanwhile, the lifeboat was slowly being reeled closer to the ship. The half dozen or so snipers, who'd set up shop at the stern of the ship, kept it in their sights, waiting. Snipers are champions at waiting. They rotated positions, three or four of them peering through their scopes for a couple of hours straight, then they'd either take a break or take a turn as spotter. They knew they could be doing this for days, and they were prepared.

The pirates weren't. As the hours passed, they became increasingly irritable. The guys on the fantail knew what was going on aboard the lifeboat because someone had brought in a Somali interpreter who was having sporadic shouted communication with the pirates. They were getting food and water delivered, but they were out of khat. They were all addicted to the chewable plant, an amphetamine-like stimulant. Add to khat withdrawal seasickness and confusion that flowed from their leader's having been nabbed during a "negotiation" on the *Bainbridge* a few days before, and you had some extremely edgy pirates. One in particular seemed to be in a hot rage. He kept screaming at Captain Phillips and periodically hitting him.

It was a tricky situation all around. Since the pirates weren't part of any known terrorist group, and, technically, weren't enemy combatants (since we weren't at war with Somalia and were in international waters), the legal authority to take them out was far from clear-cut. Lawyers in Washington were still debating. However, it had been established that members of the American military could act with lethal force against an imminent threat to self, coalition partners, or coalition civilians. This is what Jonny was discussing with his teammates as they waited. They went over and over their justification for shooting. The pirates had proven they weren't to be trusted. They'd shot at a helicopter. They'd taken shots at the ship. When Captain Phillips was showing them how to navigate the lifeboat, they'd grabbed him and kept him hostage. Walt, the SEAL officer on the fan deck with the snipers, had been granted tactical command of the situation by the commander of the *Bainbridge*. It was his decision to make. But that didn't mean he couldn't be second-guessed, potentially even prosecuted, when the smoke blew away.

Twenty-four hours into their tense and exhausting vigil, Jonny was taking his turn peering through the sight on his sniper rifle. From what he and his fellow SEALs could hear and see, the situation was deteriorating rapidly. The pirates were doing what bullies do when they get scared. They upped their aggression. The hotheaded pirate had begun to subject Captain Phillips to "mock executions," putting an unloaded gun to his head and pulling the trigger. Now there could be little question that the threat to Richard Phillips was imminent. The problem was that the only vantage point was through the small porthole windows in the covered lifeboat. Two of the three pirates had remained steadily visible, but the third, the hotheaded one, kept bobbing out of sight. If they didn't shoot—and *kill*—all three pirates at once, the survivor would almost certainly shoot the captain.

As the snipers to either side of Jonny kept the two visible pirates in their sights, Jonny kept his trained on the empty porthole. Suddenly the head of the third pirate bobbed into view, and then disappeared again. Keeping his eye and rifle steady on that spot, Jonny said to Walt, "Hey, we may not get another chance. When I see him bob up again, I need to go hot."

Walt said, "You're clear to go hot."

Within seconds, the hothead bobbed up again. Jonny had spent thousands of hours and millions of rounds of ammunition practicing on what we call pepper poppers—targets that pop up randomly and briefly that require an instant reaction and perfect aim. Now all that training paid off in a flick of the index finger, a suppressed *pfffft* from his rifle and a bullet traveled 2,550 feet per second into the head that had appeared in the porthole. The two other snipers fired virtually simultaneously.

All the pirates disappeared from the windows, but the snipers on the *Bainbridge* had heard the sharp report of an unsuppressed gun a beat after they had fired their suppressed weapons. That could only be bad news. Jonny's awful first thought was that he'd missed, and Captain Phillips had been executed. Jonny had to sit there, wondering if he'd just fucked up, while one of our other snipers slid down the tow rope from the fantail to the lifeboat—just like the "slide for life" in the BUD/S obstacle course. Every SEAL had practiced it thousands of times, and each time we wondered, "When in *the hell* will we ever use this??" It turned out that *one* guy needed it *one* time. This time. He found Phillips alive and all the pirates dead. He radioed back, "Hey, it's all good. Phillips is safe. All three pirates are dead."

As one of the pirates went down, he must have squeezed the trigger in his death throes. Phillips, who'd been trussed up like a deer by the pirates—the rope tied so tight around his hands that they'd lost all sensation and had swelled up "like clown gloves," he'd write later—couldn't see what had happened. All he knew was that the pirates were about to shoot him. He was bracing to die when he heard *BAM! BAM! BAM!* followed by a silence he hadn't heard in days. He thought maybe the pirates, who'd been increasingly at odds, had all shot each other, until he heard an American voice, the voice of a SEAL, ask, "Are you okay?"

While all this had been going on, I'd been on the *Boxer* coming up with a plan with my boss. The pirates had been asking to get towed back to Somalia where there were villages friendly to them. They wanted radios to communicate with the village elders and a ride home. We were going to give them all they asked for, but tow them a few miles north of where they believed they were going. They'd emerge from the lifeboat believing they were meeting the elders. When they showed themselves, my team and I would be waiting. It would be dark and they wouldn't be able to see us, but we'd see them with night vision and take them out.

We would have needed some pretty high clearance to get boots on the ground in Somalia. As our bosses were putting things in motion to carry out this and four alternate plans, I was sitting in the Chief's Mess getting coffee. My phone beeped with a text message that said, "We got him."

We responded, "Got who?"

"Who do you think? He's fine."

Happy Easter, Richard Phillips.

THE FIRST THING PHILLIPS WANTED when he got out of the sick bay was a couple of beers. He was a bit shell-shocked. The movie did a great job of depicting the reality. He was shaken up, as anybody would be, but happy and very grateful. They eventually brought him out to the *Boxer*, where I was, and by then I'd gotten the brief from my buddy Jonny.

When we saw Jonny, we all wanted to slap his back, but he said, "Everybody just leave me alone for thirty minutes," and walked away to the edge of the ship.

It was a big deal, what had just happened to him. He took out his Copenhagen, put in a plug, and stared out at the ocean for a while. When he came back in, I said, "You do realize that you've done the most historic thing in the history of the SEAL teams?" His response was, "That's great. Can we go home now?"

Actually, no. It took us a few weeks to get back, because no one knew what to do with us. Yet another training scar: We put so much energy into designing the hostage rescue part of the mission nobody ever thought, "How are we going to get these guys home?"

We ended up in Qatar, at Camp Snoopy in Doha, living in tents for two weeks, with no clothes. With contingency funds, the command sent us to the Arab stores that sold counterfeit Oakley stuff. We were wearing all this faux-Oakley gear, and hats and shoes that the Navy bought us, with nothing to do but work out and con our beardless military brethren out of their beer rations. The whole time Jonny was struggling. He'd said he needed thirty minutes back on the *Boxer*, but clearly that hadn't been nearly enough. He'd done something heroic, something that had made SEAL Team ▓ internationally famous in the instant it took to squeeze his trigger two times. He'd done exactly what he'd been training so long and so hard to do, and he'd done it perfectly.

But instead of feeling jubilant, what he felt was a great weight. Immediately, he sensed that some in this band of brothers who'd been more intimate with him than family for years— guys with whom he'd risked death and whom he trusted with his life—had begun to look at him with an unsettling mix of envy and distrust.

Jonny's boss had been right there with him on the fantail of the *Bainbridge*, but didn't get a shot. When we got home, we all had a little time off. When we came back to work—it was a Monday—there were already rumors: The boss wanted to fire Jonny, get rid of him, kick him out of the command. It was just a nasty vibe. I remember going over to Jonny's house with some of his fellow snipers and sitting around, wondering, *What the fuck is going on?* We couldn't understand. It made no sense at all. Jonny was the No. 1 guy out of the selection course, our first pick. I'd gone to Iraq with him. We'd had our first kills together. He was one of the best close quarters battle guys and an awesome sniper, top of the line. He took this incredible, heroic shot, and then all of a sudden, the people who weren't quite ready to shoot got pissed at him.

I kept saying to him, "Hey, Jonny, take a dip." I'd give him some of my Copenhagen. I just wanted him to hear me. I'd say,

"You're a hero. Don't listen to this shit. You're a goddamned hero. You did the best thing ever. Don't listen to them."

After a while, the head-on attacks against him died out, but the bad blood lingered. I wasn't happy about it, but it never entered my mind that someday it would all come back to haunt me.

CHAPTER EIGHTEEN

There's nothing like a new combat deployment to clear the mind. That's what we got less than two months after the Captain Phillips rescue—another return to Afghanistan to hunt high-value targets. There was a difference this time. Our team had just carried out the most high-profile mission in the history of the SEAL teams. We'd garnered worldwide headlines. And hype aside, we'd all been to Afghanistan and Iraq a bunch of times. We'd run different outstations and participated in a wide range of conflict situations, soup to nuts. We'd become the best of the best and we knew it. There were no more nerves.

New guys from other teams would approach us with a respectful curiosity—and these were combat-experienced SEALs who'd shot it out, killed lots of bad guys. Now they were chatting us up and getting excited that we were taking them seriously. You could picture their thoughts: *Hey these guys are listening.* They were good dudes who really wanted to pick our brains so that they'd get to the level they perceived us to be at.

We were assigned to a high-altitude base—Forward Operating Base Sharana in Paktika Province, an area where we mainly focused on fast-paced and exciting helo-borne vehicle interdictions. Our quarters were atop a big hill, high enough not to be so damn hot all the time. The living conditions were actually really good. The squadron before us had built it up and left us with an awesome gym with a huge seventy-inch or possibly even

257

ninety-inch flat-screen TV—all I remember was, it was *big*. We used it to watch workout videos, and after we were done working at night, we went in the gym and played video games. At the time, Guitar Hero was really big. We turned the volume up to huge, and nobody cared. We were in a gym, after all! Jonny and I would play intensely competitive games of Madden NFL—we competed at everything, including who could make the best French-press coffee—and the gym was where we had our fantasy football draft. Did I mention we had a bar there, too? It was mainly to have a place where we could congregate and talk shop, make French press, and have a dip.

It was pretty good living. We'd get missions every third day or so. Most of the truly high-value targets had moved into Pakistan, but we had a lot of intel on IED makers—and again, we loved to hunt them because they were responsible for so many American casualties. They knew our tactics now and understood they were vulnerable at night, so they'd have one house where they made the bombs during the day, then slip back into Pakistan when it got dark. We tried to hit them when they were commuting. They'd usually be on motorcycles—they could ride the hell out of those things. Our intel guys would get a bead on them, and we'd mount up and off we'd go to hunt from the air. That was the most fun I ever had conducting ops, because you knew you weren't going to be out there long, wouldn't be walking your butt off, and would get to shoot at moving targets out of a helicopter.

It was fun, like I said, but still plenty dangerous. One of our new guys found that out fast. He'd just graduated from selection training and gone on his very first vehicle interdiction. We caught up to the usual group of bad guys on motorbikes and started shooting in front of the bikes to stop them. Our Gatling-style six-barrel mini-gun could fire two thousand to four thousand rounds a minute, so it wasn't something you could ignore. One of the bad guys decided he wanted nothing to do with us. He jumped off his bike and ran like hell toward a field into the chest-high grass. I was pretty sure we'd hit him—we saw him go down—but now he was somewhere in the middle of that field in uncertain condition. We landed the helicopter in front of where we'd seen him go down and got out in a line to sweep the field. I was in the middle, and the new guy was right next to me. Our plan was to keep walking in that line until we found him. It was a dangerous tactic. At any moment, he could pop up and start shooting. But we were counting on having fast reactions.

We'd covered maybe half the distance when *blam!* something blew up just twenty feet ahead. A human arm flew out of the high grass right between me and the new guy. He followed the arm with his eyes, then turned to me and asked, "Hey, Rob, did you throw a grenade at that guy?" One of the other guys in the line said, "No, man. That's a suicide bomber. Welcome to Sharana."

One day, intel picked up four motorcycles speeding off from an IED manufacturing house. We launched in two helicopters. When the bad guys saw us, they split into two groups of two and went in different directions. I was in Chopper One, and we went after one group. Chopper Two went after the other. The guys we were chasing ditched their bikes and started running up a hill really fast into some trees so we couldn't follow from the air. We touched down on the low ground. Tactically, we shouldn't have given the enemy the high ground, but it was the only place we could get out to chase them. As soon as we hopped off, we started taking fire from up the hill. They were shooting close—the bullets zipped loudly past us.

This wasn't a good situation. It was one of the few times when we were fighting at a disadvantage. Mostly on missions, we had other teams situated in other buildings, snipers on the roof, Rangers in blocking positions, and, ultimately, air protection. This time we didn't really have any of that, and we were on the bottom, so we had to move up to them. If those dudes got set up on the high ground, it was going to be a long night.

In that moment, I was oddly aware of myself in a way that didn't often happen—it was a "how did I get here?" feeling. I felt completely calm, no adrenaline. I was a craftsman, and this was a technical problem to solve, like, "Okay, we need to get this piece of lumber level or the door won't fit." It was just, "Hand me that level so we can take this guy out."

I called my boss on the radio. "Just thinking," I said. "I'm going to take these two guys here with me on a fire team. We're going to flank."

He rogered that, so we left the rest of the team and the dog, Cairo—one of our best dogs and one I'd personally bonded with— to hold that side of the hill. I took Harp, the bomb disposal guy, and one other guy to maneuver off to the side to try to flank the shooters.

As we were moving around the hill, we got an angle on one of the bad guys and fired. He went down, apparently dead, but you never know for sure. We had to go up the hill to clear him. When I was still a few meters away, I could see he was lying on his hands. When I see someone lying on his hands, that means he probably pulled a grenade and is just waiting like the guy in the field, because he knows he's going to die anyway and figures he might as well take you with him. I stopped where I was and said, "Okay, enough of this." I grabbed Harp, the Explosive Ordnance Disposal guy, and said, "I may need you to clear him."

These EOD guys amaze me. It's a very dangerous job, but it's what they do, and they get right to it. He had no special equipment, just experience and ice in his veins. I walked about thirty meters away while he began to cut the pants off with scissors starting from the foot up, looking for any sign of a bomb. I was just hanging out while he took his time and did his tense and meticulous work. All of a sudden, he shouted, "Oh, my God. Get over here."

I was like, "No. I'm not into it, dude. Sorry."

He said, "No, no, seriously. He doesn't have a bomb. Come see this."

The bad guy may not have been packing a bomb, but he was definitely packing. Let's just say: If he'd been in America, he could have made a fortune in the adult film industry.

As we were joking about this unexpected anatomy lesson, our radio squawked: "Hey, we've got an FWIA." That means friendly wounded in action. Our moment of levity popped like a bubble. We asked who it was—we never say a name over the radio, so we expected a call sign. But this time they said, "Friendly wounded in action is Cairo."

Whenever a dog gets shot, it's just over. I remember thinking, *Oh, shit. We just lost Cairo, the best dog we ever had.*

We got the story later. As we were doing our flanking maneuver, the other half of our team sent Cairo after the bad guy. Cairo, a lean Belgian Malinois with a black muzzle, went tearing up the hill. He leaped a wooden fence and sniffed his way to the base of a tree. The bad guy had climbed into the low branches out of the dog's reach. As Cairo snapped and growled, the guy hit him with a burst from his AK-47. One bullet pierced the dog's leg and the other penetrated his working vest and lodged in his chest. Cheese, Cairo's handler, couldn't see what was happening but heard the shots and wanted to get his dog back. He used his remote to shock the dog's collar, a signal to return. Poor Cairo, conscious but critically injured, couldn't jump back over the fence, but Cheese didn't know that. Even with two bullets in him and near death, Cairo dragged himself along the fence until he found an opening. Obviously, it took him a long time. When he finally arrived, Cheese wanted to smack him for not coming back as soon as he was signaled. Then he saw the blood-matted fur.

Cairo had taken a bullet from the bad guy so one of us wouldn't have to. Now that we had the guy's position in the tree, thanks to Cairo, the team spread out around his location and shot him off his perch.

But Cairo was in bad shape. We all assumed he was dying, but Cheese wouldn't quit on him. He called another member of our team who'd been a medic, who treated Cairo exactly as if he'd been a human SEAL wounded in action. He shaved the wound, put on a chest seal, and applied pressure so Cairo wouldn't bleed out. But everyone knew the chest wound was very bad news.

They called for medevac. When the chopper arrived, Cheese and our point man, the medic, loaded Cairo in and flew with him to Bagram where they got a plane to Germany. None of us held out much hope.

Three days later we got word—Cairo had survived. He wouldn't only fully recover, but before long he'd help make history.

NEAR THE END OF OUR second month on the Sharana deployment, on the morning of June 30, 2009, we woke up to the news that an American soldier had walked off base. Completely deserted. We knew it was a desertion because before he left he'd shipped his uniforms and all his stuff back home. He was a twenty-three-year-old private named Bowe Bergdahl, and he had a reputation in his unit as an oddball, a loose cannon.

When we woke up he was still missing, but he was quickly grabbed by the Taliban. Some of the guys in our tactical operations center had intercepted a phone conversation between a local villager and a Taliban commander. It went:

Villager: "Hey, we found this American. Do you want him?"

Taliban: "What do you mean you found him?"

Villager: "We found him on the side of the road taking a shit. Do you want him?"

Taliban: "Yeah, we want him. He'll never shit right again."

We heard a lot of stories about what a misfit this kid was. Later, it came out that before coming to Afghanistan he'd told a friend, "If this deployment is lame, I'm just going to walk off into the mountains of Pakistan." But we were sympathetic. Nobody deserved what the Taliban was going to do to him. I remember thinking, *Oh, this poor kid. Man. We got to go find him.*

Everything stopped. Everything that the military was trying to do to win the war in Afghanistan stopped, and it all turned into "Let's go find this Bergdahl guy." We knew we needed to get to him before the Taliban got him across the border into Pakistan.

We took a lot of chances. Remember that our tactics called for us to land a good distance away from the bad guys' houses and walk in so they didn't know we were coming. In our haste to find Bergdahl, we were putting down these huge helicopters right in people's front yards. We didn't know anything about these people—who they were or where their sympathies lay. Another no-no, but we were breaking the rules because we knew our time—and Bergdahl's—was running out fast.

On one mission, we jumped out of the helicopter and a flood of people charged out of the house. For all I knew, they had AK-47s ready to fire. I'm so happy that my training worked and I didn't shoot anyone when they rushed us. I could have killed ten men running at me, but I held back, wanting to make certain they were threats. They weren't. They ran out not because they were bad guys trying to escape or attack, but because we'd freaked them out. They were just regular Afghans. We calmed them down and got them with the interpreter to find out what we could about this crazy Bergdahl.

We were getting so close, too. The people we were talking to knew stuff and were giving us good information. Not everyone in these villages is Taliban. All they're trying to do is live their lives. Anyway, we learned enough to pinpoint a house belonging to the locals who'd tipped off the Taliban to Bergdahl's location. When we got there we found a big wad of rupees, obviously the ransom the Taliban had paid for the information. We found it hidden—poorly—in one of the rooms, and it was way too big a stash to have been legit. I had it in my hands as we were interrogating the man of the house. I said, "Why do you have this?"

The guy was shaking, terrified because we'd nailed him. But he said, "Oh, my son works in Dubai in construction and he sent this."

I don't remember exactly how much it was, but it was obviously more than some guy working construction in Dubai could send home. I said, "Really? In packaged rupees? You're lying. I'm going to take you with me and interrogate you or you can tell me who . . ."

He eventually came clean, and pointed us in a direction, but it was already too late. Members of the Taliban-aligned Haqqani network, among the baddest of the bad guys, had moved faster than we could track them. There wasn't much more we could do. But in the first months after Bergdahl walked off the base, one of our troops that was deployed in Jalalabad made one more attempt. They got intel that the Taliban might be holding Bergdahl at a specific location south of Kabul, an hour and a half from them by chopper. They launched on the target and as soon as they landed they were immediately engaged by well-armed and very professional fighters with a machine gun. Before the SEAL team managed to kill all the insurgents, my friend Jimmy sent a dog after two of them and they opened fire. The fusillade of bullets slammed into the dog and smashed Jimmy's femur. My buddy came close to bleeding out right there, but one of his teammates who'd been a medic saved his life. The dog didn't make it.

Either Bergdahl had never been there, or the Taliban had gotten him out just in time.

The Haqqani network ended up keeping Bergdahl captive, moving him around to compounds in Afghanistan and Pakistan, for a month shy of five years. During that time he was locked in a cage, beaten with copper pipe, and nearly starved until a deal was made for his release in exchange for moving five key Taliban detainees from the American prison in Guantanamo Bay to Qatari custody.

It was a high price to pay to recover a deserter, especially when you added the price we had already paid in life and blood.

CHAPTER NINETEEN

By the spring of 2011, I'd been regularly going off to war for six years. That's six years of saying goodbye to my kids at least once a year without knowing if I'd ever get to see them any older than they were the moment I kissed them on the forehead, turned away, and walked into headquarters for yet another deployment.

It was April, and I'd just come back from a five-month stint in Afghanistan, my seventh combat deployment with my squadron. Our first post-deployment training trip was combat diving in Miami. Tough assignment, I know, but we figured we'd earned it. It was always a wise move to have a "good deal" work trip after returning from war. We'd be able to get some quality open-water dive training, work on our tactics in dealing with Somali pirate "mother ships" in the Indian Ocean, and then chill and bond in the Miami evenings.

I was beginning my second tour as an Assault Team Leader and was excited about it. I had a great crew, Two Troop, and had been working with most of the guys for a number of years. Paul was the other Assault Team Leader. He wasn't your typical SEAL, meaning he wasn't what you'd expect physically, neither especially big nor buff. But he was a fantastic swimmer, and one of the smartest men I'd ever met. He had a kind of stealth wit that snuck up on you and enlivened many a round of cocktails. He was comically proud of his bushy eyebrows and could grow one of those perfectly groomed beards that the ladies adored. My Sniper Team Leader was Jonny, my close friend and the hero of the Captain Phillips rescue. Mack, the former rugby stud with the missing tooth, was my number two. I knew him incredibly well after years of fighting together and trusted him completely.

My number three was Nic Checque. At twenty-seven years old he could barely grow a beard, but I don't think he wanted any hair on that Hollywood handsome face. Nic would prove the kind of SEAL he was less than a year later when he was part of a team that stormed a remote mountain shack east of Kabul where Taliban fighters were holding a hostage, an American doctor who'd been helping to train Afghan health workers for a nonprofit. Nic was the point man, the first through the door. He was immediately shot in the head and killed. His SEAL brother Ed Byers was right behind him. Byers shot the man who'd killed Nic, tackled another guy who was scrambling toward a gun, held him down until he was sure he wasn't the hostage, then killed him and threw his body over the hostage, at the same time pinning another attacker to the wall with a hand to the throat until another SEAL could shoot him. For that, Byers became the first Team ▆ member to be awarded the Medal of Honor. After President Barack Obama hung the medal around his neck, Byers said the medal rightfully belonged to "my teammate, friend, and brother" who "died like warriors die." Nic was posthumously awarded the Navy Cross. In my mind, he's still very much alive. I still have his cell number in my phone.

Our troop commander, Eric Roth, had also been my commander on my last combat deployment. The only commissioned officer of the group, Roth was an outstanding man and an excellent officer. He exemplified the kind of strong leadership I came to admire. He knew there was no reason to ever be a jerk and nothing wrong with being genuinely liked by your people. He did the small things, like saying please and giving praise even for a rote task assigned to the least senior man. Although that was his first deployment with our squadron, he had had four combat stints with the conventional SEAL teams and had seen more than his share of war.

Our new guy, French, was running the dive trip logistics. He was blond, tan, and ripped. At first glance, he appeared to be a cocky surfer dude, but he was quite the opposite. He'd been by far the top guy coming out of his selection course and was always looking to better himself by taking advice from older dudes and seriously studying tactics. And he was turning out to be quite adept at this logistics thing. He'd put us up at the Courtyard Marriott near South Beach. It was a great location and the perfect time of year. Guys could get up in the morning and run on the beach or take a swim in the crystal clear water. I even found myself out in the ocean—and enjoying it!—something I never thought would happen after overacquainting myself with salt water at BUD/S. The work schedule was reasonable, too, for a change.

The main work-related reason for the dive trip was our determination to get back to basic SEAL skills. Because of the two wars that had been taking up the majority of every squadron's deployment cycles as well as other global contingencies, skills like combat diving were being neglected in favor of close quarters combat, shooting, driving, helicopter training, and skydiving. It was going to be good for us to get back in the water. The fact that the water happened to be in Miami, well, we could deal with that.

One of the ways that we were able to sell the trip with such ease was the ever-growing pirate threat off the coast of eastern Africa. The *Maersk Alabama* hadn't been the first or the last commercial ship attacked, and pirates were going after private vessels, too. That meant my guys and I needed to remain in the forefront of tactical development. What kind of ladder should we bring? What kinds of weapons should we carry? In case we needed to breach or cut anything once we boarded an enemy vessel, what kind of tools would we require? All the essential gear would be bulky and weigh a ton, but we'd have to swim with it. We needed to figure out how to do that. The entire scenario was challenging, and I really enjoyed the problem solving that came with it. To be honest, it was nice to be thinking tactically about Navy SEAL stuff, not just about how to fight terrorists in deserts and mountains.

The first few days of the trip were paradise. We'd get up in the morning with the sun rising over the water. Guys would go for a run on the beach and boardwalk, swim in the ocean, or do both. It was a long way from the rigorous PT of earlier years. Our superiors trusted us to stay in shape however we saw fit. They even trusted us to relax a bit, and Miami was an excellent place to do that, as some discovered: Wake up and lazily drink coffee at a table on the patio, enjoying one of the most beautiful views on the planet. After that, showers and breakfast, then my troop would pile into our rental cars, head to the training site—a marina twenty minutes north—and begin the day's work.

Our schedule was simple: re-fit our dive gear, give each other safety checks, brief the evolution for the day, and then dive it. After a few hours, we'd have lunch on site, re-fit our gear, and then dive the plan again. Once the diving was done, we'd clean our equipment and secure the site, then head back to the hotel. Most guys would then hit Gold's Gym on South Beach, do a workout, and wait to see if Anna Kournikova showed up like she usually did. Those with no interest in pumping iron or famously sexy tennis players would go to their rooms and flip the channels until it was time for dinner. After that we'd all meet at the bar on the patio for happy hour. It was the perfect way to get back into the swing of things after an arduous winter deployment to Afghanistan. Everyone was happy, our training objectives and time lines were being met, and we were in South Florida.

Just as we were gearing up for the weekend, Paul and I received word that two positions had opened up for the Military

Free-Fall Jumpmaster Course in Yuma, Arizona. This was a great opportunity for our troop. Not only would it give us two more jumpmasters, it was a leadership qualification with serious responsibility that would greatly assist whomever we chose once the next promotion cycle came around. Promotions were getting more competitive and qualifications like this helped. The only issue was that selection for the course meant: Get on a plane, go to Yuma, and, worst of all, no weekend in Miami.

I picked Checque from my team, and Paul went with Cheese, who'd been my dog handler in previous deployments. Paul put it best when we broke the news to the boys:

He said, "Cheese, I have good news and I have bad news."

Cheese replied, "What's the bad news?"

Paul said, "You're leaving Miami, missing the weekend, and going to Yuma for Free-Fall Jumpmaster. Class begins on Monday."

"Okay, what's the good news?"

Paul waited a beat then responded, "I have no good news."

With that, Cheese and Checque packed up and reluctantly headed to the airport. The rest of us returned to the patio for cocktails, camaraderie, and scenery—of all kinds. We also wanted to brainstorm ideas about how to be the best anti-piracy team on the planet. I knew that the coming week was going to be intense, and I was right. But not remotely for the reasons I imagined.

On the evening of March 5, 2011, after a great day of training, it was once again time for a libation or two at the hotel bar on the boardwalk. I went down first, phone in hand, sending text messages to summon all the guys. Paul came down first, followed closely by Mack and Jonny. The three of us were eventually joined by most of the rest of the gang with Roth pulling up the rear. We were sitting around a table adjacent to the patio bar contemplating which drink to order when Roth's cell phone went hot. He excused himself for a few minutes and left the rest of us to ponder the many merits of tequila. We thought of several, but before we could pull the trigger on an order he returned and said he needed to talk to me, Jonny, and Paul—the three team leaders—in a separate area.

No major alarm bells went off in my mind. I was thinking one of our guys must have screwed up somehow. The four of us moved to a quieter part of the patio near the rear entrance of the hotel. There was a group of couches and we all sat, curious to know what was up. Roth said the boss—our Command Master Chief—was back home in Virginia Beach, and he needed us and Jonny, Paul, and Mack to all check out of our rooms and get back home as quickly as possible. Some sort of situation had arisen, and it required us to get a face-to-face with command leadership. That was all Roth had been told. Now this was looking like a bigger deal—especially considering that our Commanding Officer and Master Chief were supposed to have made this trip with us, but at the last minute had gone to Washington instead. Something was definitely up.

We called the rest of the troop to a meeting and told them the news: The trip would continue but without troop leadership. French had a lock on all of the logistics and had been planning this trip for about five months; he had it covered. The rest of the guys had been around long enough to train themselves and devise possible scenarios and problem solve their way through them. Plus, they had the rental boat the next day and were dying to see if they could secure it and board it. Also, they had a huge barbecue and fish fry planned once training was finished. To be honest, I don't think they were especially heartbroken to see our backs.

The five of us changed our return flights to Virginia Beach and went to our rooms to pack and arrange early-morning wake-up calls. I remember lying in my bed on the top floor of the Marriott wondering why in the world I was being recalled off a training trip so soon after finishing a combat deployment. It didn't make any sense. One of our squadrons was in Afghanistan and another was back home on standby. If there were any hostage situations in the world, they were the ones who had control for the next four months. If a high-value target poked his head up in Africa or the Arabian Peninsula, we had pieces from yet another squadron to coordinate air strikes through Air Force drones or naval aviation. There were no more targets in Iraq, so that didn't cross my mind, and if a high-level al-Qaeda or Haqqani target crossed into Afghanistan, or even got close enough to the border and we knew about it, the squadron stationed in Afghanistan would launch. Why did they want us? Why did I have to leave Miami at the best time of the year?

Could it be Libya? Just a few weeks earlier, on February 17, major political protests had begun opposing the regime of Muammar Gaddafi. It was all part of the "Arab Spring" and these protests had spilled over from Egypt and Tunisia. NATO forces were now involved, enforcing a no-fly zone after a civil war broke out. While, supposedly, this zone had been created to protect civilians, I was thinking that many people up the chain of command wanted Gaddafi dead and that the no-fly zone might be a ruse to get aircraft in the sky to locate him so he could be taken. Was this why they wanted us? I was pretty sure that Army Special Forces would be the go-to in that area of the world. They, too, had a squadron in the States standing by for global contingencies. Any way I angled it, it made no sense.

What in the world was going on?

I SLEPT RESTLESSLY AND WOKE before sunrise for my flight home. Paul, Mack, Roth, and I all managed to get on the same flight, and we had two rental cars to return. We made it to the airport without issue, checked in, boarded the flight, and returned to Virginia Beach.

After driving to the command and finding our usual, distant parking spaces, the four of us made our way up to our Team Room. Once there, we found out a few things: Almost the entire leadership of our squadron—both officers and enlisted leaders—were there, many having been recalled from other assignments.

This wouldn't have raised any eyebrows if we'd been on standby. But we were supposed to be training around the country. This was brand-new, and very odd. Nobody knew what the hell was happening. Well, the Commanding Officer and Command Master Chief did, but they weren't telling anybody yet, so we all just milled about talking in hushed voices, all with the same rising note of perplexity.

"What did you hear?"

"Nothing, what did you hear?"

"We are in our training cycle and won't be on standby for another four months!"

"Christ, we just finished deployment. What is going on?"

"Did we seriously just get recalled for some training exercise?"

"We better not miss the Thailand trip!"

As time stretched on with no new information, we began to relax a little and just shoot the shit as usual. Cheese had a funny story about his brief trip to Free-Fall Jumpmaster School in Yuma with Checque. Those two had been close friends for years and constantly made fun of each other. Even in combat. Anyway, they went out together for this course, which is considered very technical and difficult, for most units anyway. SEAL Team ▮ has an excellent track record there. People from my command are expected to pass at the top of their class, and failure is not an option.

So Cheese and Checque showed up on Monday for class. Tuesday was all classroom work as well, and so was Wednesday. But Cheese had been recalled on Tuesday night and was noticeably absent for class on Wednesday. When asked by the senior instructor where Cheese was, Checque answered with a straight face, "He quit." The rest of the class was suitably shocked. Checque never bothered to tell anyone the truth.

The familiar chatter and comfort of all being together only managed to underline the strangeness of the situation: Here we were, back in the Team Room for mysterious reasons when we should have been on the road enjoying training and liberty.

The Team Room is quite an impressive place. The main area

is a monster square space with three huge conference tables lined side by side in the middle; one for each troop. Opposite the main entrance is a huge bar with stools, a commercial sliding glass refrigerator loaded with everyone's favorite kind of bottled beer, and a stainless steel freezer. The bar is fully stocked, and we have two sinks and three microwaves. A living room next to the bar is furnished with three leather couches and a coffee table. On the wall above one of the couches are framed photos of comrades who have died, and of "Spike," a team dog killed in action in Iraq. On the wall opposite that, a huge wooden plaque bears the names of every man who has ever been a member of our squadron. The rest of the wall space is dominated by flat-screen TVs and mementos from the wars fought by the Tribe.

There's Neil Roberts's machine gun, bent at a sharp angle from impact when he fell out of a helicopter into an al-Qaeda hornet's nest on top of a ridge soon to be named for him. A bloody hood and steel handcuffs used to arrest a war criminal in Bosnia reside in a case on the wall. There is a photo from Operation Wolverine, a revenge vehicle interdiction in which our guys ambushed four vehicles containing nineteen al-Qaeda fighters as they fled the Shahi-Kot Valley trying to reach Pakistan in 2002; and a painting of the *Maersk Alabama* with the hat signed by Captain Richard Phillips. The floor cover is a 15-x-10-foot black-and-red carpet with a huge squadron emblem on it. A life-size statue of Tecumseh stands at the main entrance to greet all visitors. He has a grease-gun over his shoulder.

We continued to mill about for an hour or so until word was passed that we were to meet in the Commander's Conference Room. Once we were all inside and seated, we were given a short intro by the Command Master Chief. He read a short list of names: guys who had personal issues going on at the time and would need to remain in the Virginia Beach area to take care of them. One guy was having some problems with his wife. Another was scheduled for shoulder surgery. Yet another was still healing from a recent injury. One of the guys, Bert, was the leader for a major urban-training evolution in Los Angeles. That trip wasn't for about six months, but he figured he'd need as much time as possible to coordinate all the aircraft and logistics. He asked to be replaced so he could work on it. I'm certain that he regrets that decision.

The guys whose names had been called were asked to excuse themselves so the rest of us could be read-in. That was the first time I'd ever known this to happen. Something big was up and whatever it was, our leadership wanted it on a need-to-know basis. Even the other team leaders, Troop Chiefs, and troop commanders who hadn't been specifically recalled were asked to leave. They had to be told a few times because they couldn't believe their ears.

When they'd all departed, twenty-four of us remained. The doors were closed and our Master Chief, Willy, stood up front.

"What I'm about to tell you cannot be discussed outside this room."

We'd all heard this song and dance before, and were pretty good at heeding it. But surely they didn't mean we couldn't even tell our brothers just outside. It quickly became evident that that was *exactly* what was meant.

Willy, usually the picture of self-assurance, shifted on his feet, looking uncomfortable standing there. There had been a major earthquake in Japan, he said. Yeah, we were all aware. It had been all over the news. So what did that have to do with us? Japan is our ally and none in the room could see a need for us there. I'm sure he could sense the skepticism.

He was being uncharacteristically vague. As he talked on about the implications, no country was mentioned by name. The details were sparse, but the mission involved getting to a secluded base station that consisted of a series of buildings he likened to a large Afghan compound. It was surrounded by mountains in a large bowl. We were also told that the two dozen of us had been broken down into four teams. He read off the names and leaders for each team. I would be the team leader for Team 4.

Obviously, some part of this brief was real, but we didn't know which part. We made a religion of attention to detail. Nothing was ever glossed over like this. Things were getting downright spooky.

Willy explained that the only way to get to this target in such a sensitive area and out on time was to insert right on top of it, on the X, with all the additional risk that implied. He knew we wouldn't be happy to hear that, but he said that he and others had been in Washington planning this for the past two weeks and it was the only way. The more experienced shooters around the table frowned. It wasn't that we didn't trust our bosses—rather, it was that we shooters simply had more experience in combat. We weren't going to go into an extremely dangerous situation based on the words of a bunch of officers looking at maps around a conference table. We had questions.

Where is the target? From where will we be launching? Will we be coming from a ship or a land base? How long is the flight?

We can't tell you yet. We can't tell you yet. You'll be launching from land. We can't tell you yet.

I asked, "What type of platform will we be flying?" At this point, I was imagining the target would be some compound in Libya, and it struck me that to fly that kind of distance we'd be using a fixed-wing aircraft. I knew Ospreys—an ungainly combination of helicopter and turbo-prop—were the shiny new toy because of their ability to take off and land like a helicopter but fly like an airplane. I also knew that Ospreys had a troubled past and a tendency to crash and kill everyone on board. I may have asked the question just to prepare myself for the possibility of flying in a death trap.

Willy: "We can't tell you yet."

When I got specific about my concern with Ospreys, he said, "We won't be inserting in an Osprey, I assure you. Gentlemen, we'll be inserting to a target that is in a bowl surrounded by mountains on aircraft that are like helicopters."

Like helicopters? What the hell was that?

Willy called a break and said we'd reassemble in the same

conference room in ten minutes. He reminded us—again—that the other members of our squadron were out in the main Team Room, and we weren't to discuss a word of what we'd just been told. Every man in the room knew that this would cause a problem. The other guys would be wondering why they were not read-in and would think we were arrogant for not telling them what was going on.

Mack and I headed to the far corner of the Team Room where our computers were. I glanced at the other members of the squadron as I walked across the room. They were going on with their normal day's work: Some were typing, some were walking to the copy machine, some were sitting at the conference tables eating. Every last one was pointedly ignoring us, like a jealous girlfriend who didn't want to come out and say that she felt left out.

When we got to our side of the room, I said in a low voice, "Well, this is awkward."

"Yeah," said Mack. "Why would the headshed [our somewhat ironic term for the commanders] be so adamant about us not telling the other guys what's going on when we don't even *know* what's going on? This is getting weird."

It sure was. The guys who weren't included felt it as a judgment of their worthiness. These guys had never failed anything. They were all combat veterans, all highly decorated. Needless to say, they were alpha males and had supreme confidence in themselves. It was bad enough being told they hadn't made the cut—that the twenty-four who had were somehow better than them. The salt on the raw wound was that we clearly didn't even trust them enough to tell them what was going on. They'd been told all of this by being told nothing at all.

In fact, the seemingly puzzling selection was rooted in strategic practicality. The commanders wanted to raise as few flags as possible to avoid any chance of alerting al-Qaeda or even Pakistan that something unusual was afoot. They wanted to use one squadron, and the one that would be the most prepared and the least conspicuous. If the squadron already at war was suddenly reassigned, the locals on their base would notice. If the squadron on four-month standby in Virginia Beach left to train somewhere else the families would start talking, rumors would fly. We'd just gotten back from war, so we were still battle-ready, and we were already away training. We were the obvious choice, but only in retrospect.

In the moment, Mack and I still hadn't grasped the seriousness of what was happening, mostly because our leaders were still lying to us. Remember, the Team Room was prank central. We had always needed to have extremely thick skin because any sign of weakness *would* be exploited. Messing with the other guys was our first instinct. We came up with a name for the select twenty-four: Team Awesome—an acronym for Alienate, When Ever Suitable, Others in My Employment . . . or something like that. It never really got off the ground. Willy got wind of it and said, "The next person I hear refer to this element as 'Team Awesome' will be removed from 'Team Awesome.'"

We reconvened in the Commander's Conference Room for a few more hours. Although the target, insertion method, and reason for being there were vague (and intentionally misleading), we planned the best we could with the information given. Willy drew up a target complex on a large whiteboard and listed the four teams, 1, 2, 3, and 4, with the team leaders at the top of each list. All twenty-four of us were normally in leadership roles. Because the bosses wanted only the most experienced guys on this mission, Troop Chiefs would run teams and team leaders would do the "sled dog" work—serve as assaulters, breachers, and snipers.

Three of the teams would handle the assault on the target. My team was responsible for holding security on the perimeter. I was still assuming we were going into the African desert where there could be scores of insurgents. Holding them off would be my team's responsibility, so I wanted to go a little bit heavy. I was thinking at least three machine guns, depending on . . .

"Willy," I asked, "what kind of close air support will be available on this target? Will we have DAPs, Apaches, AC-130s, and fast movers? What about bombers?"

"No air support."

It kept getting better.

But it wasn't getting any clearer. Here we were: handpicked for a delicate mission, and all we had for mission planning was a drawing on a whiteboard. Willy had drawn up a large square off to the left of the list of four teams. Below that box, he drew a smaller rectangle and to the left of those he drew an acute triangle. He informed us that we would insert on that mysterious helicopter aircraft, my team would hold the perimeter, and the other three teams would assault the shapes. We would have the next few days to get gear together. Because command wanted to bring the maximum number of shooters in a minimum number of aircraft—four teams and only two helicopters—our normal support personnel couldn't accompany us. That meant no medics. Instead, those among the twenty-four who'd had previous experience as corpsmen would have to bone up on their medical skills, and the two officers would have to figure out a way to carry their own radios.

When someone pressed for a clearer idea of the assault teams' objective, Willy said, "They're going to assault the buildings like we always do. Go in, grab something, and bring it out. Then we leave."

"One more thing," Willy added. "Nizzro, your team will have the dog with you so make sure you save room for Cheese and Cairo. Also, there'll be one more guy who is not on the list."

"The 'terp?" I asked.

"Yes, the 'terp."

"What language will he be speaking?" I asked.

"I can't tell you that."

"That's what I figured."

Willy added, "Probably Arabic but we're still working on that."

What the hell was that supposed to mean?

At least I knew what to expect from Cairo.

"Okay, see you guys Sunday morning," Willy went on. "Once we get where we're going, we'll be read-in. There'll be VIPs there: General Thomas, the CO of SEAL Team ██ . . . possibly the Secretary of Defense . . . and the Chief of CTC/PAD."

CTC/PAD? I don't think anyone else caught that, but I did. This was the CIA's Counter Terrorism PAK/AFGHAN Desk. Libya my ass!!

We were set to leave on Sunday morning for a government facility in North Carolina, so we had the remainder of the week and Saturday to prepare. The majority of the time was spent tweaking gear that was already built and just adding additional pouches. Every guy picked for this mission had seen more than his share of combat, and each had a setup he was comfortable with. The issue was that we'd be going in with fewer people so each guy had to bring more stuff and execute more roles. Team leaders had been breachers just a few years ago, so they knew the drill. They'd only need to add a few extra pouches to carry the explosives and detonators. The former corpsmen had carried all of the medical gear in their conventional SEAL platoons before making Team ██, so they just needed to re-build. I'd carried an M60 for years at SEAL Team Two; no worries. The only thing that was eating at us was the fact that we didn't know what we were going to do. Everyone knew it was big, but exactly how big was it?

The word was starting to spread around the command. Everyone wanted to know why the bosses were planning some secret operation and including less than half of one squadron. A lot of suspicion fell on our new Commanding Officer. Some guys liked him, some even loved him, but most hated working for him. He had a reputation for overplanning everything and committing to things that weren't even remotely possible. He could work on virtually no sleep, ever, and expected the same from his men. He had a tendency to wear guys out and an uncanny ability to sell ideas to higher-ranking officers. Most shooters at the command assumed that all the above was happening again.

Guys from other squadrons were constantly pulling their buddies from our squadron aside trying to get intel.

"What are you guys spinning up on?"

"I have *no* idea."

"C'mon . . . you can tell *me*."

"Seriously, I don't even know."

And I didn't. But I was beginning to form a suspicion because of the very last thing Willy had said about the involvement of the counter terrorism/Pakistan desk. I couldn't quite believe it, though. I mean . . . *no way*.

SUNDAY MORNING, GUYS STARTED ROLLING in around 0600 and rolling out shortly after. Mack and I got in a van along with Paul and Roth. We'd loaded all of our bags onto a box-truck earlier so we had plenty of room. I was looking forward to the short, ninety-minute drive down to North Carolina because it was going to be great company. Mack drove and Paul rode shotgun. Roth and I were in the back, and we prepped for the drive south. We got coffee and grabbed some Copenhagen at some mom-and-pop gas station, along with some terrible breakfast sandwiches. On the way down, we mostly just shot the bull, and things didn't get terribly interesting until we started brainstorming about what was going on.

Roth was the only officer in the van so we figured he might have some info to which the other three of us weren't privy. We picked his brain but were wrong. He did have his assumptions, though. He mentioned some imagery he'd seen while spending the majority of our last deployment in Afghanistan. There were rumors about a target that sounded like the place Willy kept referring to. I brought up the small bit of information that nobody else seemed to have noticed in the brief. I said, "Why would the *PAK/AFGHAN desk* be briefing us today if we're flying into Libya?"

Finally, after a long silence, I just said it: "I'll tell you what, guys: I think we're going after Osama bin Laden."

Instantly, Roth replied, "That's *exactly* what I'm thinking."

Mack's voice boomed from the driver's seat, "Man, O'Neill... if we kill Osama bin Laden, I will suck yo' dick!"

It was an odd feeling, to be driving down the highway on a spring morning in such a beautiful part of the country beginning to suspect what we suspected. What would the people in all the cars passing by say if they knew what the big bearded guys in that van beside them might be on their way to do?

The hour and a half drive seemed more like thirty minutes. When we arrived at the front gate of the facility, one of the most top secret defense facilities in the country, we encountered a fog bank of confusion. No one had given a list of our names to base security, not because they forgot, but because nobody wanted a list of the shooters to ever exist. We'd been top-secreted into an interesting discussion with the guards. It took some time to sort it out, but we finally rolled past the gate.

The government facility isn't much to look at—basically, it's a lot of trees with a small airstrip in the center. All of the buildings are at least forty years old and one-story. Our destination was even less impressive than most—a small structure that looked like two doublewide trailers stuck together. Inside, in a large conference room, about eight people were milling about, setting up for a brief. Some of the people I recognized; some I didn't. Pete, our Commanding Officer, was in a conversation with some other top brass. There were several other sidebars taking place while everyone waited for the meeting to start. Most of the shooters, including me, went into the kitchen where there were several pots of coffee brewing and about four dozen doughnuts. At least there were four dozen to begin with.

After about five minutes of making small talk with friends, we were called into the room. Captain Perry Van Hooser—we called him Pete—stood in front of the crowd, which consisted of the entire assault force and a half dozen people I'd never seen before, including four women.

Pete waited as one of the men I didn't recognize closed both of the doors. They took a long look around the room to ensure that no one was in the room who didn't belong. Even the security guards were asked to remain in the kitchen area while we talked. The man in back made sure that none of the guards could hear what was about to be spoken.

"I appreciate you all cutting your training trips short and making your way down here," Pete said when the room was secure. "I know that you all had a long deployment and have just gotten back but it's time to get back after it."

He paused, and then he said it. "We have a line on UBL. This is the best intelligence we've had on his position since Tora Bora."

A man I'd figured for the Agency moved up to the front of the room as one of the four women passed out documents for us to sign. As we did, the man, Steve, who turned out to be with the counter terrorism/Pak desk, and two of the other women began the brief. This was the first time I'd ever heard the word "Abbottabad." I loved the way it sounded.

Steve said they were particularly interested in one man. He was usually dressed in white, taller than everyone else in a compound in Abbottabad, which he never left. *Ever.* He'd just walk around the interior yards and gardens day after day. They'd dubbed him "The Pacer." The Pacer walked in the garden for hours at a time, stopping to talk to children and the other men who lived in the compound. But he never did anything menial. If some of the inhabitants were gardening or digging, he'd occasionally stop near them but was never seen helping with any task. The intelligence analysts were convinced that The Pacer never interacted with anyone from the outside.

The housing structure was very large, much bigger than anything in the neighborhood, and was at the end of a road. There was a "T" intersection, but it was rarely, if ever, used. When looking at photographs of the compound, with north being the top, it looked like an upside-down triangle surrounded by a series of walls varying in height from ten to eighteen feet. The base of the walled triangle ran along an east-west road for 385 feet. The main house, three stories high, was in the center of the compound just a few feet from the northernmost wall. A front door to the south opened on a small yard.

Just to the west of the main house, still inside the main compound, was a privacy driveway oriented north-south about twenty yards long and gated on both sides. The north gate had an intercom system. The south gate opened to a garage and was connected to the southernmost structure, which was in a secondary compound inside the main compound. The second structure was thought to be the guesthouse. The garage was only big enough to fit one car completely. Intelligence analysts told us this was extremely fortunate. The residents owned two cars: They could always tell when someone had left, or when everyone was home. When both cars were there, one would stick partially out of the garage into the driveway.

To the west of the driveway, a large, roughly triangular-shaped yard contained two small structures on the wall bordering the driveway. They were assumed to be animal pens and storage. It also appeared that this enclosure was where trash was burned. To the east of the three-story house was a large garden, also surrounded by a wall. A gate on the northeast wall appeared to open to the exterior street, but it was actually a decoy, which I would personally discover in a few weeks. Off to the east of the garden was yet another triangular yard, surrounded by walls but containing nothing.

The three-story house was a bit of a puzzle. There was definitely an entrance on the south side facing the wall and there could have been one on the north. Because of how close the north side of the house was to the wall, though, it was impossible to see. The Pacer had never been seen coming out of the visible door, so it was assumed there must be a northern entrance. This also led to questions about the interior layout. We assumed three families lived in the entire compound: one in the guesthouse and probably two in the main house. If The Pacer only left through a northern door, maybe it was accessed directly by stairs from the second or third story, meaning the main house was actually two separate residences. The analysts believed that The Pacer lived on the third deck, again, because of an oddity in the architecture: A balcony on the third floor's south side had been completely enclosed by a seven-foot-high privacy wall. No one from the ground outside could see in nor could anyone in any of the neighboring houses.

This was a common theme for the entire compound. The guesthouse had an exterior stairway on its southeast side that led to the roof and served as a balcony. It also had a privacy wall built around it. While the majority of the exterior wall was twelve to thirteen feet high, this small portion was eighteen feet high, high enough to block every possible view from the outside. The entire exterior wall was covered in barbed wire.

The Pacer had clearly arranged things to keep the world out, and himself in. He never left the compound—pacing endlessly in the garden or out of sight inside. The other residents also contributed to the suspicious pattern. Analysts were able to determine that the vehicles, a car and a van, were used differently; the van for local tasks and the sedan for chores that required several hours of travel.

The sedan had been the key for getting us to this point: The man who drove it the majority of the time was named Abu Ahmed al-Kuwaiti. AAK was a Kuwait-born Pakistani Pashtu who was bin Laden's most trusted courier. Our intelligence had learned al-Kuwaiti's name and also that he'd taught computer skills to one of the 9/11 hijackers so he could communicate clandestinely with terrorist leaders. Al-Kuwaiti had been with bin Laden at the battle of Tora Bora in December 2001, which had been the closest we'd gotten to killing him. Both men escaped and were believed to have remained in close contact from that point on.

Al-Kuwaiti was extremely careful about any kind of electronic communication. He'd only turn his phone on when he was at least ninety minutes away from the compound by car, and he'd always turn it off at least ninety minutes before returning.

Cautious, but not cautious enough. Our intelligence agencies had been able to track him driving back to Abbottabad. Once they got a look at the odd security features of the compound he'd returned to, they knew they might be on to something.

To be honest, the briefing went on so long—six hours—that we all began to get restless. I realized that if I were ever tempted to divulge classified information, I wouldn't because it's so boring. I think all the shooters were thinking what I was: *I don't care how you found him. You say he's there. Let's go kill him.*

About that: The briefers mentioned that we were *not* the No. 1 option. One option—"the right thing to do" from an international law standpoint—was a multilateral mission where we'd tell the Pakistanis that we knew bin Laden was there, and we'd go in with them. Everyone in the room simultaneously thought, *Yeah, right. You can take that off the table because once we tell the Pakistanis that we know he's there, he's gone.*

Another option was an air strike on the compound with a B-1 or a stealth bomber. Some Air Force dude had calculated that to make sure the strike killed him—to leave absolutely no doubt—it would require something astonishing, like thirty-two two-thousand-pound bombs. It was insane. With that payload, you'd kill everyone in the city almost. And we'd never be able to recover any DNA, so we'd never know for sure anyway.

A third option was what we called the hammer throw: Arm a drone and wait for The Pacer to pace into the garden, then just chuck one bomb at him. But even if it was a direct hit, we'd seen people who had entire houses collapse on them walk away unhurt.

Then, they said, "There's you." The unilateral, boots-on-the-ground option. The riskiest in terms of negative repercussions. And of course, the riskiest in terms of American lives. Our lives.

Admiral William McRaven, the top commander of the Joint Special Operations Command, who gave his account of the mission for the first time five years after the raid, recalled in an interview with CNN that in early April 2011, he presented a plan to the president and his senior advisers in the White House Situation Room for a helicopter raid into the compound. Obama said, "Can you do this?" McRaven recalled.

He replied, "Mr. President, I won't know if we can do this until I have an opportunity to bring in the SEALs and the helicopter pilots from the 160th (Special Operations Air Regiment) and re-hearse it." McRaven said he'd need about three weeks to be sure.

Obama said, "Okay, you have three weeks."

CHAPTER TWENTY

A life-size replica of the Abbottabad compound had been constructed using CONEX shipping containers, with fencing that could be removed so it would be less likely to be picked up in satellite imagery. All the measurements were exact, or close to it. Our training would be unusually realistic. They brought in conventional Black Hawks, and we went out every day, fast-roping out of the hovering choppers.

The preferred plan looked like this: When we arrived at the compound, my helicopter, Dash 2, would drop external security just outside the north gate. That would consist of me; two snipers, Jonny and Robby; Mack with the machine gun; Cheese, the dog guy; Cairo the dog; and an interpreter. Cheese, Cairo, and Robby would loop around the compound as the helicopter lifted back up above the main house. That team would fast-rope to the roof, and then jump down to the third-floor balcony, which is where we thought bin Laden was. Jonny, Mack, and I would hold security where we were, looking east and west. The other helicopter, Dash 1, would fast-rope the primary assault team into the courtyard between the main house and the guesthouse. Snipers looking out both doors of the chopper would cover from above as the team roped in. This was the most vulnerable spot of the operation, as Dash 1 could be hit from any angle while hovering.

Of course, the interior of the house couldn't be exactly

replicated because it was unknown, but we had no problem with that. We don't want to know the interior. Just get there, see what it looks like, and let our tactics take over. Anticipating exact layouts can just confuse the issue. Go in, respond.

As team leader for external security, I was never supposed to be in the house. But as I was watching the scenario play out in training, something seemed off. I talked to Willy, my Master Chief, about it. "This is bin Laden we're talking about, and we've only got a couple shooters. We need as many as we can get in there," I said. Jonny, who was one of the two snipers on security, was already a team leader. "He doesn't need me out there to lead him. I need to be on the rooftop team."

Willy thought that maximizing the number of shooters inside the compound—sharpening the point of Neptune's spear—made sense. He moved Jonny to security team leader and put me on the rooftop assault team.

Even though we'd assaulted hundreds of compounds much like this one, we trained on this like no other—hours and hours with the sun up and hours more after the sun went down to get used to doing it with night vision—even though darkness had become our native element. To be honest, we were overtraining. I developed tendonitis from fast-roping so much. It was a little frustrating because I knew if it got much worse, I was going to have to pull myself off the mission. We already *knew* how to fast-rope. We didn't need to keep doing it. I managed to tough it out, but years later when my biceps just blew up one day while I was bowling—*bowling*—I was convinced that I had that excessive fast-roping to thank for it.

After we finally called it quits for the day/night, we'd go back to these crummy little barracks. No flat screen—in fact, no TV at all. But there was a nice little game room with Ping Pong tables, pool tables, and a couple of video games. It wasn't like our regular deployments. We weren't joking around like we usually did, and nobody felt like drinking. We all believed that the Abbottabad compound, and the main house in particular,

was almost certainly going to be rigged to blow as soon as we
touched down. I started calling our team, only half-jokingly, the
Martyrs Brigade, because if the house blew up when we were
on top of it, we were fucked.

That's if we even *got* to the house. There was a good chance
Pakistani air defense would bring us down before we even hovered in sight of it. Or maybe we'd be surrounded by Pakistani
troops and end up spending the rest of our lives in a Peshawar
prison, which would be worse than dying.

We talked about it: "This is the last thing we ever do, so let's
get our shit together."

I got into a discussion with the guy who'd end up being the
point man in the assault on the third floor of the compound—of
course, we didn't know that then. We talked the way SEALs never
talk: "Once we go on this mission, we aren't going to see our kids
again or kiss our wives. We'll never eat another steak or smoke
another cigar." We were trying to get down to the truth about
why we were still willing to do this when we pretty much knew
we were going to die. What we came up with was that we were
doing it for the single mom who dropped her kids off at school
and went to work on a Tuesday morning, and then an hour later
decided to jump out of a skyscraper because it was better than
burning alive. A woman whose last gesture of human decency
was holding down her skirt on the long way to the pavement
so no one could see her underwear. *That's* why we were going.
She was just trying to get through a workday, live a life. She had
no desire to fight and no ability to defend herself. Now we were
going to fight for her. We were going to fucking kill this guy. We
started getting fired up just talking about it.

I don't think any of us had even a momentary doubt. Everybody wanted to go. This was the big one. This was why we'd
signed up. We figured we were all going to die eventually, so
why not go out doing something noble?

And who knows, maybe we'd somehow make it back.

In the common room, there was a model on a portable cart, an exact small-scale replica of the compound. Everything down to the trees was identical. We'd stand over that and just run through possibilities: "Okay, here's the plan, but what if this happens? What if a car leaves the compound? Which helicopter's going to chase it?" We'd just talk through everything over and over, get some sleep, then start running the scenarios for real, over and over, the next day.

We tried to plan for all the things that could go wrong. Of course, the most obvious was that we'd get shot down as soon as we crossed the Pakistan border. We were invading a country with nothing more than two helicopters. But the higher-ups seemed less worried about that. They said, "Just chill out."

Okay. But what if the Pakistani police or military showed up while we were inside? If we could avoid it, we sure didn't want to get in a gunfight with them—we'd be on their soil. Our first plan was that we'd produce bin Laden's body and a high-level diplomat in Islamabad would negotiate: "We told you, if we found bin Laden we were coming to get him. That's what we did. We didn't hurt any of your guys doing it. Now we want our guys out."

Of course, they probably would have just tried to arrest us. I wasn't in the meeting, but as our training was nearing an end, I heard that when President Obama was presented with that possibility, he nodded his head and said, "Okay, that's interesting." Then he looked at the Air Force chief of staff and said, "What do you need to rain hell on Pakistan—because my guys aren't surrendering to anybody."

I was so proud of him. Our guys tend to be extremely conservative politically, but he could have gotten a lot of votes from us that day.

AS THE DAYS PASSED, IT began to seem like the president was leaning toward using us as his option. He even authorized staging more helicopters with another thirty or so SEAL Team guys and some Rangers nearby to serve as a quick re-action force in case things went south. I couldn't know for sure, but based on what I was hearing at the time about the president's resolve, I assumed our military had fighters ready on the Afghanistan-Pakistan border, and probably bombers overhead, in case there was no other choice but to fight our way out of Pakistan.

We continued training from Sunday through Saturday evening, then we all hauled ass back to Virginia Beach. We'd been training so hard we couldn't wait to get to the ready room for drinks. We had Saturday night and Sunday off before we flew out to Nevada.

There, we all had to sign a bunch of documents that said not only were we not allowed to discuss what we saw here, we weren't allowed to discuss what we *thought* we saw. We actually did stay there, in some barracks. The base didn't have a gym, but I ran every day while listening to Pearl Jam, which I hadn't done since just after high school. For some reason, I felt I needed a blast from the past, so I cranked up "State of Love and Trust," "Corduroy," *Ten*, and "Alive." One of the choruses on "Alive" goes, "I, I'm still alive/ Hey I, but, I'm still alive/ . . . / Hey I, I, I, I'm still alive."

At that point the lyrics struck me as wishful thinking.

Finally, we got called to a briefing on the famous mystery helicopters we'd be flying into the compound on. We turned a corner and saw them for the first time. I started laughing. Someone asked, "What's so funny?"

I said, "Well, I used to say it was a ninety percent chance that we were going to die. Now I think it's about an eighty percent chance we're going to live because I didn't know they were sending us to war on Transformers." They were some of the coolest things I'd ever seen, and I won't get more detailed than that. We'd all been grimly determined. Now just looking at them made us far less grim and even more determined.

We only trained there for a few days. Mostly, it was just to get used to the frame of the aircraft. The seats had been removed to make each craft lighter, and there was more room inside than we were used to, so it was kind of refreshing. And they flew great. The mission planners assigned the four best pilots in the Army to fly them—two for each bird. We did a few training runs, and on the last one hit the training target with every explosive we had. We wouldn't need it again anyway. It was literally and figuratively a blast.

The following Saturday, April 23, we flew home.

"Go be with your families," the commanders told us. "We haven't been given the green light yet, but we're going to Afghanistan to stage. We want to be ready when they call."

So we had a couple more days with our kids. When I got home, Nicole knew something was up. I'd never been able to tell her much. On deployments, I'd had to send emails from a fake email account, and I couldn't even see the pictures of our kids she posted on Facebook because I wasn't allowed to be on Facebook, or Instagram, or Twitter. So my leaving on mysterious missions was old hat. But she knew this one was different. I couldn't explain why I'd abruptly returned from training and why I was flying out when other teams were already deployed. I could see her registering all that. It was odd. We'd never really had a heart-to-heart about the chance that I'd die doing my job. Even though no one on my team had ever been hurt, we'd lost a lot of friends; a lot of her friends' boyfriends and husbands. So we both understood there was a chance. But all of that remained unspoken. I knew what was going to happen, but she didn't, and that made it harder.

Meanwhile, I had just over a day to accomplish a lifetime of loving gestures. Hopeless, obviously. I didn't want to scare the girls by seeming overly serious or hovering over them, so I went shopping. What do you buy a seven- and a three-year-old in that circumstance? What gift says, "Sorry, your dad's about to die"? I don't even remember now what I did get them, just that it wasn't enough.

As I was leaving the mall, I noticed a Sunglass Hut right there in the middle of the concourse, and I walked up to it. I don't know why. I looked down and there was a pair of Prada sunglasses for $350—at least $300 more than I'd ever considered paying for sunglasses. I was looking at them and thinking, *You really shouldn't. You're an E-7 in the Navy. You can't afford these things.* With the extra pay for jumps, dives, demolitions, hazardous duty, and housing allowance, I made quite a bit more than conventional forces—but it still wasn't enough for Prada. Then I thought, *Hell, a week from now I'll be dead. Or maybe I'll live through the raid after all and have to steal a car and drive to the embassy in Islamabad. Shit happens. The sun's going to be out and I'm going to need sunglasses.*

I put them on my American Express card. If I never came back, American Express could afford the loss.

The next day, my older daughter went off to school, and I took my younger daughter to Chick-fil-A for a goodbye outing. She was about to turn four, and happened to meet a girl just her age there. Of course, they became instant BFFs. While they played, I sat with the girl's grandma and made small talk. She had no idea who she was talking to. My attitude was like, *I'm just going to finish this chicken sandwich with waffle fries and go try to kill bin Laden.* It didn't seem real—even to me. Nothing was sinking in. All I wanted to do at that moment was get it over with. I didn't want to be there anymore. I wanted to go.

I took my daughter home and waited for her older sister to get back from school so I could say goodbye. My about-to-happen departure had me feeling so much respect for my wife. I could kiss the kids and hold it in for the thirty seconds it took to get to my car, then cry the whole way to work. But Nicole had to stand there with these two little blond girls looking at her for strength and not cry. *Ever.* And she didn't.

The surreal feeling continued when I got to work. Nobody else there knew why we were going overseas, including high-ranking officers who were somewhat pathetically trying to get involved even though they didn't know what it was they were trying to get involved in. They just knew it was big and wanted to get their fingers in it. The guys running our op weren't having it. We boarded the big C-17s, and the commanders wouldn't let anybody not involved on board, even though our destination could be disguised—we were stopping in Germany first, just as we always did for deployment. We got off at Ramstein, had breakfast, then hung out until it was time to take off for Afghanistan. At Bagram, we switched from a C-17 to a C-130 and made another short flight to Jalalabad. It was weird at first because a SEAL Team ▇ squadron was there already, in the middle of their deployment. I'm sure they guessed what we were there for, for the same reasons that we had guessed it. They obviously thought they should have gotten the assignment, and they might have been right about that. If I'd been in their spot, I would have been pissed off and probably shown it. But they were good to us.

We had to use alternate barracks that were outside the normal compound, but we worked out in the same gym as them, played poker with them every night, hung out with them, and just shot the shit. As it turned out, they wouldn't be left out of the mission after all. As we started to build out our plan, because of the president's aggressive stance we were given the authority to beef up everything. We decided we'd bring the already-deployed squadron across the border with us, about forty strong. They'd wait in the forward staging area on a mountain thirty miles from the compound, in case we needed them to come bail us out of a jam.

WE KNEW THIS WAS THE ultimate mission, and the mood was a lot more serious than normal, but not to the point where we were upset. We still joked a lot, did all the things we'd normally do on deployment. If there was unusual anxiety, it was not because we might go, but because we might not. The better part of the week went by and we were still waiting for a green light. The days dragged. On Friday, we got called to a brief. Pete, the top SEAL Team ███ commander, was sitting at the head of the table. Walking in, we knew it would be one of two things: We were going or we weren't. Not going meant we'd get to go home soon and see our families. And live. Not going also meant that we'd miss out on the chance to make history. We didn't have to wait long to find out which it was going to be. Without much of a preamble, he said, "The president's authorized you guys to launch. It's either going to be tomorrow or Sunday."

It felt as though an electric charge had surged around the table. Now we were definitely going. The possible launch nights were the two nights that month with zero illumination from the moon. On Saturday, the mission was pushed to Sunday. The official cause according to the commanders was inclement weather, but we all knew the weather was fine. The real reason was that Obama had been scheduled to attend the annual White House Correspondents' Dinner, a high profile event broadcast live on C-Span. He didn't want to cancel at the last moment, or get up and leave in the middle of it, which would have attracted worldwide attention and tipped everyone that something big was up.

So on Saturday night, Obama behaved as if the Correspondents' Dinner was just an ordinary event in an ordinary presidential weekend. He sat at the head table in his tux while Seth Meyers of *Saturday Night Live* gave a hilarious roast. Meyers spent the first few minutes poking fun at C-Span for being unwatchable and unwatched. Then he said, "People think bin Laden is hiding in the Hindu Kush, but did you know that every day from four to five he hosts a show on C-Span?"

The camera panned to Obama, and his reaction, which you can see on the Internet, is priceless: He slouched his shoulders at a comfortable angle, threw back his head—a handsome smile spreading from cheek to cheek—and chuckled amiably as if this were the best joke of the night. Nobody in that audience could have guessed what must have been going through his mind at that moment. Within twenty-four hours, the world would know either of America's great triumph in eliminating its most bitter enemy, or its abject humiliation in trying and failing to do so.

If it had been me, I probably would have said to Meyers, "Fuck you, we're going to kill him tomorrow."

But I wasn't in Washington, I was in Jalalabad ready to step up into a badass Transformer and fly through the night to Pakistan and whatever fate awaited me.

I left the briefing intent on doing something I dreaded but now couldn't avoid: writing letters to my kids, the kind that would only be delivered if I wasn't ever coming home. The pages would be mostly filled with apologies for missing their weddings and not being around for any of the good and bad times, as well as thank-yous for taking care of each other and their mom. I went to the administrative office to get legal paper and a pen, and as I was walking back I ran into the woman intel analyst who'd basically been the one to track bin Laden down to the compound. She'd been with us through those first briefing sessions in North Carolina and throughout the training, and had flown over with us. Now she was outside pacing tensely. She was an attractive woman, though not exactly Jessica Chastain, who would play her in the movie.

I said, "Hey, why are you so nervous?"

She kept pacing. "What the fuck you mean, 'Why are you nervous?'"

What she meant was: "Isn't it only too obvious why I'm nervous? We're about to invade the country of a nuclear-armed ally to take out someone we're only guessing is there based on years of my work. Why *shouldn't* I be nervous? Why aren't *you* nervous?"

I nodded, searching for the right response. "Well, I'm just going to do what we always do. We're going to get into a helicopter, fly somewhere, fuck with some people, and come back. The flight's just longer. We do this every night."

I thought about it for a moment then said, "You know what, *you* have to be right, though, so I understand why you're nervous. Have a great night."

Then I walked off.

Admiral McRaven, the Joint Special Operations Command (JSOC) chief, would later say that the intelligence that bin Laden was in the compound was presented to him as "at best fifty-fifty." But as I prepared to board the helicopter that would take me there, I had no doubt about who I'd find once we made our way in. And I owed that certainty to having gotten to know this intel analyst. *I* was 100 percent convinced bin Laden was there because she was. Although my guess now is that she was probably just 90 percent positive, hence the pregame jitters.

The way that I decided to deal with the fact that we were launching in less than twenty-four hours was to get on the treadmill and do a long run. As I pounded the rolling belt into submission, I was watching the NFL draft on TV, waiting for the Redskins to get their pick. Yeah, sue me, I'm a Redskins fan. Anyway, I was thinking, *Who are they going to pick, are they going to go with a lineman?* And then another thought broke in: *What does it matter, I'm going to be dead anyway.*

So I wasn't nervous, just fatalistic.

I went off and wrote those letters to my family. It was difficult and painful, and I really had to struggle through it. When I finished, I realized I couldn't give them to a friend because all my friends were going on the mission with me, and we all might die. I had to go searching for someone I sort of knew, and trusted. I came up with a Navy intelligence guy. I gave him all these complicated instructions regarding who got which letter and where to find them. And, of course, I told him that if I lived I wanted those letters right back, because shredding them was the first thing I wanted to do.

That night—actually it was morning, because we were on a reverse cycle, but it was night for us—we played poker again. I didn't want to play at first because I thought the guys might break out some beer. We weren't allowed to drink, but if the beer was there, it might happen. And I wanted to be absolutely clear on this mission. I ended up playing, and not drinking. Maybe that's why I didn't win. I had fun anyway.

After the game we all took Ambien to sleep because everyone was pretty pumped. We usually get Ambien before a mission, but this time we made sure everyone took it. We all needed to be rested. We were sleeping in an open bay area, and that makes it hard to sleep with all the coughing and snoring and whatever, but the Ambien did the job.

We woke around dusk on Sunday. I had a big breakfast and went to what I knew was going to be a historic brief. It was in a huge hangar, and we had a big crowd for such a super-secret mission—the air crews and mechanics, all the SEALs, the Explosive Ordnance Disposal (EOD) guys, all the Agency people. Admiral William McRaven stepped up and instead of giving us a bunch of technical information, he just spoke off the cuff. He said he had watched *Hoosiers* the previous night, one of his favorite movies. He talked about a scene in the movie in which tiny Hickory High is about to play for the state championship in a gym bigger than any they've ever seen, with bleachers set up for thousands of fans. The Hickory High players are all farm boys used to tossing balls in bushel baskets and shooing cows off the court. They're looking around at this huge arena with their jaws dropping. The coach tells the smallest kid on the team to get up on the shoulders of the tallest kid and stand in front of the hoop. Then he gives him a tape measure and asks, "What's the height?"

"Ten feet, Coach."

Now he tells them to measure from the back of the rim to the free throw line. "What's the distance?"

"Fifteen feet, Coach."

The coach says, "Those are the exact same measurements as your gym back in Hickory, it's just a bigger building. More people are watching. That's it. Otherwise it's the exact same."

Then McRaven said to us, "You guys do this every single night. This time the world will find out about it, it's a bigger stage, but it's exactly the same."

It was the perfect message to send us at that moment. Hearing those words, I loved the guy. McRaven was Navy after all, which is probably one of the reasons *we* were there instead of Army Special Forces, and why the operation was called Neptune's Spear—the SEAL trident. The guy had been born to give that speech.

I was also thinking, *I really doubt he watched* Hoosiers *last night.* But I appreciated the analogy. It always seemed to come back to basketball for me.

After the briefing, we walked back to our individual cubicles and suited up. I hadn't changed my usual kit for this mission, which I'd pared down over the years for minimum weight and maximum utility. I no longer even carried a knife or a pistol. I had my ceramic body armor, Nalgene water bottle, two protein bars, and my Heckler & Koch 416 automatic rifle with three extra magazines. Even in that hour-long gunfight near the Pakistan border I'd only used one and a half magazines—forty-five bullets. Let's just say, running out of ammunition wasn't high on my list of concerns.

I'd elected *not* to use the now-famous panoramic night vision goggles. They were new, with four tubes instead of two, and I wasn't used to them. So I went with PVS-15 night vision goggles. This wasn't an op for testing new equipment.

Dressed for battle, we walked out to the fire—a big fire pit where the shooters had congregated from both squadrons. The fire pit had a pyramidal chimney. On its four sides, someone had cut the emblem of each of our squadrons. Cool.

This time, there were none of the usual jokes and sarcastic taunts. There were hugs and fist bumps and guys saying, "Have a good fight. See you in a few hours." It was serious for all of us. Even though we had a squadron in reserve—they'd follow forty-five minutes behind us and wait at the staging area during the raid— we knew they might get shot down on the way in. We were the ones with the super-stealth birds. They were flying conventional Chinooks, the kind that got shot down in the Korengal Valley.

If reinforcements for al-Qaeda showed up or a big gunfight ensued, we weren't going to get into a *Black Hawk Down* scenario. Those guys were a Quick Reaction Force to make sure of that. And if *our* choppers didn't get through, or if we all got taken out somehow, they'd make a run on the compound and try to get bin Laden. We weren't going to miss this time.

Some buses rolled up and their doors hissed open. They were going to transport us to the secure hangar where the modified Black Hawks were warming up. There was just one last thing I had to do. I stepped into one of the B-huts—the cheap plywood housing units—to make a phone call.

"Hey, Dad," I said after hearing his familiar hello on the other end. He told me he'd just parked at Walmart to pick up a few things. "Just getting ready to hop on a bird," I said.

It was late at night and pitch black in J-bad. In Butte, it was about twelve hours earlier, so almost noon. I'd made a ritual of calling him before I left on my missions. I could tell he was always happy to hear my voice, and that put me in the right frame of mind for what lay ahead.

He'd always say, "Hey, I wish I was going with you."

I'd say, "Yeah, I wish you were, too, Dad."

He said it again now. "I wish I could go with you."

This time I said, "Don't worry, Dad. I'm with some great guys."

He instantly sensed the difference.

"Everything okay, son?"

"Yeah, everything's good. Hey, Dad, I just wanted to say thanks for everything. Thanks for teaching me how to shoot free throws. Thanks for teaching me how to be a man. It's nice that we got to know each other as adults."

My dad knew I couldn't tell him what was up. But he knew *something* was, and it scared him.

Later, I found out that he sat in his truck for twenty minutes after our call, poleaxed by a feeling of dread.

"Hey, Dad," I said. "I've got to go to work."

He ended the call with, "I love you." I told him I loved him, too, then hung up and jogged out to the bus. Jonny had been looking for me. I gave him a thumbs-up. He gave me the finger.

The stealth Black Hawks were at the airfield a mile away. Huge stadium lights had been stood up all around them, the blinding beams facing out so nobody could see the helicopters inside. It worked amazingly well. We all took our last piss—you didn't want to be thinking about a full bladder in the hours to come—and boarded in teams, with my team in Dash 2, the trail bird. Dash 1 would lead us in. Finally, we lifted off and headed northeast, as if we were going to Asadabad, which was a flight we'd made often. But instead of turning left, which is the way into the Korengal Valley, we turned to the right.

By the time my dad made his way through the noonday crowd at Walmart, I was flying fast and low in a chopper on a moonless night across the Pakistan border.

CHAPTER TWENTY-ONE

Now that we knew we were in Pakistan, we also knew we could get shot down at any minute. Thoughts start running through your mind: *How does it feel when a helicopter blows up? Do you die instantly or does it crash and you're falling and something cuts your head off? How long does it take to die?* You're just thinking all these weird, jumbled thoughts. I tried to get my mind off it by looking around and just observing everything around me. We were sitting on these camping chairs, the kind that fold out into little tripods and sell for like $9.99 at Walgreens. I was facing forward. The pilots were behind a solid wall, so unlike in a normal helicopter, we were in the back by ourselves. Cairo and Cheese, his handler, were right beside me, on my left. Cairo was always happy to be working. If he hadn't been wearing the still-bloodstained vest with the bullet hole in the front, you'd never know he'd been nearly killed in combat. He looked completely relaxed, like the family dog in the front seat of a pickup truck on the way to a camping trip. Too bad he couldn't stick his head out the window.

Some of the other guys were asleep, which impressed me. No way could I have slept. We were ninety minutes out from the compound. To keep my mind from spinning off somewhere I didn't need it to go, I started counting. I learned that as a sniper. Counting keeps you cool, keeps your mind engaged, but in idle. I counted zero to a thousand and a thousand to zero, zero to a thousand and a thousand to zero. I must have done that a dozen times before we banked to the south about eighty minutes into the flight. Now we were on our attack run, and as I was counting, just between random numbers, I began to repeat, "Freedom itself was attacked this morning by a faceless coward, and freedom will be defended."

It was the first line of President George W. Bush's address to the nation on the morning of 9/11. I have no idea where that came from, or how I remembered it verbatim, but I just started saying it in my head, over and over.

I could almost hear President Bush's voice over the whirring rotor above me. And I was thinking, *Holy shit, this is really it. I'm on this mission and we're going to kill this son of a bitch.*

We made another slight turn to the right, and the helicopter door opened. We were two minutes out, looking out at a city—a city with no idea we were coming. We passed very close to a golf course, just out the door, and I thought, *How strange.* There sure weren't any golf courses in Afghanistan. The sight drove it home somehow—*we were invading a country with golf courses.* This was no exercise.

The compound came into view, looking almost exactly like the training setup. It was dark, as if the power was out, and I had a fleeting thought that maybe our Agency guys had made that happen somehow. The two helicopters split. Dash 1 headed for the point between the two houses where an assault team was going to fast-rope from both sides. This involved sliding down thick, braided ropes, attached to bolted ends inside the helicopter. There are no safety harnesses, we just slide down grasping the rope with our gloves. The heavier guys sometimes use their feet as well. This is dangerous, but allows multiple people to slide down the rope simultaneously, one above the other. As we slid, snipers would be aiming down out of both sides of the aircraft, anticipating resistance. We flew to our designated spot on the north side to drop off our external security guys. The snipers, Cheese, Cairo, and the interpreter jumped out, and we immediately began to lift up, headed to the rooftop. Then we thumped right back down.

Our pilot had seen Dash 1 try to hover inside the walls above the courtyard and fail. According to two US officials who praised the skill of the pilot, the chopper lost the lift necessary to hover because it entered a "vortex" condition. At least two factors were at play, they said—hotter than expected air temperature and the compound's eighteen-foot-high walls. In our North Carolina simulations, the walls, although to scale, were essentially fences, allowing air to flow through them. The solid walls in the compound created a bowl effect that affected the aerodynamics just enough to make a critical difference in the lift of the aircraft. Whatever the cause, the Dash 1 pilot felt the loss of control and adeptly spun the nose to the right, put the tail on top of the southwest wall and eased the nose into the dirt; a controlled crash landing. Had he *not* been one of the two best pilots in the world, he might have tried to power up, which could have been catastrophic. That would have rolled the bird and killed everyone on board. He made this life-and-death decision instantly. Our pilot saw this and knew that if Dash 1 couldn't hover inside those walls, neither could we. So he just put us back down. Talk about effective nonverbal communication.

We hadn't seen any of this. We'd only overheard the radio transmission, *"Dash 1 going down,"* but had thought the pilot was saying, *"Dash 1 going around,"* which we assumed meant they'd taken fire and done a racetrack—a loop up and back for another pass. All we knew for sure was that we were back on the ground, which meant scratching the perfect plan and starting over from right there. We'd rehearsed exactly this. We knew the compound like we knew our own front yards. There was a gate near the northeast corner right in front of us. We'd blow that and enter there. It was just a few steps to the gate. Within seconds of jumping from the chopper, the breacher had attached a seven-foot charge of C-6 right down the middle and blew it. The metal gate peeled open like a tin can. Behind it was a solid brick wall. The breacher said, "Failed breach. This is bad."

"No, this is good," I said. "That's a fake door. That means he's in there."

We said we were going to blow the carport. The radio crackled to life.

"No, don't blow it, we'll just open it."

What the . . . ?

I thought, *Okay, it doesn't matter how they got in there. I'll find out later. Let's go.*

The door opened, and an upward thrusting thumb appeared, the universal signal that these were the good guys. As we entered, I looked to the left. We were walking down the carport, and it was all dawning on me: *Holy shit, we're here, that's bin Laden's house. This is so cool. We're probably not going to live, but this is historic and I'm going to savor this.*

I could hear gunfire: the distinct sound of an automatic AK-47, and the suppressed semi-automatic 5.56 of the good guys. Some of the shots were closer than others but several of my guys were shooting. I came around the corner to see one of our guys in the aftermath of a gunfight in front of the main house. The fight had only lasted two seconds. He shot through a window, and a man and woman were down inside. He was still looking at them while clearing the room as best he could from the outside. I could see them lying dead together.

He looked concerned. "I just killed one of the women, too," he said. "She jumped in front of him right as I was shooting. Am I going to be in trouble?"

"Let's not worry about being in trouble," I said. "Let's finish this mission."

Okay, I thought. *Now the women are martyring themselves. This is definitely the right place.*

I didn't think the dead man looked like bin Laden, but I couldn't linger. We still had an entire house to clear. We entered through the front door of the main building. A few of my guys were already ahead of us and were making their way down the hallway, clearing the rooms as they did. Some guys stayed back to search the two bodies. It was standard tactics and we were all experts. The floor was a long hallway with rooms off to the sides and a barricaded door on the far end. In a spot like this, you clear the rooms, in order, and spend the least possible amount of time in the hallway. Bad guys will "spray and pray" down hallways. Even though Allah isn't always around to guide their bullets, they do get lucky sometimes. On all sides, we could hear women and children crying—we later learned that living with bin Laden in the compound were three of his four wives and seventeen children—but that level of habitation was no different than in many of our targets.

There were four rooms. I entered the last one on the far right of the hallway. A little girl was in there, obviously terrified and alone. Even in this tensest possible situation, we couldn't just ignore her. One of the guys took her arm and led her across the hall and into another room already filled with women and children where he handed her over to one of the women. We were in a fight and looking for the world's most wanted man, and he was making sure a young girl was as safe as possible under the circumstances. He came back into my room, and we were looking down the hallway where two of our guys were breaching the barricaded door. After failing to make sufficient headway with a sledge, they stopped to put charges on it. The door obviously led to stairs up to the next level, so we had to just stand in the room and wait until they got it open. I heard the guy behind me say something about a helicopter crash. My immediate thought was that one of the Chinooks carrying the reserve squadron forty-five minutes behind us had been shot down, so I said, "What helicopter crashed? The reserve team?"

"No, dude," he said. "*Our* helicopter crashed in the front yard. You walked right past it."

I thought, *Well, shit, now we're never getting out of here because we only have one helicopter. We better get up there and kill him before they blow up the place.* All along we'd been scanning the ceilings, looking for hanging bombs—which is how the bad guys set up a lot of their booby traps, intended to bring the entire house down. We were surprised we hadn't seen any. Yet.

The breachers blew the charges on the stairwell door and it split open. As we made our way up the stairs I was five or six guys back. The woman intel analyst had told us that when we got to a set of stairs we should expect Khalid bin Laden, Osama's twenty-three-year-old son, to be there, armed and ready, his father's last line of defense. "If you find Khalid," she told us, "Osama's on the next floor."

The stairwell was in total darkness, so unless Khalid or whoever was up there had night vision, they could hear us coming but not see us.

We could see *them*, though. As we were moving up, a figure popped out just above us on the half landing between the first and second floor. We saw him for just an instant before he darted back behind a banister. He was armed with an AK-47. The point man stopped dead and pointed. I should have grabbed a couple of guys and pulled them back down the stairs to let the advance guys handle the situation in case whoever it was tossed a grenade down on us. The setup risked all of us dying at once. But it was such an awesome moment, I couldn't obey my tactical instincts. Here were two grown men trying to kill each other, separated by ten inches and a nice thick banister. In that supercharged instant, it would have been easy to forget that *we* could see and he couldn't. But the point man thought it through beautifully: Khalid knew somebody was nearby but he didn't know we were Americans for sure. In no more than a whisper my guy uttered a phrase he'd learned before the mission began. He said it twice, in both of the languages bin Laden's son spoke, Arabic and Urdu. "Khalid, come here."

Khalid, confused by hearing his name called, poked his head around the banister and said, "What?" That was his final word. The point man shot him in the face. The bullet entered above the chin and exited out the back of his head. Khalid dropped where he stood. Blood pooled around his head and soaked into his bright white blouse. The train started moving up the stairs to the second floor with me in the back. Each man stepped over Khalid on the way up, and everybody except the point man started clearing the rooms to the right and left on the second floor. The point man kept his gun trained on the top of the stairs to the third floor, which was right in front of him with a curtain hanging over the entryway. At some point before I got there, he took a shot at a tall figure behind the curtain, but couldn't see the result. I moved up behind him and put my hand on his shoulder. There were only two of us left. This was it.

The point man stared down the barrel of his gun, never letting his aim leave the curtain. My hand rested on his shoulder. I could halt him or tell him to advance with a touch.

At this point, we were spread way too thin. It was just the two of us there. Whoever was on the third floor knew we were coming, and they were probably putting on suicide vests—as many other, lesser al-Qaeda leaders had done in the past—and barricading themselves in fighting positions with weapons. Our tactics said we should wait for more guys, or go down and get Cairo to run up ahead of us. But we didn't have time. The occupants of the third floor were getting ready to make their stand, and we needed to get up there.

The point man was aware of this, and he started to speak, only knowing one of his guys was behind him, not who it was.

"Hey, we got to go, we got to go."

I knew what he was thinking because I was thinking it, too: *Okay, this is where the suicide bomber's going to hit us.*

And then I had a thought so clear it was like a voice in my head. *I'm tired of worrying about it, let's just get it over.* It wasn't bravery, it was more like fatigue or impatience—*I'm fucking done with waiting for it to happen.*

I squeezed his shoulder.

We swiftly moved up the stairs to the curtain, and he pushed it aside. Two women stood there screaming at us. The point man lunged at them, assuming they had suicide vests, tackling both and landing on the floor on top of them. If they blew up, his body would absorb most of the blast, and I'd have a better chance of surviving and doing what we'd come there to do. I turned to the right and looked through a door into an adjoining room. Osama bin Laden stood near the entrance at the foot of the bed, taller and thinner than I'd expected, his beard shorter and hair whiter. But it was the guy whose face I'd seen ten thousand, a hundred thousand times. He had a woman in front of him, his hands on her shoulders. In less than a second, I aimed above the woman's right shoulder and pulled the trigger twice. Bin Laden's head split open, and he dropped. I put another bullet in his head. Insurance.

The woman, who turned out to be Amal, the youngest of bin Laden's four wives, kind of fell on top of me. I carried her over to the bed. Her calf was bleeding. She'd seen the point man coming up the stairs, leveling his gun at her husband, and jumped in front just as the point man pulled the trigger. She didn't seem to be seriously injured, but was almost catatonic. I don't think we even cuffed her.

For the first time, I noticed a little boy, bin Laden's youngest son, a two-year-old, tottering on fat little legs in a corner of the room. He'd watched the whole thing, but it was so dark and he was so young, he didn't know what was going on, except that it wasn't good. He was crying. I thought, *This poor kid had nothing to do with this. He's just in the middle of a shit storm right now, poor guy.*

I picked him up and put him on the bed with the woman. Now other SEALs began making their way into the room. I stood there and, kind of frozen, watched my guys do the work I'd seen them do hundreds of times. One of the guys came up to me and asked, "Are you okay?"

Was I? I felt blank. "Yeah," I said. "What do we do now?"

He laughed and said, "Now we go find the computers."

I said, "Yeah, you're right. I'm back. Holy shit."

"Yeah, you just killed Osama bin Laden."

We went downstairs and found what looked like some kind of hastily improvised office, with work stations in three different rooms. At that point, our guys were doing what they normally do, picking up the big computer towers and slamming them down. The hardware opens as if by magic and out comes the hard drive. We were stuffing everything that looked important into big net bags, filming everything.

I bent down to look under a bed and saw some huge duffel bags. I pulled them out and opened them up. They were filled with what looked like freeze-dried, vacuum-sealed rib eye steaks.

"Wow," I said. "They were in for the long haul, they have all this food." We kept finding more of these huge bags, all filled with freeze-dried meat. Then someone said, "Wait a minute, this isn't beef, this is opium."

They had many hundreds of pounds of the drug squirreled away there.

Not only had we just ended the life of bin Laden, we'd stumbled on what appeared to be al-Qaeda's central bank as well as an intelligence jackpot. We were rushing now, trying to shovel as much of the intel haul as we could into the bags to hand off to the predesignated guys who'd carry it all back.

By this point, we'd overstayed the thirty-minute window we thought was our limit for getting in and out without coming into conflict with some element of the Pakistani military. Admiral McRaven would later say that, at this juncture, he was starting to sweat. He knew that Pakistani MiG fighter jets had been scrambled and were hunting for us.

When I went back upstairs, the one guy we'd brought along from the reserve squadron because he'd taught himself Arabic in Iraq was interrogating two of bin Laden's daughters, asking who the man dead on the floor was. They lied at first, but eventually one said, "That's him, that's Sheikh Osama."

The point man and two other guys had put him in a body bag,

but they hadn't closed it yet. One was standing over the body with a camera—we wanted to take digital photos to confirm we'd gotten who we knew we had. Bin Laden's head was a mess, split wide above his eyebrow like a melon dropped on a tile floor. I bent down and pressed the head back together, trying to restore the features to recognizable condition, and our guy with the camera snapped a lot of pictures. We needed to get them to the Ground Force Commander who, we hoped, could pass them to command in J-bad. Most urgently, though, we needed to tell him that we could confirm bin Laden was dead. Once he got the word, seventeen to eighteen minutes after our boots had first touched ground outside the compound, he radioed Admiral McRaven and said, "For God and country, Geronimo, Geronimo, Geronimo, EKIA."

Geronimo was the code word for finding bin Laden, and EKIA means Enemy Killed in Action. I thought "for God and country" was a bit much, but on the other hand, *why not*?

We zipped up the bag, and all four of us carried al-Qaeda's dead leader down the stairs and out the front door, where we took a right down to the carport. Jonny the sniper was there.

"Hey, here's your guy," I said.

Jonny just looked at me a minute.

"You got to be shitting me."

"No," I said. "Let's go home, man."

I ran back into the house. It didn't need to be said, but I said it. "We have to go. Now. Forget about these women and children, forget about the interrogations, we're leaving."

The interpreter told the women they needed to stay in the house until morning, or watching aircraft would fire missiles. A lie, but we knew the Pakistanis would be there before then. We hustled everybody out of the house, and sent the EOD guy and one of the breachers over to the downed helicopter to fix timed charges to blow it up. The pilot protested. He said he thought he could fly it out, but we weren't taking chances. We called in the Chinooks.

Dash 2, the helicopter I'd come in on, was already on the way back from a designated waiting area in the mountains to pick up the team from the downed bird, and the body bag. It was a bit delayed—just under twenty minutes—because it needed to refuel, but I assumed the brass wanted the "proof of death" transported in one of the special birds. Meanwhile, the rest of us had been assigned to wait for another Chinook in a field to the east of the outer wall. I turned to the guys who set the charge and said, "Hey, what's that time fuse at?"

"About thirty seconds."

Just then we heard the helicopter coming right for the compound, directly over the courtyard. The radio guy and I had a brief but intense conversation.

"Abort! Abort! Abort!"

The pilot pulled up sharply and circled away just in time. The timers clicked and the charges went off, creating an immense blast that would have taken down the incoming Chinook. Disaster avoided.

Just then, I looked up at one of the neighboring homes and noticed a guy standing there, tapping something into his cell phone. Turns out, he was the guy who'd become famous around the world for live-tweeting the raid, blaming it on the Pakistani military.

The chopper came back around, and we got on. I was sitting next to another SEAL who asked the question that every SEAL asked every other SEAL when they found out what had happened:

"Who got him?"

That's when it started to sink in.

"I did," I said.

He kind of straightened up and said, "On behalf of my family, thank you."

Jonny the sniper—the guy who took the shot that saved Captain Phillips from the pirates—was sitting on my other side, which was interesting, because of the seven billion people on the planet, he might have been the only one to even come close to understanding what I was feeling. He also remembered how, when he'd been struggling with the glare of the spotlight that came with what he'd done, I kept trying to calm him down with a plug of my Copenhagen.

Now he returned the favor. His Copenhagen can appeared in front of my goggles. "Here, take one of mine," he said. "Now you know what it's like to be a fucking hero."

CHAPTER TWENTY-TWO

Ninety minutes would give us a shot at another fifty years of life.

We weren't in any stealth bird now, and we'd just raised holy hell in a less-than-optimum location. Abbottabad is the site of Pakistan's elite military academy—essentially, their West Point. So none of us on that chopper would have placed odds on making it back to Afghanistan before the Pakistani air defense woke up and rained missiles on our victory parade.

Seventy minutes to go, still flying. I could see it in everyone's eyes, but nobody was saying anything because they didn't want to jinx it. It was like watching a perfect game being pitched in the seventh inning. I wasn't saying a thing because the second anybody said anything we were getting blown up. I was trying not to even form the words in my head.

Sixty minutes to go.

Forty.

Twenty.

When I think of it now, it reminds me of when the super-underdog USA hockey team beat the Russians in 1980. In the old TV clips, you can see the tense crowd counting down the last minute, afraid of the hope rising in their hearts, afraid they want it too much and that their very desire will somehow guide a desperation slap shot past their goalie into the back of the net, a last-second thunderbolt that will kill their dream. But no

Russian finds an opening. Ten seconds, and the USA fans start counting down, almost timidly at first, but louder and louder until they're all screaming. *Three . . . two . . .* You can see what they're thinking, which was pretty much what we were thinking on that chopper: *This could happen. We might live.*

Five minutes.

Those final three hundred seconds stretched out like Silly Putty until the very idea of a second wore itself out. The span didn't so much end as screech to a halt with a voice popping up on the radio. "All right, gentlemen," said one of the pilots. "For the first time in your lives, you're going to be happy to hear this: Welcome to Afghanistan."

Holy shit! We'd done it. We'd lived!

The remaining stealth bird, Dash 2, was still a little bit behind us. When they landed a few minutes after we did, I ran into the point man. He pulled me aside and asked, "Hey, was he hit when you went in the room?"

"I don't think so. No," I said. I saw it again in my mind, bin Laden standing there behind his wife, his hands resting on her shoulders, no sign of injury, fear, or pain in his eyes. He was just kind of frozen, the classic deer in the headlights.

The point man slapped my shoulder.

"Well, you own this," he said. "You got him."

And then he tilted his head quizzically. "Where *was* everybody?"

I knew he was asking why it had been just the two of us going up those stairs to the third floor.

"Guys were busy," I said. "We didn't have a lot of guys in this mission to begin with."

"All right, cool, okay," he said. Then he looked up. "Hey, there she is." He was pointing at the CIA woman. "You got to give her something, man. You killed bin Laden."

We walked over to her, and I pulled the magazine out of my gun and held it out to her.

"Hey, do you have room for this?"

There'd been thirty bullets in that magazine when I'd left Afghanistan that night. Now there were twenty-seven.

She looked at me, and I could see it sink in. "I think I can find a space in my backpack," she said, taking it from me.

In the movie *Zero Dark Thirty*, a SEAL walks her character over to the body. She sees it for the first time, then walks away. She waits until she boards the C-130 to tear up.

That's not her at all.

What really happened: The point man and I walked her over to the body bag, which had been opened again, revealing that familiar but now ruined face. Below the neck didn't look too pretty, either. As I watched her look him over, I was thinking, *This is historic. Here's her life's work; she just found the most wanted man in history, there he is, it's all her doing. What's she going to say?*

Stone-cold, stone-faced, she said, "Uh, I guess I'm out of a fucking job."

And then she walked away.

I admired her brass, but for my part I was starting to feel the euphoria. I was alive, and I'd done this thing that seemed part dream, part Hollywood movie. People were coming up asking, "Who got him?" and everyone was pointing at me. Admiral McRaven came over and put his hand on my neck, like a proud father almost. I admired the guy. When Dash 1 went down before the entry into the house had even begun, it would have been easy to panic. It could have been the beginning of a historic fuckup. But in that moment, it wasn't going to help to have the people in the White House freaking out. So he'd gotten on a video teleconference with Washington and said, "Okay, there's an issue, but my men are prepared, so don't worry."

Turned out to be true, too.

Anyway we were all standing around laughing and slapping hands and bin Laden was just lying there at our feet through it all. The president had asked McRaven to confirm the body was bin Laden's. The intel guys hadn't had time to get DNA comparisons yet. McRaven unzipped the bag and took a look. He knew that bin Laden was tall, about 6′4″, a respectable altitude for an NBA shooting guard. He decided to measure the body right there, just to make sure it was the correct height. It took a few minutes for us to realize that nobody had a tape measure. McRaven looked around until his gaze settled on a particular guy. "Son, how tall are you?" he asked.

The guy replied, "Well, sir, I'm about six-two."

"Good," McRaven said. "Come here. I want you to lie down next to the remains here."

"I'm sorry, sir. You want me to do what?"

McRaven repeated his request.

The guy stretched out next to the body. Sure enough, he was a couple of inches shorter. When McRaven reported back to Obama, the president said, "Let me get this straight, you can destroy one of my two-hundred-million-dollar helicopters, but you can't afford a ninety-nine-cent tape measure?" Guy's pretty funny. I heard he later gave McRaven a plaque with a tape measure on it.

Eventually, we zipped Osama back up and put the body on a C-130, then we all flew up to Bagram where everything was laid out—the body, all the intel we'd gathered, all the photos we'd taken on our iPhones. The intel experts—CIA, FBI, and probably some agencies I never even knew existed—were swarming all over it. There was a big TV tuned to Fox News and we were keeping an eye on it. The media had all been recalled to the White House, which was especially odd on a Sunday, so the speculation started going through the roof. Everyone was calling their sources, including some of us, but we didn't want to confirm it yet. Our bosses were laboring over the final reports from the raid, going through every-body's stories, trying to nail down all the facts—how many EKIA, how many women were hurt, how many were okay. The White House didn't want to put something out there and have to go back on it.

As it was, an early report from the White House said bin Laden had been armed and used his wife as a human shield. That was quickly retracted. We only saw his guns—an AK-47 and a pistol hanging above the door of the room where I shot him—*after* he was dead. According to a Pakistani government report, when local authorities showed up at the compound just about fifteen minutes after we blew up the downed bird and left, Amal told them that bin Laden had been reaching for his gun when American soldiers appeared on the third-floor landing. According to the report, Amal said they'd been awakened by our helicopters, which she at first thought was the rumble of a storm. As she got up to turn on a light, bin Laden shouted, "No!" He knew we were coming for him. Why he hadn't managed to grab his AK-47 in the ten to fifteen minutes between the time the chopper landed and the time we arrived on the third floor is a mystery, and will remain so.

I also don't know if he was using his wife as a shield or not, but if he was, it wasn't an effective strategy since he was at least a foot taller than she was, and I had a clear shot right over her. There was no question I was going to take that shot. This was bin Laden. We had every reason to believe he was wearing a suicide vest and posed a threat, and were fully authorized to take him out. If he'd fallen face-first on the floor with his arms out in front of him where we could see them, I would have cuffed him and put him on the chopper back to J-bad. But that's about the only way that would have happened.

Anyway, before long some reports began popping up on TV that the mysterious recall of the media to the White House might be about bin Laden. It was confirmed—I don't know how—before the president even had a chance to speak. We all began looking up at the TV now. Some Army guys brought in big green tubs of food. I grabbed a great big breakfast sandwich with eggs, cheese, and hot sauce, which tasted incredible. I'll credit that more to my state of mind than the chef, though. I was standing there chewing this delicious sandwich, watching the president of the United States make a surprisingly long walk down a red-carpeted White House corridor to a podium in front of the camera. "Tonight, I can report to the American people and to the world that the United States has conducted an operation that killed Osama bin Laden, the leader of al-Qaeda, and a terrorist who's responsible for the murder of thousands of innocent men, women, and children."

As I heard him say Osama bin Laden, I turned my head from the TV and looked at Osama bin Laden. I thought, *How in the fuck did I get here from Butte, Montana?*

One of our guys piped up, "Hey, Mr. President, would you mind mentioning that no one was hurt, because our families are all watching this." It took Obama a couple of seconds more, but then he said, "No Americans were harmed."

We were all thinking, *Thank you, now we're good.*

I know now that the instant my dad saw the news alert, he knew I'd been in the middle of it. This time he was certain, and not just that I was involved. When he heard the president say bin Laden had been killed, he *knew*: It was me. He didn't guess it. He didn't believe it. He *knew* it—he possessed inexplicable certainty that not only had I been on the mission to get bin Laden, but that I'd personally fired the shot that accomplished the task.

I didn't get to call Dad, though. We didn't have access to phones and didn't want to break mission silence yet. We went back to one of the buildings on the base, a huge chalet-style place with a big pizza oven outside. The cooks made us pizzas, and we just stood around talking about how awesome it all was. There were computers there, so we were checking out all the news sites. The words "SEAL Team ███" were everywhere. We had no idea we'd be linked to the raid so quickly.

It was very strange. SEAL Team ███ had been a relatively obscure entity before Captain Phillips. That perfect-for-the-movies rescue had put us on the cultural radar. But this? This was something else entirely. The fascination with who we were and what we'd just done exploded all around us.

At the same time, the cone of silence was descending. We weren't allowed to debrief anybody. Days later, the secretary of defense, Robert Gates, came to the command in Virginia Beach to meet us and they wouldn't let anyone in except the guys who'd been on the raid. Everywhere we went it was the same. We were all awarded Silver Stars (sorry, Mom!).

We flew to Fort Campbell, Kentucky, to meet President Obama. As he was being debriefed by our Ground Force Commander, we were sitting in rows of chairs waiting. One of the guys from the helicopter command who'd flown us in, the 160th, came over in front of everybody and gave me a stiff salute. I wanted to say, "Come on, dude." I knew the other guys would be pissed about it. It was the Somali pirate situation all over again. Jonny had been right. I was learning what it was like to be a fucking hero. Guys closer to me than family, guys who I assumed would be my best friends forever, were giving me the stink eye. I could feel the tension escalating by the minute.

Suddenly this dynamic, impossible-to-miss voice was saying, "Hey, everybody!" I came out of my funk instantly, thinking, *Hell, yeah, the president's here.* Vice President Joe Biden came in right beside him. Obama gave a quick talk, basically saying how proud he was of us and how proud he was to be an American, then he presented us with a Presidential Unit Citation.

We had a gift for him: a framed flag that we'd carried on the mission. We'd all signed the back of the frame, using our call signs rather than our names. It was cool, because we could tell that he totally didn't expect it. He was speechless for a minute, then he said, "What do you think, Mr. Vice President? You think I can find a special place to hang that?"

Biden said, "Yeah, I know a certain presidential library where that would look good." Obama replied, "Oh, no, this is going in my bedroom."

It was a nice moment and totally broke the tension. Unfortunately, the good vibes didn't last. I began to hear secondhand comments, guys talking about me and saying, "With all the extra attention, why is he bragging about it?"

Bragging was the last thing I wanted to do. It would be absurd to brag. We all knew that any one of our guys would have done exactly what I had done, and just as effectively, if he happened to have been in my position. In fact, the point man did something far *more* heroic than I when he tackled those women we believed to be wearing suicide vests. He'd been willing to sacrifice himself for the success of the mission. But all anyone wanted to talk about was "who got him?" and the word spread so fast there was no way to put a lid on it. I was getting calls from all over the country from people who wanted to thank me, saying things like, "Great shot." I felt hugely uncomfortable in the spotlight. I'd been part of a team with a code of silence, and now we were known worldwide and I was being singled out. From my teammates, I felt jealousy and disapproval. It just sucked.

I started getting pulled in by my bosses almost weekly. They'd say, "Hey, what are you doing? Who are you telling?"

All I could say was, "I don't know where this is coming from, man. I just want this to go away."

As the summer wore on, I was beginning to think that the only way that would happen was if *I* went away. I'd intended to stay in the Navy for thirty years, but I regretfully started planning to retire after fifteen—which would leave me with no pension and wondering what the hell I was going to do to support my family. That was especially ironic when I got word that there'd been a meeting of our squadron in which people were bashing me for "trying to cash in," saying I'd already signed a book contract for seventeen million dollars.

It wasn't true, and I shouldn't have had to prove myself to anyone. But I was beginning to feel that I needed to prove *something*. I considered going on one more combat deployment just to show, *Hey, I'm like you guys. I'm going back to war. I'm not writing a book. I'm not cashing in.*

* * *

ON THE NIGHT OF AUGUST 5, 2011, in Wardak Province, Afghanistan, a platoon of forty-seven Army Rangers set off in two helicopters to kill or arrest a Taliban leader named Qari Tahir.

The Rangers were inserted into a landing zone in a valley not far from the compound believed to be Tahir's residence. As the platoon approached, aerial reconnaissance observed two groups of Taliban fighters leaving the compound. One was engaged and eliminated by Apache helicopters. The second group managed to take up defensive positions. Tahir was suspected to be among them. The ground commander decided to send a reserve of seventeen operators to pursue and eliminate the survivors. The SEAL contingent, a military dog, thirteen other Americans, seven Afghan government troops, and an interpreter flew into the valley in a Chinook helicopter, code named Extortion 17. One minute from touching down, RPG grenades hit the chopper, destroying the rear rotor and bringing it down. All thirty Americans, and all thirty-eight men aboard, plus the dog, died in the crash.

It was the worst loss in the history of Naval Special Warfare, and the worst loss of American lives in a single incident of the entire Afghan conflict. So many of my friends had died in an instant it was impossible to process. As a command, we went from planning operations to planning funerals.

I was especially haunted by a memory of one of the fallen SEALs, my friend Robert J. Reeves. His friendship was especially meaningful to me in the summer after the bin Laden mission when I was struggling with all the resulting complications, and uncertain of my future. He and three other SEALs had this big fancy house in Virginia Beach we called "the boy band house" because all of these guys were so damn good-looking. He also had an absolutely gorgeous and extremely sweet girlfriend who always called me her "other Robert J." One night, Robert and I were sitting at his big dining room table, and he poured himself a glass of wine and offered me one. For some reason, I was in a healthy phase and wasn't drinking anything so I turned it down. As he sipped alone, he looked at me and said, "You know what? One day a lot of us are going to die on one of those helicopters."

I know it's the wrong thing to obsess over, but I'll always regret not having that last glass of wine with my friend. After the funeral, his girlfriend called me to say, "Now you're my one and only Robert J." It just about killed me.

The losses tore us apart—not only personally, but tactically. We knew that that level of combat experience could never be replaced. Senior operators would need to be shifted to different squadrons to backfill leadership positions. I left the squadron I'd served with such pride to go to another, and volunteered to extend my service until August 2012. The new squadron was a breath of fresh air, a chance to get away from the jealousy and recriminations and to remember why I loved being a SEAL again. I even began to reconsider my decision to leave the Navy. Right before Thanksgiving, we left for a deployment in Afghanistan—at Forward Operating Base Shank located up in the mountains to the east.

We stayed in the very same rooms as the fallen, and we overlapped with the squadron's surviving members, those who purely by chance hadn't dressed out for the doomed mission. It just sucked to see what the permanent loss of beloved friends was doing to these guys. I'd gone through the selection course with one of them. He was sitting alone reading a book—which, considering how SEALs usually spend their downtime, was a definite sign of depression. I didn't even want to try to talk to him about the guys he'd lost, but I hoped I could lighten his mood a little by joking with him. "Hey, Adam," I said. "Why don't you have an iPad? Why are you reading a book?" He looked up without a glimmer. "I don't know. I just like the feel of a book." That's all he said to me the entire time. He'd lost so many of his guys, he couldn't even be there.

So it was tough to begin with, and other things made it worse. Dead of winter in Afghanistan, especially at an altitude of six thousand feet, is fiercely cold. Plus, conditions in Afghanistan had deteriorated. The Forward Operating Base was hit with mortar fire from insurgents every day, and there were "Green on Blue" attacks—assaults on coalition forces by the very Afghan troops we'd been training and supporting.

It was demoralizing to see that so much of what we'd accomplished and sacrificed for had started to come undone. And it was even sadder to realize I'd be spending my second Christmas in a row in Afghanistan, away from my girls. I watched an online video my wife had made of Santa sending our daughters personal greetings. I could so easily imagine the faces and shining eyes of the girls as they watched it. I pictured my oldest daughter enjoying the video with a tolerant smile on her face, only half-believing it. She was in second grade and only seven years old but ahead of her time as far as critical thinking goes. And I could imagine my youngest, who'd turned four a few months before I left for Afghanistan, watching Santa with some concern. The video really played up the whole "naughty or nice" theme, and we all knew the truth: She had her moments. I was sure the naughty/nice calculation would create a minuscule iota of doubt in her mind, but none whatsoever in mine. She has a huge heart and loves to share. I knew she'd get exactly what she wanted for Christmas. Except for her daddy being there to open gifts with her.

I thought about them all the time and worried, too. We had FaceTime and used it often, but means of connecting only went so far. I'd promised them that we'd go to Great Wolf Lodge when I got home, and I knew they couldn't wait. But they'd have to. I'd told them I'd be home after Christmas, which was true, but only because March was "after Christmas." The four-year-old would never grasp that I'd stretched the truth, but my oldest daughter could look at a calendar and know that Christmas was just around the corner. Her mother told me she'd packed a suitcase and insisted on leaving it by the front door so she'd be ready to go when I got home "after Christmas." I couldn't wait to be done with this and take them to the Lodge. They'd been dealing with my absence all of their lives, but that didn't make our separation any easier.

I was getting too old for this. Walking down the hill to the showers—the steep, slippery, icy, and brutally cold hill—feeling every day of my thirty-four years, I nearly ran into a young Ranger emerging from the two-story complex in a towel. He was twenty-three and had about 7 percent body fat, just a complete stud. He saw me and said in a thick Boston accent, "Oh, you guys are the new SEAL Team ▇ guys in town. Right?"

I admitted as much.

He said, "Cool, you can play us in a game of tackle football for Thanksgiving. SEALs versus Rangers."

"Are you fucking kidding me? You guys will destroy us. There's no way, man," I said. "If you want to talk tactics, I'll teach you guys some tactics. But I'm not going up against a bunch of Rangers in a contact sport."

It was so cold and uncomfortable—for the bad guys and for us—that we didn't work much. The few missions we did come up with had a different feel. This was our first time working with the CST, the Cultural Sensitivity Team. The team is made up of junior Army officers, women. They'd go out with us and make sure we didn't unnecessarily trample on Afghan cultural niceties. On target, we paid much more attention to things like respecting the Quran, because to be honest our first few deployments, we didn't give a fuck. We started to realize how serious these Afghan Muslims were about their holy book and their women. Having female personnel with us who could speak a little bit of the language made things a lot less incendiary when we were rousting suspected bad guys. The CST officers could search the women and talk to the kids.

There's debate now about having women in combat roles. I believe any woman who can get through the same training as the men is fully capable. I remember walking through miserable frosted-over swamps with a woman named Amy who was maybe 5-feet tall and up to her waist in muck. She never once complained, and never fell behind. On this deployment, we got in a few gunfights with the women. There was one I worked out with a couple times. We'd go on five-mile runs, and she'd beat me. Granted, I'd gotten fat, 230 pounds, but she could run her ass off. Truth is, most SEALs bitched a hell of a lot more about conditions than these ladies did.

The female officers were good to have around, but it all contributed to this growing sense that I'd done my time, and my time was passing. Even when we had bad guys to go after, it wasn't the same. We'd do an offset insert, several kilometer hike, climb a few fences, blow the doors off. Occasionally, we'd think we were going after what we'd call a high-value target, but in Afghanistan by this point there was really no such thing. We were going after thugs mostly, not terrorists. In our minds, we were building them up into something they weren't. The real bad guys were all over in Pakistan.

Our missions had become what we called "strike to develop." We'd be sitting there for six or seven days, doing nothing but working out and playing Xbox. We'd find a target more out of boredom than a real sense of mission. I always disagreed with that—if there were no missions, there were no missions.

I guarantee that nobody will remember or care who the alleged high-value target was in the Extortion 17 mission. The bad guy was meaningless. We lost all those men because someone got bored.

My very last mission as a SEAL came out of one of those slow weeks. The intelligence people had been going over film from one of their drones, just looking for something to target. They noticed a group of guys in a shitty little mountain village—what we call MAM, military-age males—who were obviously armed. They could see that these guys had rocket-propelled grenade launchers—from the air it looked as if they were carrying 2 x 4s. These guys would load up their weapons and drive out of the village, winding through mountain passes on this miserable little road making their circuitous way to neighboring villages. They thought that by taking this remote road they wouldn't be seen. That's where they guessed wrong.

The intel guys saw them do this one day, a Monday, and told us it was highly suspicious. We weren't impressed. Then they did it again. Same thing. Same spot. They were obviously waiting to ambush a convoy. We still didn't want to launch. We didn't want to waste our time sitting out in the middle of nowhere waiting for something that *might* happen. They did it again Thursday, and now we were starting to summon some interest. We said, "All right. If they do it again on Friday—their day of prayer—then for sure they'll be doing it on Saturday."

Friday came, and they sure as shit did it again.

So now we made a plan. We knew their pattern. Saturday morning they'd say their morning prayer as the sun came up, load up the car, and drive out to their ambush spot on the side of the mountain. We'd be waiting for them, staging a little ambush of our own. It's called an L ambush, because you set up one line perpendicular to the bad guys' route of travel, then another line parallel to the route and at ninety degrees to the first line. It's one of the oldest military maneuvers in the world. Soldiers have been doing L ambushes for two thousand years.

We presented our plan to our Army bosses—the Army was running this FOB. We said, "We're going to insert one kilometer away from this point right behind the mountain and we're going to walk in while it's still dark. We're going to hang out until the sun comes up. When it does we're going to hide behind this rock, and we're going to station these guys here. We're going to set up an L ambush."

The Army officer said, "L ambush? What's that?" I looked at him disbelievingly. "You're serious? An L ambush is the second thing they teach you when you join the Army. The first thing is, 'There's your bed.' The second thing is, 'This is an L ambush.'"

"Explain it."

So I explained it, pointing at the map. "These guys are going to get out here. We're going to get out here. I'm going to be the team leader on this spot right here with one guy to my left flank, and I'm going to move out there when the cars come up."

He said, "How are you going to stop them? You don't speak Pashto."

I said, "I'm going to point my gun at them. Everybody speaks gun."

Then he asked, "What if he doesn't stop?"

"I'm going to fucking shoot him. Where did you come from?"

We finally talked the Army guys into it. They even assigned a manned aircraft to watch the guys in the village. We set up a series of pro words—words to say over the radio conveying necessary information without giving anything away. We used colors this time, a modified traffic signal. Black was baseline, then red when the enemy started out, yellow for when they were on the way, followed by green. Green was when we'd step out from the rocks and speak gun.

Saturday, a few hours before dawn, we flew out to the mountain and hiked up to the spot. We set up behind some rocks so the enemy wouldn't be able to see us as they approached in their cars. The leg of the L, the maneuver element, set up, and our snipers climbed high on the mountain with their MC24 .30-caliber sniper rifles, about two hundred meters out from the target. For them at that distance it's like, "Which nostril do you want the bullet to go in?" The sun came up and nothing happened. There was a mountain between us and the village, a total visual block. So we were out there smoking cigars and bullshitting with each other. Here we were, armed and ready to kill these five insurgents, having a little cigar social.

The guy in the observation plane was keeping us updated, and sure enough, the guys came out from their prayers with their rocket-propelled grenade launchers and started loading up the car. Then we got word that the fucking car wouldn't start. We were still smoking. We knew it would take them fifteen minutes to get there, assuming their lousy car ever started, so we just chilled. They messed with their car for another twenty minutes, and then the pilot reported that they actually put the RPGs and machine guns down so they could push-start it.

So now it was pro word yellow; they were on their way. We smoked for another five minutes, and then figured it was time to get all Navy SEAL and hide behind the rocks. We'd just take a few more tokes on the stogie, then kill these five dudes. No adrenaline whatsoever.

Finally, we stubbed out the cigars and waited. An engine wound up the grade just out of sight. We leveled our guns at the spot where it would emerge. This is the funny thing about war: Our targets had been driving the only vehicle that had been on this road for months, because it was barely a road. But our eye in the sky piped up. "Hang on! Wrong car." A blue van emerged from the mountain and rolled past. I could see inside: a mom, a dad, and some kids going who knew where. Jesus. I'd come within seconds of going hot on the Brady Bunch.

This was taking forever. Those guys must have been driving like ninety-year-old ladies. It started to snow. We heard the whiny little Nissan before we saw it. Five of us walked out from behind the rocks, forming what we call the line of death, the base element. As the car came up to us, the "L" part of the deal would sweep through, leaving them no escape.

I was standing there in the road, staring straight at the driver. At about twenty meters, he braked. I saw him push the Nissan into reverse. His face creased, and his lips moved. I swear he was saying, in English, "Fuck. Fuck. Fuck." He stomped on the accelerator, and the bald tires whaled helplessly in the snow. Stuck.

I shouted, "Hey, get out of the car. You need to get out of the car."

Now this was the point where tensions rise rapidly. The passenger-side door slammed open. A guy hopped out holding a belt-fed machine gun. He ran toward the trunk. One of my line of death guys fired and the machine gunner went down like a sack of cement. Almost at the same time, the driver's head exploded. One of the snipers had decided, "Fuck this. They're moving." So he took the guy's head out. The guys in the backseat started scrambling for the exits and the whole thing just turned into a shit storm, everybody on the line firing their weapons. The two guys in the back fell out of the car and the shooting stopped.

As we cleared the scene, we found more belt-fed machine guns, AK-47s locked and loaded, grenades stuffed into pockets. We were thinking, *Wow, we just saved a lot of lives, look at these fucking people,* when one of our Afghan partners—every mission was now nominally "Afghan led"—came running up holding the grenade part of the RPG in his hand. It was green and shaped roughly like one of those toy rockets you fill with water, pump with air, and shoot off into the sky. In fact, this guy was as excited as a kid with a new toy. As we watched him approach with dawning horror, we noticed that there was a goddamn bullet hole through the shaped charge.

We all yelled. "Put that fucking thing down. Jesus. What's wrong with you?"

That was my last mission ever. At that point, we had all become so used to war, none of it was a big deal. That was part of the reason I was getting out. I knew I was getting complacent. If I kept at it, the next destination was sloppy, and sloppy kills.

CHAPTER TWENTY-THREE

I'd completed four hundred combat missions, walked through minefields, flown a hostile mission through the missile defense system of a nuclear power, been pinned down by a superior force in a dead-end valley. But the scariest thing I ever did was leave the Navy.

After sixteen and a half years, I had two Silver Stars, four Bronze Stars with Valor, a Joint Service Commendation Medal with Valor, three Presidential Unit Citations, and a Navy/Marine Corps Commendation Medal with Valor. I also had a mortgage, no pension, no college degree, no job.

I went to talk to the Navy exit people and asked, "What's the grace period? How many months after I get out can I keep my kids on my health insurance?"

They said, "You get out on 24 August. Health care for your kids ends midnight on the 23rd."

Thanks for your service. Now beat it.

Four other SEALs and I had put together a plan. We'd all get out and start a consulting firm. Security. Leadership. Team building. Or maybe we'd just make gear and sell hats. We didn't know. We'd been in the SEAL bubble so long we had no idea what we were doing, no sense of the real obstacles. I was the first to get out, and they were going to come right after me.

It didn't happen. Someone heard what we were doing and a particular group started giving the guys who were getting out with me a bunch of shit, calling them sellouts. Predictably, perhaps, the pressure caused them to cave. The SEAL bubble was all they knew.

One thing I've learned since becoming a civilian is that being a Navy SEAL is only part of your life. High school is a part of your life and it's the most important thing when you're in it. Then it's over. For me, for over a decade, being a Navy SEAL was everything. Those hard-as-nails instructors at Coronado and the officers I served under in the years after taught me to meet, and rise above, challenges I wouldn't have imagined. And my SEAL brothers—they taught me a sense of comradery that I still consider priceless. But to keep growing, we all have to move to the next phase. That's life.

Guys who are still in sometimes have difficulty appreciating that. Some pay too much attention to what others in the squadron room say about them. They get caught up in the alpha male bullshit. And that's a shame.

When we were in combat—before all the absurdly restrictive rules of engagement, before we'd killed anybody famous—being a SEAL was the best experience in the world. I was able to go to work with people who were better than me. I was never a "cool guy," I simply worked with cool guys, walked behind cool guys. Sometimes, by chance, I found myself in the front, would turn a corner, and do something cool myself. That's how I found myself in Osama bin Laden's bedroom; I arrived on the shoulders of giants.

And because I did, I have this ability to influence, and I plan to use it to do as much as I can for others. There are veterans out there who had much more dangerous jobs than I did. The soldiers who spent months on end in the valleys of Afghanistan, the Marines who patrolled through minefields day after day, the everyday soldiers rolling through the IED-strewn streets of Iraq—all had tougher jobs than I had. My fellow SEALs and I had the ability to fight on *our* terms; those other guys didn't.

Now I have a platform and they have nothing. Some are in the same position that I was, leaving the military before meeting the retirement requirement, no pension waiting for them. I want to raise awareness and help.

There are also the thousands of people most affected by 9/11.

I got to meet some of those who lost loved ones in the 2001 attacks for the first time in the summer of 2015. I'd been asked to donate something I'd worn on the mission to the National September 11 Memorial & Museum in New York. I agreed, with one condition: I'd do it anonymously. My name wouldn't be on it. They agreed, and even gave me a private tour of the place before it opened. At the end of the tour, I entered a room filled with 9/11 families. There was a politician speaking to them, and she brought me up on stage. "Just say a few words to these people."

For once, I wasn't at all prepared. I just started talking about the shirt I was donating, and I could see something happen in the eyes of all these people whose wives and husbands, fathers, mothers, sons, and daughters went to work one crisp September morning and never got to see their loved ones again. I felt this powerful connection, and I just kept talking, for the first time publicly telling my story of the bin Laden mission. After, people crowded around me to say how much hearing my story meant. One woman said, "I'm not afraid anymore. I've lived the worst nightmare imaginable, and because of today I'm not afraid anymore. There's a face with this, and you're telling me the truth. All the conspiracy theories are gone and he's dead."

A man came up with his grandson. His son, the boy's father, had been one of those who through no fault of his own ended up dying on 9/11. The man said, "Every single day, my grandson has asked me, 'Why did God do this?' and I always say, 'God *didn't* do this. The devil did this.'"

He looked up at me, a tear running down his cheek and a defiant gleam in his eyes. He said, "You, sir, killed the devil."

Since the early hours of May 2, 2011, I've had many moments when I've wondered if being the one who killed Osama bin Laden was the best thing that ever happened to me, or the worst. I'm still trying to figure that out. It's a difficult position to be in, one that has caused anxiety and sleepless nights. I'm confident, though, that this all happened for a reason. I'm committed to making the most of it.

ACKNOWLEDGMENTS

This book is a collection of incredible but true stories set in places and circumstances in which I was fortunate to find myself. Hard work and a positive attitude contributed to a good result, but I would never have been able to accomplish what I did without the people I was and am so fortunate to have in my life.

To my kids: You showed up in the middle of the adventure but have been my inspiration through the wars and after.

Jessica: Your courage, honesty, and immeasurable love have all had immense effect on this outcome and many others. You're my little soldier.

Dad: Thank you for always being there and always having my back. Even when I'm wrong.

Mom: Even though I never told you everything, thank you for your undying support and love. We're all here to do something special.

Family: The foundation we forged growing up remained so strong throughout. From graduations of all types to today, thank you for always being so honest and helpful.

To every teammate, instructor, mentor, analyst, pilot, and soldier with whom I've ever shared a moment, an op, a flight, or a fight: Nothing would have been possible without the team and the heroes you all are.

Rhonda Bentz: Thank you for giving me honest, well-thought-out advice and insight into pretty much every facet of business, communication, brand, and, well, life.

To my agent, Howard Yoon, and the Ross Yoon Agency: Your tireless work and professional commitment to excellence afforded me the best of all opportunities. Thank you for helping us all make this work.

To the Scribner publishing group and especially executive editor Rick Horgan: I could not have been more fortunate with this outcome. "Thank you" is not enough.

To my team: Rick Alcalde, Ashley Kern, and Matt Jones, and my attorneys at McDermott Will & Emery: Steve Ryan and Lazar Raynal. Thank you for making crucial introductions and decisions at the right times.

Finally, to Tom Shroder: You helped me turn a lifetime of experience and years of war into this book, and I cannot thank you enough. I'm proud to call you my friend.

INDEX